To Steve —

Please enjoy my
unique new book !

Best Wishes —

[signature]
2013

Pro's Pros

Extraordinary Club Professionals
Making Golf Great!

Joel Zuckerman

For information, contact Saron Press, Ltd.
608 Boyd Creek Drive, Ridgeland, SC 29936.

www.saronpress.com
info@saronpress.com

First Printing, January 2013

PRAISE FOR THE GOLF PROFESSIONAL FROM THE WORLD'S GREATEST PROFESSIONAL GOLFER:

When I think of great club professionals, it's not hard to understand that the first person I think of is the late Jack Grout. Jack gave me his friendship for nearly four decades, serving as both my golf instructor and, after the premature death of my father in 1970, as a second father to me. Jack gave a great deal of himself to me as my only golf teacher from the day I first attended one of his junior golf classes at Scioto Country Club in Columbus, Ohio, right up through my final major championship victory in the 1986 Masters.

Jack Grout was truly a pro's pro, someone who deeply loved and lived the game, and spent his adult life passing on his love and knowledge so others could also gain great enjoyment from golf. Great club professionals add so much to our wonderful game. They encourage, inspire, mentor and teach. They are often under the radar. But it is the hardworking, dedicated club professionals, found in every corner of our nation, that are in so many ways the lifeblood of golf and the caretakers of our game. ---*Jack Nicklaus*

ALSO BY JOEL ZUCKERMAN

- *Golf in the Lowcountry---An Extraordinary Journey Through Hilton Head Island & Savannah*

- *Golf Charms of Charleston*

- *Misfits on the Links*

- *A Hacker's Humiliations*

- *Pete Dye Golf Courses—50 Years of Visionary Design*

- *Kiawah Golf—The Game's Elegant Island*

DEDICATION

This book is dedicated to Eddie Ambrose and Eric Nadelman, two fine young men who have never met, but share more in common than just their first initial.

Both are former golf professionals, though neither chooses to make his current livelihood in that business. But they are personable, very likable, hard-working, ambitious and intelligent. And take it on face value when I claim that 95% of all avid golfers would be greatly served in exchanging their own game for either Eddie's or Eric's, and be much better for it.

Every book project begins with an idea, and it was Eddie who initially gave me the notion of doing a book about one of the more prominent subjects contained herein. Speaking to Eric on a related subject a short while later, he suggested I expand the idea to include a wider range of top-notch pros, instead of focusing on just the one.

So it was Eddie who hatched the idea and Eric who sharpened the focus by urging me to widen the lens. My gratitude goes out to both of them.

ACKNOWLEDGEMENTS

My thanks go out to all thirty professionals for their time and participation. I specifically want to acknowledge Mike Harmon, who is not only the Old Pro, but my Own Pro. Also Bob Ford, who has more connections than AT&T. It was these two gentlemen in particular who helped lay the groundwork to identify and contact many of the pros I came to know in the writing of this book.

Thank you to John McNeely, a fabulous host at his remarkable facility Diamond Creek. Dana Rader for the same reasons in Charlotte. Same can be said for Phil Owenby in Richmond, Rick Vershure in Scarsdale, Brad Worthington and Suzy Whaley in Connecticut, and both Rick Rhoads and Jim Langley in Northern California. Also Laurie Hammer in Florida, and Mark Brenneman in Las Vegas. Mark is correct in his long-held assessment. It doesn't get much better than leaving his 19th hole for the limo with a "Rhonda-Rita" to go.

"My Three Sons" was a popular sitcom in the '60s. My Four Sons are Rick Castillo, Kevin Hammer, Kevin Rhoads and Brennon Langley, all of whom were generous with their time in speaking glowingly about their fathers.

Thank you also to John Marsh at Secession Club, and Tod Ortlip and Jan Hensel in Columbus, Ohio. Nicole Weller and Amanda Workman in Savannah, Ray Greyhofsky on Sea Island, and Dennis Satyshure in Baltimore.

Publisher Paul deVere of Saron Press Ltd, book designer Elizabeth Gauthier, cover artist Caryn Wheeler, cover models

James Wohler and PGA Professional John Phillips, and photographer Dick Hochman.

Lastly to my wife, Elaine. Regrettably a non-golfer still, even after my seven books on the subject. But now, with all these new friends in high places, perhaps she'll deign to take a swipe or two, instead of always repairing to the tennis court. Hope springs eternal, anyway.

Joel Zuckerman
Savannah, Georgia
January, 2013

TABLE OF CONTENTS

Introduction

S ay the words "PGA Professional" to the average sports fan, even the casual golfer, and they will quickly envision Tiger Woods, Phil Mickelson, Freddie Couples, Ernie Els, Bubba Watson or Rory McIlroy. But there are professional golfers and then there are golf professionals, and to borrow an expression long favored in the United Kingdom, these entities are as different as chalk and cheese.

The great game of golf does not exist because of the exploits and derring-do of high-flying, highly compensated Tour players who travel the world on private aircraft, wielding their clubs like rapiers in pursuit of oversize cardboard checks, gleaming silver or polished crystal trophies, and annual compensation of seven figures and beyond.

No, the true heart of the game, the fabric of golf, is stitched by the club professional. It is the club professionals who give lessons, run clinics, facilitate tournaments and club competitions, interact with members, patrons and guests, and generally do whatever possible to ensure that golfers who come into their orbit have a positive and enriching experience.

It's no secret that the last two decades have been a rocky time for the game of golf. A moribund economy, uncertain job market, lack of leisure time, and myriad other potential distractions have conspired to make golf less of a priority than it might have been for generations past. Participation has stagnated, rounds are down, and golf course closures continue to outpace new course construction. Just as troubling is the fact that the younger generations, persons currently in their mid-20s to mid-40s, are playing far less golf than those in the same age bracket did twenty and thirty years ago. The future of golf isn't necessarily bleak, but it is somewhat uncertain.

Into the fray step the 27,000 men and women who make up the membership of the PGA of America. It is their job to grow the game, teach the game, and help enrich the lives of those who choose to play. It is these golf professionals who can spark the flame in a newcomer or bring back to the game someone who long ago relegated their clubs to a dark basement corner. The PGA professional helps unlock the sheer joy of golf. In so doing, he or she contributes mightily to a multi-billion dollar enterprise that employs many tens of thousands and is an important part of the lives of millions of Americans.

If every PGA professional worth his or her salt was given their due within these pages, this volume would make the Encyclopedia Britannica look as insubstantial as a dime store paperback. Suffice it to say that hundreds upon hundreds deserve recognition, but space and economic constraints limit the number included here to thirty. These profile subjects aren't meant to be one-in-a-thousand in comparison to their peers. An entirely different set of thirty pros, or totally different thirty after that, could have been featured. While decades of tenure, a trophy case bursting with industry awards, and an affiliation with marquee resorts or blue-ribbon private clubs describes many if not most of those featured here, some traits are endemic to all: an abiding work ethic; sound business sense; respect of their peers, admiration and affection from their members and customers; a winning personality; an even-keeled disposition; and great love of and for the game.

You can call them the best of the best, the top of the pyramid or the crème de la crème, and you wouldn't be wrong. But the best description of all might simply be: the pro's pros.

Ron Branca
Salt Lake City, Utah

The great state of Utah is, if not an insular place, certainly self-contained. Here are two examples, only about two miles apart. To the wider college football-loving world, "The U" means just one thing— the University of Miami, former national powerhouse, and consistent producer of NFL-caliber talent. But around Salt Lake City, "The U," understandably, is the University of Utah. And "The Country Club" brings those who love golf's history and its most esteemed venues

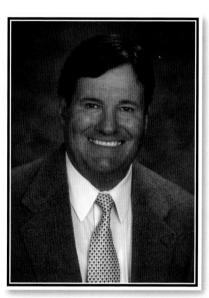

Ron Branca--2011 Utah Section PGA Professional of the Year

immediately to mind of Brookline, Massachusetts. This leafy venue outside Boston is the site of Francis Ouimet's extraordinary US Open triumph a century past, the Ben Crenshaw-inspired Ryder Cup comeback in 1999, and other indelible moments in the game's history. But 2,000 miles from Brookline in the Salt Flats of the Utah Valley, lies a club of great distinction in its own right, with a history nearly as long as its like-named Massachusetts neighbor. And a great part of that history is inexorably tied to the Branca Family, where Ron has served as the club's head professional for nearly 20 years, following his father, Tee, who held the same post for more than half-a-century.

The Country Club was founded in 1898, moved to its current location in the eastern part of the city in 1920, with its distinctive, red-roofed clubhouse originally built in 1922. The golf course was originally designed by Utah native George Von Elm and Scotland's Willie Watson. Von Elm was the 1926 US Amateur champion who beat the great Bobby Jones in the final, after losing to Jones in the final on two previous occasions. Watson was a renowned architect who created magnificent courses like the Olympic Club and Harding Park in San Francisco, among other highly-regarded designs. The golf course has been remodeled three times over the years, most recently by John Harbottle.

Over its more than 90-year existence, the club has played host to presidents (Taft, Harding) major celebrities (Hope, Crosby, Babe Ruth) and of course, numerous golf luminaries. (Hagen, Palmer, Nicklaus, Casper, Player, Miller, Trevino, etc.)

Tee Branca began as a caddy at The Country Club in 1923. He worked his way through the ranks, and after completing his military duty, became head professional in 1944. He held the job until 1995, when his older son Ron took the reins. "Never mind the 51 years," begins Ron Branca, with a shake of his head, "he also opened and closed the shop seven days a week, first person here and last one out the door. My brother Don and I used to joke we would really feel sorry for the poor guy who followed him in this position. We had no idea it would eventually be me!"

Tee Branca was an active member of the PGA of America for 65 years, from 1930 until 1995. Only the great Byron Nelson was active in the association for that length of time. He is a member of the Utah Golf Hall of Fame, and a four-time winner of the Utah section's Professional of the Year.

His father died when he was a small child, and his mother, a saloon dancer in Idaho who could barely speak English, moved scrawny Atilio Branca and her five other children down to Salt Lake City in search of work. He dropped out of school in ninth grade to earn money for the family, and despite the fact that both of his parents had been born in Italy, like his Scottish forbearers, it seemed a natural for him to drift from sheep herding to golf. It was a combination of affinity for the game, embarrassment about the strange ethnicity of his given name and his extremely slender build that made it easy for those around him to refer to him originally as Tei, which some years later morphed to Tee, which eventually became his legal name.

"He started out left-handed," couldn't afford or find many lefty clubs, so out of necessity became a right-handed player, and a very good one at that," marvels Ron Branca.

Ron and Don, only a year apart in age, became excellent players themselves. The Country Club wasn't their boyhood stomping grounds; they honed their games at the Bonneville Municipal Course just a few miles away. Both were stars at nearby Highland High, and the Branca Brothers were in the middle of an incredible run in which their team went undefeated in winning the Utah State Championship for eight consecutive years. Later in life, Don won the Utah State Amateur Championship in back-to-back years. Their father coached them with what little time he had to spare, Ron joking, "Sometimes we wouldn't see him for days at a time, because he left for work before we got up, and came home after we were asleep."

Ron Branca, who has always lived in Utah, played collegiate golf at "The U," where he tangled with age-contemporaries the likes of Tom Watson, Gary Koch and Andy Bean. "I was quite a strong player locally, but never made much of a splash nationally." Turning professional after graduation, the recent alum came back and coached golf for many years at the University of Utah while serving concurrently as the head professional at a municipal golf course near the Salt Lake City Airport called Rose Park.

There were several years when Ron Branca's work schedule was even more hectic than his father's. "I spent 17 years at Rose Park while coaching golf at The U. I also was the head professional at a nearby course under construction called Wingpointe, and held all three jobs for a few years concurrently. I moved to the new facility fulltime, and several years later, had to give it up to assist my dad, who by now was somewhat elderly and having health problems."

When the legendary Tee Branca was ready to finally step down, at age 83, it seems a given his oldest son would be named successor. After all, he had been around The Country Club his entire life. He and his brother worked in the bag room and assisted in the shop when needed as children, and then Ron returned as an adult with some 20 years of experience as a head professional, helping his dad run the always-busy operation for several more years. But that's not quite the way it worked out.

The Country Club conducted a nationwide search for their new head professional, and received more than 300 applications from all corners. While few golfers residing outside of the Intermountain West are aware of the club's excellent reputation, it's no secret within the golf profession itself.

'I thought of it as a 'mercy hire,' particularly when they only offered me a one-year contract at the beginning," continues Ron

Branca, chuckling at the distant memory. "There was amazing interest in the job, and some extremely qualified professionals were hoping to get it. Even though I was very familiar with the operation, had a solid resume and decades of experience, some applicants had even more experience than I. Honestly, if it wasn't for my father I doubt I would have been given the chance, but he cast a massive shadow over this club, and I guess they decided to give me a shot."

Nearly 20 years later, "the long shot" has apparently paid off. Now past 60 but still tall, broad and with a shock of thick, dark hair, Ron Branca will be stooped and silver-haired long before he could hope to replicate his father's remarkable tenure at the club. Not that he's aiming to, anyway. "My brother and I realized long ago we could never hope to duplicate what our father did, it would be impossible. He was a legend not just in Utah, but also nationwide. I imagine there are members who think I'm not the man my father was, but at least they don't say it to my face!" So laughs the 2011 Utah Section PGA Professional of the Year.

Don Branca is uniquely positioned to comment about the different challenges that both his father and older brother had to deal with during their respective tenures. "The profession has changed so much. My dad was an elite person at the club, almost a father figure, or a member of the family, which was typical in the "old school." But now head pros are often considered businessmen first and foremost, and are under greater scrutiny from the membership than might have been the case a generation or two in the past," states Don, who was a long-time head professional himself at several clubs in the Salt Lake Valley before changing his career course.

"Ron does a great job at The Country Club, he is very personable and well-liked by the membership. My sense is the membership is more demanding now than it was when my dad held the reins, he did things without anyone really questioning him. Ron is held to an accountability factor that didn't exist 30 or 40 years ago, things are more competitive in the golf business now, as they are in most any business, and I think he does a wonderful job in an environment that has changed dramatically since he and I were kids, or for that matter, even starting out as young professionals ourselves."

Amedee Moran is the club's longtime general manager, and his tenure has spanned both generation of Branca pros. "Though the business has changed so much in the 30 years I've been here, I first think of the similarities between father and son," offers Moran, who began as a dining room busboy. "Tee was and Ron is a perfect gentleman, at the club, away from the club, and on the course. Tee was a Utah golf treasure, one of a kind. In his era the pro was basically an independent contractor, who owned the shop, the range, the cart revenue, etc. Ron his done a wonderful job of bridging the gap between the eras, where now the head pro is part of the management team. In my opinion, The Country Club has been extremely fortunate to have these two men as head professionals over the last 70-plus years."

Continues Ron Branca, "We have more than 400 golf members here, and I would estimate that only about 10% of our current members were also members when Dad retired, as it's almost a generation ago. But they all know of him, through his reputation, through stories told by members, through the honors and accolades he's received. He had a great personality and people loved him. He turned pro at 18, and stayed in the business, at this club, in one capacity or another, his entire life. He was a fine

Tee Branca strikes a pose amidst the Wasatch Mountains

player, teacher, the club's chief recruiter and best ambassador. The club dedicated a bridge to him on the golf course and unveiled the plaque honoring him on a weekday afternoon. 300 members came out to the ceremony."

For Ron Branca and his long-serving staff, it must sometimes seem that nearly that many members and their guests roll through the shop or onto the course on particularly busy summer days. Reprising the same work ethic that served his father so well, he states, "We are here from light until dark, which is fine. I enjoy being a professional in a snowy climate, where we have what amounts to a nine-month season. I'm not sure how my colleagues manage it in locales where they play year round."

Branca manages with a staff that's been with him since Day One in the mid-90s. He gave up his coaching duties at The U as requested, hired three assistant professionals, and none of the trio has ever chosen to seek greener pastures. In fact assistant Wayne Fisher's association with Ron Branca predates The Country Club, as their relationship initiated as coach and player at The U. All told, they have been working together for nearly 40 years. "Part of the reason is the lack of good golf jobs in the region, and part of it is the fact that an assistant's job here is better and in some cases more prestigious that a head job elsewhere." What's left unsaid is the fact the Ron Branca must be an exceptional boss.

Exceptional is a word that also describes The Country Club's location, in the eastern portion of the Salt Lake Valley, but less than 30 minutes from the Wasatch Mountains. Not only is the club flanked by imposing peaks, but in springtime, individuals so inclined can ski morning through midday on sun-softened snow at world-class resorts in Park City, then drive a short distance to the valley and enjoy 18 holes in shirtsleeves.

Speaking of Park City, half-a-dozen golf clubs have sprung up in or around town in the last decade or more, each of them commanding considerable attention due to the course architect, topography, scenery, amenities, clubhouses, surrounding real estate communities or some combination thereof. Each offers competition to The Country Club, and some longtime members have either defected to one of the newcomers, or at least taken on a second membership in the higher elevations.

"We are managing to hold our own," concludes Ron Branca. "It's because we have a totally revamped infrastructure, both the golf course and clubhouse. It's because we have always attracted many of the prominent residents of the city, because we have a longer season down in the valley than they do in the mountains, and finally, because of our history."

With father and son combining for nearly 70 years in the head professional's job, which adds up to more than three-quarters of the club's existence since 1920, it is as unique a history as virtually any other golf club in the United States.

CURRENT OR FORMER HEAD GOLF PROFESSIONALS WHO WORKED FOR OR WERE COACHED BY RON BRANCA INCLUDE:

- Mike Bicker
- Scott Brandt
- Devin Dehlin
- Steve Elliott
- Wayne Fisher
- Clark Garso
- Jeff Green
- Brad Hansen
- Matt Johnson
- Craig Mackay
- Reed McArthur
- Gene Munk
- Eric Nielsen
- Paul Phillips
- Mike Richards
- Doug Roberts
- Steve Sharp
- Jeff Waters

Ron Branca's tip for fellow golfers:

Most amateurs don't seem to have an understanding of how important their alignment is relative to the target. Bad alignment can be the source of bad technique. Take the time to align/aim the face of the club to the intended target. Then simply keep the toe of your shoes parallel to your intended line. This parallel toe/body position allows the club to swing on the target plane.

The second problem seems to be that both men and women golfers never seem to use enough club for the required shot, they regularly come up short. I explain that in most cases when hitting an approach shots or when chipping, the more club you use, the less swing you need. The smaller the swing, the fewer things there are to go wrong. Good balance is usually the first benefit of using more club with less swing. Better balance leads to more consistent shots. Be sure to use enough club to get the job done!

Ron Branca's tip for fellow golf professionals:

I have had the honor and privilege of growing up in family that was totally involved in the golf business. My mother was state amateur champion and my father won many professional events and was a PGA member for 65 years. I have enjoyed my life in the golf business and have spent some 40 years as a PGA member. I know that those of you that have spent many years in the business have learned many valuable lessons. These are a few of my thoughts that might be helpful to professionals with less time in grade!

We all know how crazy and sometime frantic this business can be. I have learned not to take myself so seriously! I can now enjoy some of the craziness by talking through and attempting to calm potentially volatile situations. People want to have fun and sometimes it takes extra effort to help them do so.

I have a wide range of experience from owning and managing a club repair shop to serving on many rules committees and playing in local and national events. This versatility has kept me the expert at my clubs which I feel has been the difference in keeping or losing the top jobs. Keep fresh with continuing education and keep your golf game in respectable shape! Keep up on rules and changes and even put a grip on once in a while. Make time for yourself and family. This has been the hardest aspect for me. I always felt that I could put that off until tomorrow. Those tomorrows are running out. Regret is the worst!

Find a way to balance work with family. It is the most important thing you can do for a happy life in this business. When the time is right, try to give something back to the business. If you can do some of these things I know you will enjoy the ride, because it goes by way too fast!

Mark Brenneman
Las Vegas, Nevada

Mark Brenneman at Shadow Creek

Shadow Creek. It's a golf course as alluring and mysterious as its name. Visiting this verdant desert oasis is the province of a privileged few, most visitors to Las Vegas, even those who enjoy golf, don't even know it exists. It's a wonderful course in a magical setting, unlike most anything a first-time visitor has ever encountered previously. In that way it mirrors the eclectic career of its general manager and PGA professional Mark Brenneman, whose path to the position, much like his golf course, is one-of-a-kind.

Certainly not all, but the majority of golf professionals get into the business early on. They work in clubs or at courses growing up, gravitate to the business after college graduation, or shortly thereafter. Brenneman is an anomaly, and it's safe to say that there's not a single golf pro working in the world right now that came to a position of prominence using the blueprint that he did. His doesn't really resemble a career arc; it looks more like a career EKG.

Brenneman was a high school All-American, and was recruited to play on the golf team at Furman University in South Carolina. But he only lasted a year, as he felt golf was making him too one-dimensional as a person. He gave up the game, transferring to the State University of New York at Cortland, not far from his Syracuse roots.

He graduated with a BA in Economics on a Saturday, and began working on Wall Street at Dun & Bradstreet the following week. These were the 'dark years,' golf-wise, as Brenneman pursued and obtained his MBA, eventually becoming an international banker for Standard Chartered Bank. It was more or less an eight-year self-imposed hiatus from the game, through most of the 1980s.

"Just as I felt that golf made me too one-dimensional, I eventually began to feel the same way about banking and the financial markets," continues the pro. Trying to tap into his creative side, and fulfilling a long-term desire to live on the water, Brenneman moved to picturesque Sausalito, at the northern terminus of San Francisco's Golden Gate Bridge. He bought a sailboat, which was both his residence and weekend diversion. Tapping a connection he had made as a banker, he became an art dealer, selling paintings on commission in a San Francisco gallery. "It was a totally different world, not just the cross-continent location or my new living arrangements, but also the wholesale change from the security of a big banking job to living on my sales commissions."

When he wasn't sailing or selling, the once-and-future golfer began to slowly rediscover his love for the game, courtesy of the weekly skins games at the famed San Francisco municipal golf course, Harding Park. "I was holding my own against some strong players, and it reawakened my former desire to compete." Then in his early 30s, Brenneman figured it was 'now or never' in terms of competitive golf, and in the same bold fashion that saw him leave Wall Street for a San Francisco sailboat several years prior, he decided to move to Scotland, the better to focus on making a run at the European Tour's Qualifying School.

He based himself at the famed, yet isolated Machrihanish Golf Links, in the far western portion of the country, and began to play weekend competitions throughout Scotland and beyond. His six months overseas were fruitful, but the harsh reality of what he was up against was brought home to him in dramatic fashion. "One weekend I was paired with a fellow who shot 65-65. He told me he had just changed his putting grip from conventional to left hand low the day before! I was shooting 78-78, and realized I was out of my league, or as they say over there, I didn't have 'the bottle.'" His Q-School goal deemed unrealistic, the weather turning nasty in autumn, he returned to California.

Back in the Bay Area, the operative question for Brenneman was, "now what?" Reluctant to return to finance or fine art, he took a job as an assistant pro at Shoreline Golf Course down in Mountain View, California, in the heart of Silicon Valley, a full 45-mile drive from his home. These weren't banker's hours (nor art dealer's hours, for that matter.) If he was tasked with closing the shop at dark and opening at first light, rather than spending the better part of two hours driving to and from, more often than not he'd open his car's hatchback and sleep, however fitfully, in the parking lot. The nascent pro couldn't help but notice these peculiarly-named companies ensconced in modest strip mall office buildings as he made his way to and from the golf course. Little did he realize his career was about to take off also, maybe not on the same trajectory as Google and Yahoo, but in dramatic fashion nonetheless.

On the advice of a guest speaker in one of his PGA seminars, he sent out his resume to the ten finest clubs on his career 'wish list.' He never heard from Augusta National, Pine Valley, Merion or most of the others, but Spanish Bay, just a couple of hours south on the famed Monterey Peninsula, offered him an assistant's job. Thankful to be spared another cross-country move, and delighted that the facility reminded him greatly of the Scottish courses he so enjoyed, he quickly moved through the ranks at the Pebble Beach Company.

Within two years, Brenneman was named the head professional at the Del Monte Golf Course, the original of what eventually became four courses owned and operated by the Pebble Beach Company. "One of the reasons I got the job is they seemed to like my answer regarding how I would celebrate the club's centennial, which was in 1997," recalls the pro. "Having been exposed to so many old-line clubs in Scotland, I suggested a week-long celebration where we invited other hundred-year old clubs from around the world to come to the Peninsula and celebrate with us."

While Del Monte is a charming and historic venue, and the wellspring from which the other courses followed, (little-known fact: The original name for Pebble Beach Golf Links, which debuted in 1919, was slated to be Del Monte #2) when Brenneman was offered the top job at Spyglass Hill a few years later he didn't hesitate.

This was a higher profile position, and at Spyglass Brenneman was host pro at both the PGA Tour's ATT National Pro-Am and the 1999 US Amateur in short order. A bellwether day, not soon to be forgotten, occurred in June of 2000, shortly before the US Open was contested at Pebble Beach. The pro went out and caddied at Spyglass for six-time Major Champion Nick Faldo, and Microsoft founder Bill Gates. It was an eerie portend to the call that came to his office that very afternoon. "A headhunter called me and asked me to come to Las Vegas to interview for a job, but he couldn't tell me the name of the prospective employer," continues Brenneman, amused at the memory. "With no more information forthcoming I told him I had no interest, but he asked for my resume anyway, so I sent it along. When he called back the next day, he admitted it was Shadow Creek."

Though intrigued by the prospect of an interview, Brenneman wanted to hold off for a few weeks, until the Open furor had come and gone. The casino brass insisted he visit post haste, promising him he could be out and back the same day. So figuring it might be his only chance to see the legendary course, Brenneman took them up on their offer for a quick visit, and when it was offered shortly thereafter, took the job.

The differences between the quaint and cozy Peninsula and the garish excesses of Las Vegas were as dramatic as the temperature difference when the pro arrived for his interview. It had been 55 in Monterey. Vegas had 'double-downed'; it was 110. But the strange new world that the small-town Syracuse product had stepped into was evident on his first day on the job. He walked into the locker room at Shadow Creek to find but two souls: Michael Jordan and Charles Barkley. "It was so ironic that I spent four hours with Faldo and Gates the very day I got the call from Shadow Creek," reflects Brenneman, who took the reins as Shadow Creek's GM in August of 2000. "Lots of golf professionals, particularly those at higher-profile clubs, meet, shake hands and take a quick photo with luminaries as they come through. It's what I refer to as a 'dog-and-pony show.' But to have the chance to spend quality time with the types of gifted and successful people who visit us is definitely one of the highlights of the job."

Brenneman with former President George HW Bush

"I consider Mark to be one of the great club professionals I've met in my life," states influential Hollywood producer Jerry Weintraub, one of the heavy hitters regularly found in Brenneman's orbit. "He's a great companion, and an interesting man. He's not only wonderful to be with on the course, but you want to have lunch with him after that, and have a drink with him after lunch. I've been playing for more than 50 years," continues one of the first producers to be honored with a star on the Hollywood Walk of Fame. "I have memberships at numerous golf clubs at home and abroad, and am deeply involved in a business partnership that owns many more high-end private clubs. I have been exposed to hundreds of golf professionals over the years, and Mark is as good as they come."

Discretion is one of the operative words of Brenneman's post, so he prefers to speak in generalities. "I've been lucky enough to meet four presidents and one First Lady, and been honored to play golf with three of the four. I've played with Oscar winning actors and directors, and hall-of-fame athletes in all the major sports. There has been a wide array of newsmakers, celebrities, pop stars, rock stars, what have you. It's a unique situation I'm in, because these types of people are used to being the center of attention wherever they go. But when they come out here, because we are so limited in our play, and the environment is so relatively spacious, they are on their own, nobody knows who they are."

Shadow Creek still has the reputation of an invitation-only playground for the casino high-rollers. However in addition, the general public enjoys limited access, regardless of any proclivity they might or might not have about wagering massive sums at the green felt tables. The $500 green fee keeps most window shoppers at bay, despite the caddy fee and limo ride to and from the course included in the tariff. "We get more inquiries from potential visitors than we are prepared to allow on property," admits the pro. "The important distinction is we are an amenity to the casino, and don't run as a typical golf course operation per se. We are probably one of the very few golf facilities anywhere <u>not</u> looking to attract more customers, increase rounds played or boost revenue."

At most courses foursomes are the norm, but Shadow Creek sees plenty of twosomes and singles on property. Not hard to understand, as a round here is a real indulgence for many, and with so little pressure on the course it's easy for groups of any size to play without undue delay. "Our appeal is rooted in the fact we are the polar opposite of the environment most visitors are coming from," continues Brenneman. "The casinos are often busy, with lots of noise, and numerous distractions. Out here we offer a very quiet, relaxing, back-to-nature experience, with twenty thousand trees on property, all sorts of wildlife and birdlife on a meticulously maintained golf course. We are peaceful, tranquil and intimate, which aren't often the first three words that come to mind when you think of Las Vegas!"

"I don't think there's another job quite like this in all of golf," concludes Brenneman, who by virtue of his distinctive resume and background, is not quite like any other golf professional himself.

CURRENT OR FORMER HEAD GOLF PROFESSIONALS WHO WORKED FOR MARK BRENNEMAN INCLUDE:

- Chuck Dunbar
- Jin Park
- John Pietro
- Bill Sendell
- Dale Taylor

Mark Brenneman's tip for fellow golfers:

In his very English, Victorian accent actor Hugh Grant once told me, "Golf isn't taught very intelligently, is it?" The monthly cover of most every major golf magazine confirms this. I don't suggest those who teach golf deliberately try to mislead, nor are those who learn golf particularly slow. Still, why is golf so difficult to learn? If we can put a man on the moon, why can't we play the game with a reasonable amount of confidence? Why do some improve and others don't?

Perhaps after the fundamentals are realized (i.e., grip, stance, alignment and address) we tend to move too quickly from tip to tip to tip and this becomes confusing. I am not interested in adding to the confusion. Instead, I propose we move toward the physical sensation of swinging a golf club. It's a golf swing after all. By the simple act of swinging a club back and forth, back and forth, back and forth, a lot of things fall into place and other things, like position-related thoughts, which only serve to increase tension, fade away. People who do this find the game becomes fresher and they become more self-reliant. This seems to me to be a pretty worthwhile outcome.

Mark Brenneman's tip for fellow golf professionals:

Part of being a PGA member includes promoting the game of golf. And yet for those of us who are around golf courses on a daily basis, how many actually play less today than yesterday, less this year than last? There are reasons not to play which taken singly are negligible although when combined seem staggering. But to promote something we don't actually participate in is somewhat hollow and even hypocritical. Furthermore, the feeling and sight of just one well-struck shot simply will not go away. What are we waiting for? Disappointments, frustrations and obligations are all valid – just as valid as a high, soft fade into a setting sun. And this seemingly inconsequential moment has within it the potential to change our entire manner of living. Why would we not want to share this? Play the game.

Ron Castillo, Sr.
Oahu, Hawaii

Compared to other luminaries showcased within this text, the larger-than-life club pros with half-a-lifetime spent at marquee venues, Ron Castillo Sr. has a resume that at a glance appears a bit shallow. He spent a decade as a head professional at a semi-private facility, then another

Ron and Dorothy Castillo

decade as the owner of a retail golf store. But peer just slightly below the surface and it will quickly become apparent that Castillo has a rich and deep golf legacy, as deep as the waters of the blue Pacific that's surrounds his native Oahu, in the Hawaiian Islands.

Despite the accolades he's received, the awards he's won, his position as one of the grand old men in Hawaiian golf history, Ron Castillo Sr. has a living, breathing legacy: His five children, Rick, Lori, Ron Jr., Michael, and Joey. They are all accomplished players, highly regarded, and are either currently or have previously been, like their father, consummate golf professionals.

Rick is the oldest of the five siblings, and has had the most traditional and enduring career as a golf professional. He followed his dad to the Waialae Country Club on their home island of Oahu, where he worked during high school and college, and then spent more than 25 years at Wailea Golf Club on Maui, including nearly two decades as their head professional. "Even now in my 50s I often ask myself, 'what would Dad do?' as a father, as a husband and as a golf professional. Even though my decisions can differ from Dad's the question is still a reflex. I suppose it reflects my respect for his knowledge and wisdom," explains Rick, currently the Director of Golf at The King Kamehameha Golf Club and Kahili Golf Course on the island of Maui. He is quick to point out it's not just the Castillo Clan that seeks out knowledge from their father.

"When it comes to the history of golf in Hawaii, Dad is the first person that much of the golfing community and I would seek for information. He's now past 75, but his memory for facts and storytelling is among the best of our elders," continues the former PGA Merchandiser of the Year. "Because he is one of the founders of the Hawaii Golf Hall of Fame, to ensure continuity I also joined the selection committee, and have served as chairman for many years. Dad still serves on this committee, and needless to say, his opinion carries the most weight in the selection process. I have a duty to uphold his standards."

No one has held up the family's playing standards to the degree of Lori Castillo, a three-time USGA Champion, who eventually followed her dad into the Hawaii Golf Hall of Fame. "Our parents had five kids in six years, so this kept them very busy and resources did not allow them to spoil us with costly activities," recalls Lori, who currently serves as University of Hawaii's women's golf coach.

"Dad introduced us to golf, one by one as time, money, and opportunity permitted. I remember my parents taking us to the beach one day a week and then the park to shoot baskets or throw a football other times. Sports and physical activity were a part of our every day life. We all played sports (baseball, volleyball, basketball, football) through middle school. And when we got a bit older it was time for dad to bring us to the course and finally introduce us to golf."

"When he was a working golf professional, we were invited to tag along on weekends, holidays, and summer to the course. With five of us there, we were put to work doing odd jobs around the clubhouse and driving range until the tee opened up at Hawaii Kai's executive course. We played that course over and over and really honed our short game skills. Together I'm not sure how many holes-in-one were made but I made five on my own," reminisces Lori, a former U.S. Girls Junior Amateur Champion who also won the U.S. Women's Amateur Public Links championship back-to-back in 1979 and 1980. "I'm sure many daughters feel this way about their dad, but my father is an extraordinary man."

Ron Castillo Sr. returns the complement to his Stanford-educated daughter. "Lori is successful at everything she does. I think if I had five Lori's and formed a company, I'd be a millionaire. She's meticulous. She crosses all the T's and dots every 'I.' She doesn't skip any of the steps. It doesn't come easy for her, she just works harder than most people."

Spoken as someone who knows a bit about hard work himself. He's a Hawaii native, but not a native Hawaiian, as his dad was born in the Philippines, and is not of Polynesian descent. "My father was a golf nut, and introduced me to the game. I became a caddie, and in those days we had very limited access to the course. I became good enough to captain the high school golf team, but that was the extent of my on-course achievements."

Not quite the case, according to his namesake. "Dad was a great local player," offers Ron Jr., the middle child. "He won lots of tournaments on the islands, and played in a half-dozen Hawaiian Opens. He and I completed a rare feat in the Aloha Section. We both won the stroke play and match play championships in the same year! I caddied for him when I was a teenager, and then he caddied for me more than 25 years later when I won them both myself," explains the Kauai-based teaching professional. "But beyond trophies, it was the golf culture he established in our house. Dad surrounded himself with other passionate golf enthusiast, both friends and acquaintances. Years later, when I ventured outside these golf circles, I was astonished how people were disconnected from the game. For the first 15 years of my life I thought everyone played golf or knew someone who played, or their family played golf. Golf was and still is a lifestyle with our family. It's just something we enjoy without question."

Before the kids arrived, Ron Castillo Sr. had a short stint at the University of Hawaii, which preceded four years in the Air Force, then a couple of years as a Honolulu policeman. After that he became the general manager of his dad's extensive chain of barbershops before finally getting into the golf business several years later.

He began as an assistant pro at a military course called Fort Shafter, where he had previously worked as a caddie and pro shop clerk, then moved to a similar position at Waialae Country Club, longtime home of the PGA Tour's Sony Open. It was after three years as an assistant when he received his first, and what was to be his sole head pro position, at Hawaii Kai golf club. A decade later he became the proprietor of a retail store called Golf Action Hawaii, which he ran for another decade prior to his retirement. Since selling his golf store, he has remained close to the game by giving lessons to a loyal cadre of students.

All five Castillo kids make their living in the golf business

Castillo Sr. was one of the founders and served as first president of the Aloha Section of the PGA of America, once they broke away from the southern California chapter where they had long been enmeshed. "There are 41 sections in the country, and ours was the last to be recognized by the PGA, back in the mid 70s." He was the first member of his section to be a member of the PGA Executive Committee, he has also been the Aloha Section Player of the Year, Professional of the Year, and one of the founders of the Aloha Section PGA Hawaii Golf Hall of Fame, and was inducted as a member of the hall some 25 years later.

Above and beyond everything he has done for golf in the 50th state, what he has done for his five offspring is equally impressive. "I was a little kid, but I can still remember the day my mom drove me to the golf course for my first 15-minute lesson with dad," offers Joey, the youngest sibling, who covers the entire state of Hawaii as a longtime field representative for PING golf equipment. "I didn't know it at the time, but he was setting me up for wanting more. This was my very first lesson in golf about planting the seed correctly. He told me that day that I should only play this game if I'm having fun, and I use that same philosophy to this very day with my junior golfers and their friends."

"My Dad has been a great father, leader, teacher and number one golf instructor," continues Joey, a longtime PGA member. "I've been fortunate to have had the opportunity to play golf with him twice a week for nearly a decade and watch him shoot his age regularly. He always insisted we play the game for ourselves, not for anyone else, never quit, play against the course, and give your best effort. These basic guidelines have given me a large network of friends, a free education, and a career that I love."

The family patriarch has played in five Major championships throughout the continental United States, many significant events in Australia, but appreciates his native Hawaiian courses as much as anywhere else in the world. "It's always warm, it's almost always sunny, the trade winds are usually blowing. But how magical Hawaii is as a golf destination isn't really for me to say, I grew up here, so this is what I am used to. I will leave it to visitors to comment on the thrills of playing golf in these islands."

What has to thrill Castillo Sr., or at the very least give him a feeling of deep satisfaction, is how all of his children decided to follow his example. "I guess it is a very nice complement to me that my children all decided to get into the industry. I suppose they looked at me, and liked what they saw."

While there have been thousands of accomplished players who have played in a smattering of important events through their lifetimes, the list of those who exerted such a complete and comprehensive influence on the succeeding generation is far shorter. Explaining how he turned five kids into lifetime converts, all of whom are making their livelihood from golf, Castillo Sr. offers, "I had a reputation as an excellent instructor, and served for a long time as the vice-president of the Hawaii Junior Golf Association, so I saw plenty that was good, and plenty that wasn't so good between parents and their children. My rule of thumb was simple: I wouldn't give advice to my children unless they asked. I only requested that they conducted themselves honorably, and act like gentlemen and gentlewomen on the course. Whether they decided to go into golf or not, I only requested that they become an asset, not a liability, in their chosen profession."

Michael Castillo marvels at the deep entrenchment he and his siblings have in the game, even though their dad never pushed them. "I have pre-teen daughters, and they have a very casual interest in golf," asserts the former Director of Golf at two of Hawaii's iconic resorts, Princeville and Poipu Bay. "Even though it was stressed that we were to play golf for ourselves, and nobody else, in the back of our minds we were trying to impress our dad, and I suppose we all got into the business because we looked up to him so much."

Michael, now an assistant professional on the mainland at prestigious Big Canyon Country Club in Newport Beach, California, theorizes the family's fascination with golf was only partially due to dad's charismatic influence. "When we weren't in school or playing other sports we went to the golf course. But my kids and their cousins have far more distractions. Back in the 70s, we could find the same entertainment value in an empty cardboard box as kids today find with their iPad or smart phone!"

Ron and his wife Dorothy have eight grandchildren and one great-grandchild, but, agreeing with Michael, he admits that the golf gene hasn't really proceeded to the third generation. "I don't know why, other than the fact there are far more diversions available to young people today," concludes Castillo Sr. "But golf has become a way of life in my family, and a passion for my children. I suppose I have something to do with that, and I am very pleased with the way they have all turned out."

Ron Castillo's tip for fellow golfers

Golf is a unique and special game. It is the only game I know where you are expected to call an infraction of the rules on yourself, even if the result could be unfavorable. I know of no other sport where your behavior is critical to personal image. Your persona is a reflection of your character.

Success in this game is more than managing tactics and technique. It is more about managing yourself and all the emotions that come with expectations and disappointments. Golf is a challenge that will last a lifetime. The joy that comes with one good shot makes up for all the others.

Ron Castillo's tip for fellow golf professionals

The head golf professional is the "shepherd of the flock." He's the mentor to his staff and the role model for how the game is played. Therefore, he should strive to be the authority on all things concerning the industry of golf. He is a major influence in the integrity and traditions of the game.

John Dahl
Fargo, North Dakota

North Dakota winters have much in common with the type of chocolate nutritionists recommend: Both are dark and bitter.

It's not easy being a golfer in the so-called Peace Garden State. (And a more obscure state nickname simply doesn't exist.) Arctic conditions prevail from Halloween 'till Easter. The springtime snowmelt means the rivers rise and serious flooding is a distinct possibility across the northern plains, flat as a

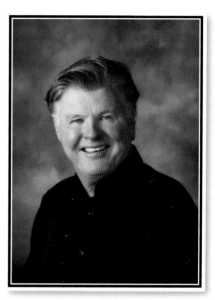

John Dahl--Fargo's Finest

cookie sheet. Yet golf survives, even thrives at places like Oxbow Country Club in Fargo, where head professional John Dahl has been ensconced for more than 30 years.

Though he didn't take up the game until he was nearly 40 years old, John's father Obert Dahl worked himself down to a 3-handicap, and was decades ahead of his time in terms of "video analysis." "In the late 1940s my mom used an old-fashioned movie camera to film dad's swing as he hit balls into blankets in the basement," begins the esteemed pro, chuckling at the memory. "Golf and golf instruction was part of the conversation at home from when I was just a small boy, and being able to play was a privilege," states Dahl, who has given in excess of 30,000 lessons. "I spent two full years on the range before my dad allowed me on the course, from ages eight to ten, just practicing with a cut-down 4-wood."

Dahl has a reputation as a 'tough-love' type of teacher, making a point of telling his students not what they want to hear, but what they need to hear. The technique is remarkably effective, as fully half of the 300 members at his Fargo club maintain single-digit handicaps. It's impressive on any level, but more so in the northern hinterlands where the golf season takes its sweet time to commence and where an icy curtain brings the year to an abrupt close. But he came by his no-nonsense attitude honestly, as the Dahl Doctrine was passed down from father to son.

"I was a serious hockey player in high school, and was recruited to play at the University of North Dakota. But I took 50 stitches to the face my senior year, had severe shoulder injuries, and my dad, knowing I had no NHL future, told me I couldn't play, that my future was in golf, and I should get to it before I ruined my body. He called the hockey recruiter, and told him not to bother even coming to the house," recalls Dahl, who despite the autocratic manner in which he ran the family, admired his father's unwavering work ethic. Obert Dahl worked on the railroad for nearly 50 years, and never took a sick day.

It was the same nose-to-the-grindstone mentality that elevated John Dahl from a mid-70s shooter to a par-breaker in a grueling winter of hard work. John played golf at North Dakota State, and turned pro after his junior year. As newlyweds in 1975, he and his wife Rachel, also a Fargo-area native, moved to Naples, Florida, with $600 to their name. "We drove my Pinto down, got an apartment for $115 a month, with no telephone or television.

Rachel was making a dollar an hour waiting tables at Pizza Hut, and I took $400 of our money to join a local golf club."

At a glance it sounds like grounds for a quickie divorce, but Rachel knew her driven husband would work dawn 'till dusk to hone his game, which he did. A local pro named Bill Lewis provided Dahl with some pointers, and when Dahl returned to Fargo the following year with four or five shots excised from the scorecard, he was now a force in the local section. It's instructive to note that going from 85 to 80 is exponentially easier than going from 75 to 70, but that is what Dahl accomplished during his Florida foray.

"I spent three years playing mini-tours, knowing my future was as a club professional and swing instructor," explains Dahl, named eight different times as one of GOLF Magazine's Top 100 Teachers. "I wanted to be a well-rounded club professional, and knew that playing in tournaments under pressure would advance me in all aspects of instruction."

He spent three years as head professional at Watertown Country Club, in the South Dakota town of the same name, before taking the job at Oxbow, ten miles south of his hometown, in 1982.

Dahl paints a vivid picture of the typically avid North Dakotan. "Everyone knows the season is short, so they are raring to go once we open. They play with gusto, they play often, some of our members post upwards of 80 rounds annually, which is impressive in a year-round climate, never mind in a six-month season." He also defers some credit for his expansive stable of accomplished players. "Maybe it's the fresh air, the wide open spaces, the Scandinavian heritage of so many residents, but whatever the reason, I seem to get lots of good athletes as students, who are strong, coordinated and flexible. Improving their games is easier than those who are less physically gifted."

Dahl laying the groundwork for another potential college scholarship

He might well be describing his daughters, both of whom earned full-ride golf scholarships. Erica, now pursuing a PhD, played at Iowa State. Her sister Jeana, in law school, played at Wisconsin. John and Rachel Dahl's two dolls opened plenty of eyes in Fargo, and well beyond, and provided proof positive that spending constructive time on the lesson tee was a recipe for saving tuition money, and lots of it. Dahl estimates his younger students have earned in excess of a million dollars in college scholarships. "It got to the point where I was telling eager junior high and high school students and their parents that they wouldn't be paying for college if they could get their swing speed up over 90 mph, which translates into increased distance."

There was no distance greater than the young gal from far-off Williston, North Dakota, who drove seven hours each way with her mom several times a summer to take lessons from Fargo's finest. She met Dahl at a mid-winter golf clinic as a pre-teen, and when he complimented her on her swing, she was insistent her parents book lessons with him as her birthday present. Apparently the cost of replacing the car tires due to all that excess mileage was well worth the golf scholarship she eventually won to Grand Valley State in Michigan.

"John has a great eye, and a true passion for teaching. He helped me improve beyond my wildest dreams," offers his good friend and longtime student Mike Podolak. Before they began working together, Podolak managed to qualify for the 1981 US Amateur, then was devastated by his sky-high rounds of 78-90 at the treacherous Olympic Club in San Francisco. What a difference a couple of years make. Working diligently with John Dahl, the Fargo insurance agent improved to the point of winning the US Mid-Amateur in 1984, playing on the 1985 Walker Cup Team and earning an invitation to the Masters in 1986. "Although he's particularly adept at improving tournament-caliber players, he can also help anyone improve. We've been working together 30+ years, and I'm still a 'plus' handicap. He's one of the finest golf instructors anywhere."

Despite his reputation as a teacher, Dahl points out he's not wearing out a trench on the range every day. He takes care of his shop, takes members overseas, does the super-popular "Mystery Bus Tour" with his eager flock of golfers every year, where they gather in the parking lot with clubs and an overnight bag, and head off to an only-revealed-at-that-moment golf destination. "I usually only teach three lessons a day, but I do plenty of five or ten minute fixes also, in the shop, in the grill room, wherever I'm asked."

He admits with a candor uncommon to his profession that part of his great success as a teacher feeds his own ego, almost like a power trip. Like a Svengali, he can methodically transform a timid, uncomfortable and awkward high-handicapper into a competent golfer that plays the game and interacts with peers in a confident manner. "I promise that new member, that 25-handicapper, if he is willing to jump in the cage with me, and work on his game in the manner prescribed, he will drop to an 18 that first year, then down to 12 the next season, and then single digits after that. I make the promise because I've never been wrong, and the member invariably gains confidence immediately, because they know positive results are in the offing, and their skills are bound to improve. So it has a short term, and a long term effect."

Despite the lack of downhill skiing available on this oft-frozen tundra (as the humorous billboard says crossing the state line: Welcome to North Dakota—our mountain removal project is complete!) Dahl, himself a skier, sees the corresponding analogy as valid. Just as a beginner is limited in who they can ski with, sticks mostly to the bunny trails and has to scrutinize the trail map to insure they don't find themselves on a trail beyond their ability, so too does a beginning or lesser skilled golfer. They are intimidated by the course, their inexperience and the better players at the club. Once a degree of competence and confidence is instilled, much like an advanced skier who needn't consult the trail map constantly, the improving golfer is less concerned with who they play with, and how they'll perform during the round.

For 25 winter seasons, Dahl wielded the same unique power as the head teaching professional for a private golf school called Executive Golf Limited, which conducted classes in warm-weather locales like Hawaii, California and Florida. "It was a great opportunity given to me by friend and respected professional Jim Ahern, who founded the operation, but I was regularly in the firing line."

As the school's name implied, it was the province of power brokers, and the clientele included upper management types from blue chip and Fortune 500 companies, including the occasional president or CEO. "These are people who are used to telling others what to do, and not being told what to do. It might have been a slight exaggeration, but to set the tone early I would begin lessons by telling them, 'I know everything about golf, and you know nothing.'"

His brash personality in combination with his expertise was a breath of fresh air for many of these business titans, surrounded as they are by 'yes men' all day. It was no wonder that Dahl developed a loyal following, all sorts of repeat business and genuine friendships with a range of different heavyweights.

For the last decade or so Dahl has spent winters teaching at a lovely facility well north of Scottsdale called Quintero, in a little burgh called Peoria, Arizona. Some of the Oxbow Country Club faithful have followed him to the southwest, as there are smatterings of North Dakotans who, like Dahl, want to escape the Big Chill, and purchased memberships at his winter retreat.

"Above all else, teaching is my thing," continues the three-time Teacher of the Year in the Minnesota PGA section. "Whether it's helping high school kids improve and get a scholarship, helping women who can barely get the ball in the air learn to enjoy the game, or assisting strong players take the next step and become more competitive. What perplexes me is when I see golfers who are clearly not enjoying themselves, sitting morosely in the 19th hole post-round, yet don't seek out help."

He pauses for a beat, and then finishes by saying, "I wish I could make them all understand that instruction doesn't have to be difficult or intimidating. I can really help them have more fun, hit the ball better than they can imagine and lower their scores. All they need to do is ask."

CURRENT OR FORMER HEAD GOLF PROFESSIONALS WHO WORKED FOR JOHN DAHL INCLUDE:

- Bob Cahill
- John Hamilton
- Greg Hiller

John Dahl's tip for fellow golfers:

It's long been said that golf is a game of opposites. You hit down to make the ball go up, you swing easy to hit the ball hard. Here's an "opposite" you've probably never heard: The more a player's head drops down during the set up, the higher their handicap goes up.

The main reason for the incorrect positioning on the top of the backswing is that the golfer's head is often poorly positioned at address. When you watch a professional or a very good golfer from a front on view, you will be able to see a good portion of his or her face. On the flipside, when you watch a higher handicap from the same position, the top of their head is visible, but their face can't be seen. Unfortunately, this inverse relationship is so harmful it destroys any chance of making a good backswing. If your head is buried into your chest in the set up, it is almost impossible to move behind the ball as needed during your backswing. As a result, your upper body is either stuck on top of or in front of the ball at the completion your backswing. It is this undesirable position that creates poor shots—tops, fat shots, pull-slices, and pull-hooks, among others. Therefore, next time you stand up to the ball, try glancing down at the ball with your "face showing" like a good golfer versus staring down at the ball with your "face hidden" like a bad golfer.

John Dahl's tip for fellow golf professionals:

I truly believe that "a single picture is worth a thousand words." Therefore, I rely heavily on video feedback when teaching. I teach enough that investing in video equipment makes sense. But for golf professionals who can't justify the cost, there is a simple and easy answer—the iPad. The iPad has made recording swings fast, easy, and affordable. For roughly $500 dollars and a couple of $5 apps, you can do everything that previously cost a few thousand dollars.

The iPad has even changed the way I teach. For instance, when I finish teaching a lesson, I send each student a collection of swing highlights, which focus on chipping, pitching and putting. That way the student can download the swing clips onto their home computer and can easily refer back to them. I also save a copy of the students swing for my reference. That way I can pull up the swing during our next lesson if needed.

Not only do I use the iPad to record swing clips of the students I teach, I also use the iPad to capture and catalog video clips of perfect grips, set up positions, backswings and follow-throughs. Lastly, I have found that the iPad makes it easy to capture some candid on-the-course moments during a tournament or on men's day. After taking some video, I can plug in my iPad to the 70 inch flat screen in the bar-and-grill and play back all of the good swings, great shots and a few humorous moments. Not only has this new device brought about fun, I know that using this multi-model form of teaching with my students has forever changed the learning curve associated with learning to play golf successfully. I am convinced that even a golf instructor with little experience will feel much more confident with this simple and useful tool.

Bob Ford
Oakmont, Pennsylvania

"I was in the right place at the right time. Twice."

So begins the estimable Bob Ford, who uses little more than ten words to explain his unique employment situation, and in so doing showcases the self effacing wit which is just one of the many positive traits that has lead him to the apex of his profession.

Ford is the head professional at two of the most acclaimed clubs in all of golf. Oakmont, outside of Pittsburgh, and Seminole, in the

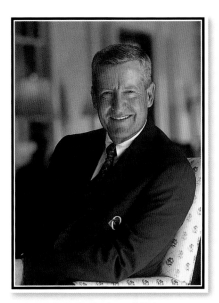

Bob Ford---Ace of Clubs

South Florida town of Juno Beach. When he turned 50 some years back he longed to add a third job to his resume, but his attempt to qualify for the Champions Tour never came to fruition. It has been an ongoing theme of frustration in an otherwise-charmed professional life, the close-but-not-quite gestalt that has kept him from consistently competing in the game's highest echelon. Ironic, considering his place in the highest echelon of the game has long been secure.

Originally from the Philadelphia area, Ford moved west with his family to Pittsburgh just after his high school years. An avid player, Ford tried to land any job at all at Oakmont in time for the 1973 US Open, just to soak in the ambience. The teenager found three weeks of temporary work at the club that summer, and was first exposed to legendary Oakmont pro Lew Worsham.

Worsham began at Oakmont in the spring of 1947, took a bit of time off that summer to win the US Open by beating Sam Snead in a playoff, and continued his club pro duties for 32 years. Between running the Member-Guest and selling sweaters, Worsham found time to win nine other PGA Tour events, was the Tour's leading money winner one year and went undefeated on a Ryder Cup team. So it's not hard to understand Ford's never-ending desire to make it as a Tour pro—his role model came to work every day in the same shop.

When he graduated from the University of Tampa in 1975, Ford went to work full-time as an Oakmont assistant. "I had never considered being a club pro, it never crossed my mind. I always wanted to play for a living," states Ford. "I figured if I couldn't play at the Tour level, being at a club like Oakmont would possibly lead to a member offering me a job to sell steel, or insurance."

When Lew Worsham retired in 1979, the club's board chose Ford as his successor, bypassing the pro's son Rick, who had far greater tenure than the relative newcomer. Explains Ford, "It was an awkward situation, but Rick, who now owns a driving range in North Carolina, and I have remained friends to this day."

The differences between his summer and winter jobs are quite distinct. Oakmont, despite its incredible historical significance, reflects Pittsburgh. It's a lively, full-service country club, lots of kids and families, pool and tennis an important part of the equation. Seminole, by contrast, is solely a golf club.

Oakmont has hosted as many important championships as it has holes on the course. 18 separate times the game's finest players have gathered for US Opens, US Amateurs, PGA Championships and the like. Three particularly incandescent moments would include Jack Nicklaus winning his first Major, besting hometown hero Arnold Palmer in the 1962 US Open, Johnny Miller's incredible final round 63 to come from well behind and win the 1973 US Open, and Bob Ford's 26th place finish as the host pro in the 1983 Open. More on that last one in a moment.

Seminole has only hosted high level amateur competitions. Though one could effectively argue that any run-of-the-mill club event at Seminole is a high level amateur competition. Its membership roster is peppered with former USGA champions, and those who compete internationally at the game's most prestigious levels. It is long standing tradition that dictates all persons must be off property at 6 PM, and if there's two hours of daylight left, a player is on the 17th green with a chance to set the course record, or at least record his or her best-ever score, more is the pity. The club serves lunch only, no dinner, no breakfast. There is a gorgeous pool overlooking the course, but it's innately understood that it's not only off limits, it is also not to be lounged around.

Long before he ended up at Seminole and 30-odd years ago, the host pro owned the US Open concession, and Ford knew it would soon be Oakmont's turn to host in 1983. Just a year after he took over the top spot in 1979 he qualified for the 1980 Open at Baltusrol in New Jersey, and when he wasn't playing or practicing, he was actually working in the merchandise tent for host pro Bob Ross. "I picked his brain on merchandising, and wanted to learn as much as I could." Ford did the same thing (working the tent, not playing) in the succeeding two years, and was ready when the Open returned to Oakmont in 1983. "My innovation was the mail-order concept. We ran ads in various golf publications, using Bobby Clampett as the fashion model. The sales results were so impressive it didn't take long for the USGA to take over the mail order business for themselves."

Ford also qualified for and played in that home Open, finishing 26th. When asked which was a greater windfall, the 26th place check or the receipts accumulated from all of that mail-order merchandise, Ford cracks, "never mind my top 30 finish. The concession, including the innovation of the mail order, was worth more than the first place check they gave to Larry Nelson!" The Open returned to Oakmont in 1994, and Ford was denied entry to the field by a whisker, losing in a playoff. He describes it as "one of the worst experiences of my competitive life." He was assuaged somewhat in being the last host pro to ever own the merchandising tent, even though he was by now sharing profits with Oakmont.

Better news was on the horizon about five years later, when Ford was asked to become the head professional at storied Seminole. "There are several Oakmont members who are also at Seminole, and being invited down to golf with them over the years allowed me to meet many other members. Conversely, there were plenty of Seminole members who visited Oakmont, so I really started to become familiar with the club," recounts the 1987 PGA Professional of the Year.

When after 28 years on the job Jerry Pittman (who spent many concurrent summers as the head pro at esteemed Saucon Valley in central Pennsylvania) decided to retire as Seminole's head pro in 1999, Ford was asked to take over. There was no formal interview process, no resume submission or executive search. The club lost a quality man, and had no reservations about who was the best candidate to replace him. Following in the footsteps of Tour-

Johnny Miller watches Bob Ford in action

hardened pros seems to be Bob Ford's lot in life. "One year as a club pro Jerry played in all four Majors," says Ford with admiration, "and that same year finished in the top ten at The Masters. His resume as a player was very impressive." The Oakmont brass renegotiated his contract to reflect the fact the Ford would be spending six months in both Florida and Pittsburgh going forward.

"Oakmont is a 24/7 job, open every day, for breakfast, lunch and dinner," continues Ford, outlining the differences in his two posts. "We have 400 families, which means about 600 or 700 members, and they play tennis, shoot skeet, have a swimming pool that's actually in use, that sort of thing. The biggest difference is the governance. It's a typical democratic system, with board members being elected to three-year terms to sit on the various committees. It's the normal hierarchy. At Seminole, there are no committees at all. Everything is decided by one man."

Ford is referring to the 'benevolent dictatorship' concept, the most well-known examples being the decades-long tenures of Clifford Roberts at Augusta National, or John Arthur Brown at Pine Valley, two of the finest private golf clubs in existence.

Ford spells out some of the other disparities between his two jobs. "Oakmont is much busier, we do twice as many rounds as Seminole. At Oakmont you can show up in the late afternoon, grab a cart and go out and play six or eight holes. That doesn't happen at Seminole, where you generally come out to play a full round, and walk with a caddy. It's a short day, because members don't come on property until 8:30 in the morning, and must be off property by 6:00 in the evening."

Another difference is the type of member each club attracts. Other than fifty national members, Oakmont's membership comes almost exclusively from Pittsburgh. While there are scads of excellent golfers at Oakmont (they have to be; considering it's one of the world's most demanding courses being a member is a real trial-by-fire) Seminole draws a national, even international set of serious, competitive players. There are some 20 USGA champions on the membership rolls.

Early in his career at Oakmont, before the PGA Tour went to its all-exempt format in the mid-1980s, Bob Ford spent significant time and energy during wintertime trying to Monday qualify for that week's Tour event. "The club was always very generous and supportive of me," he recalls. "They never begrudged me my desire to try and play competitively, and not once did anyone question me regarding the time I was putting into my golf game." Not surprising, considering the understandable pride the club had taken in the success of Ford's predecessor. "But I realized after a few years and repeated attempts and repeated failures to make a go of it that I had made the right decision in becoming a club professional."

Which is not to say Ford, who was the PGA Club Professional Player of the Year in 1988, doesn't know which end of a club to hang onto. Never mind the repeated US Open, Senior Open, PGA Championship and Senior PGA Championship experiences he's enjoyed, which helped to sate his thirst for top-level competition. A vignette that shows his ability and humility concurrently occurred one memorable afternoon several years back at nearby Latrobe Country Club, the western Pennsylvania course not far from Oakmont that Arnold Palmer grew up on, set the course record on, and now owns. With three holes left, Ford needed three pars to shoot 59, and best Palmer's course record by a single stroke. But when he won his match on the 15th green, he chose to walk off the course, rather than go for the record. When asked how the record would have been considered official since it was conducted at match play, and included conceded putts, Ford quips, "there were no concessions. All of the putts went in, which is probably always the case when you are on pace to shoot 59!"

Arnold Palmer has long appreciated all the positive attributes possessed by Ford, up to and including the fact he left his Latrobe CC record alone. "If you set out to describe the ideal golf professional, you couldn't select a more fitting person as a role model than Bob Ford," says Palmer. "I have known Bob since his days on Lew Worsham's fine staff at Oakmont Country Club and through the many years since then that he has served Oakmont and more recently Seminole as their head professional. He has a wonderful warm, low-key personality that reflects itself in the way he treats everybody he comes in contact with all the time. In fact, he often goes out of his way to make appearances at sports and club functions throughout the area. Let's not forget the fine playing record he has compiled locally and in national PGA club pro events, either."

Besides his playing record, Ford takes great pride in the copious number of young men he has mentored, and then sent off to run clubs of their own. 'I have had a huge advantage," he adds with a grin, "because I have been sending them off from two clubs, not just one!" He is equally pleased to have raised his family in a mostly normal fashion, despite the unusual job pattern. "For 25 years I lived on the 18th hole at Oakmont, the only house on the course. When I got the Seminole job the three kids were little and they came down to Florida for three months through winter, and were home-schooled by my wife, Nancy. Now that they are in their late teens and early 20s, with two away at school, we make our home down in Florida. While we are in Pittsburgh we live in another home in the town of Oakmont. The club uses our former home as a guest house."

"But if I were to pick the single best thing about these jobs, about being the head golf professional at these two wonderful clubs, it is being able to meet and befriend not only these distinguished members, but also many of their guests. It's really been a "Who's Who" experience, and the types of people I've met through the years have been incredible."

It is far easier to catalogue those luminaries whom Ford hasn't rubbed elbows with, as opposed to who he has. Elvis and the Ayatollah haven't been in his orbit, he's hobnobbed with a

Kennedy, but thankfully nobody named Kardashian. Suffice it to say that a red carpet roster of ball players, billionaires, power brokers, politicos, business titans, movie stars and jet-setters of all stripes have made their way to these golden realms in Pittsburgh and Palm Beach. In this digital age the desk-top Rolodex has gone the way of the buggy whip, but if Ford had one, it would be the size of a bowling ball, and carry the same weight.

"I wouldn't know what to do with myself if I didn't get up every day and come to one of these two jobs," concludes Ford. "I'm kind of one-dimensional. Other than my family, my whole life is golf."

And what a life it is.

CURRENT OR FORMER HEAD GOLF PROFESSIONALS WHO WORKED FOR BOB FORD INCLUDE:

- John Aber
- Billy Anderson
- Steve Archer
- Tim Bennet
- Adam Brigham
- Colin Campbell
- Jack Druga
- Sean Farren
- Matt Frietag
- Ryan Garrity
- Tom Gilbert
- Bill Hall
- Scott Jenkins

- Eric Johnson
- Adam Kushner
- Greg Lecker
- Anthony Malizia
- Jason Marciniec
- John Marino
- Rick Martino
- Chris Muldoon
- Gary Nye
- Michael O'Connor
- Nathan Olhoff
- Dave Pagett
- Paul Ramee
- Tony Romansky
- Don Sargent
- Andrew Shuck
- John Spelman
- Scott Sundstrom
- James Swift
- Steven Wright
- Joe Zinchini

Bob Ford's tip for fellow golfers:

Every golfer wants to shoot lower scores, but needs to be realistic with goals relative to the time commitment allotted to play and practice. In other words, 20 or 30 minutes on the range once a week isn't often going to lead to vast improvement. The best way to improve one's game is to seek the knowledge and friendship of a respectable PGA Professional in your area. There are a lot of people who gravitate to golf and will try to convince you of their teaching credentials, but be careful. There is a lot of misinformation out there.

On a related note, if you are a member of a club or frequent visitor to a public or resort course, take the time to introduce yourself to the professional and their staff. They will bend over backwards to satisfy you.

Bob Ford's tip for fellow golf professionals:

One of the most important but overlooked skills that golf professionals need to develop is accurate and comprehensive record keeping. This becomes especially significant over the course of a long career, and even more so if there are several job changes that occur over time.

You should use your lesson planners as your diary. Write down everything you did that day, including who you taught, who you played with, and anything unusual that might have happened. You will be amazed how many times you will refer back to it. Keep detailed records and file them by year. Keep track of staff, committee and board meetings and minutes, educational seminars, resumes, tournament results, and things of this nature. Be sure to take a staff picture each year and start an album of all of those you worked with.

These suggestions take very little effort, but over time will provide a comprehensive and accurate look at your entire career, and all the important people who were part of it.

Laurie Hammer
Boynton Beach, Florida

Most club pros approach their careers the way an accomplished chess player looks at the chessboard; they are continually anticipating their next move.

Laurie Hammer wasn't wired that way. Though other opportunities came his way from time to time, he chose to spend more than 40 years at Delray Dunes in Boynton Beach, Florida, before retiring in 2010. His was and remains a rich legacy; of professional

Laurie Hammer---"First" among equals

accomplishment, enduring friendships, personal satisfaction, wonderful memories, but tragically, also a deep sense of loss.

When you think of Laurie Hammer the word "first" quickly springs to mind. There are few professionals who compare with the commitment to excellence demonstrated by Laurie throughout his career. He was a first team All-American at the University of Florida his senior year. He was a successful graduate of the first-ever qualifying school, or Q-School class in 1965, where he obtained his PGA Tour card. He might be the first club professional to appear on the front and back cover of Golf World Magazine simultaneously, the former for a big tournament victory, and the latter as a fashion model. (And back in the day you would have thought you were looking at a doppelganger of actor Jeff Daniels, albeit decked out in a wild pair of 70's era golf trousers.)

Above and beyond all that, he was the first professional at Delray Dunes, built the first house in the development, which was, keeping with the theme, located on the first hole. Is it a stretch to say that Hammer was "first" among equals?

In his three-and-a-half year stint on the PGA Tour that preceded his life as a club professional Hammer won one event, an alternate-shot competition with close friend Dave Stockton. "I did fair, but not great," begins the distinguished, silver-haired pro. "When a friend of mine from college named Jack Cabler offered me the chance to become the head professional at Delray Dunes, where we also got in on the ground floor of the development, we decided to do so. In my mind I was committed to three or four years on Tour to see if I could make it, and when I didn't I was ready to walk away. I left the Tour with no regrets."

Certainly the greatest regret of his life was the untimely passing of his two-year-old daughter Cynthia, who died accidentally after falling off of a railing at the Atlanta Tour stop in the spring of 1970. More than 40 years later, Hammer still becomes visibly emotional about that awful day.

"I was leaning towards leaving the Tour anyway, and when Cynthia died it sealed the decision," continues Hammer. Adds his wife Marlene, "We lost our taste for the Tour life after that."

The home they built was the first of what eventually became 310 houses in the community, and Hammer's college teammate Bob

Murphy and his wife built directly next door. Murphy is a former U.S. Amateur champion who also amassed 16 total victories on the PGA and Champions Tours. "The Hammers are wonderful people and great neighbors. We've lived next door to each other ever since the beginning so that pretty much sums it up," states Murphy, a longstanding member of the NBC golf team. It was both couples first housing purchase, and neither has ever felt the need to move elsewhere. They have remained next-door neighbors for nearly 45 years.

There are a number of reasons Laurie and Marlene Hammer couldn't be convinced to leave Delray Dunes. These include the effortless commute to the office, (30 seconds by golf cart) their friendship with the Murphy's, their close relationship with golf course designer Pete Dye and his wife, Alice, who lived nearby and were part of the club's social fabric, and also the fact that their children Kevin and Julie were so happy and established.

In a situation that is highly unusual in the private club world, owing to his early real estate investment in the community, Laurie was actually a member of the club where he was employed as the professional.

Technically it means he could have played in the annual Pro-Member as a single, but in actuality, the Hammers enjoyed and still enjoy not only their membership, but also membership in the mutual admiration society at the club. After all, Palm Beach County is full of private club members with sizable bank accounts and matching senses of entitlement. But no such superior vibe existed at Delray Dunes.

"We have always been committed to treating our unique relationship with the Dunes with respect and we have enjoyed decades of friendships and professional satisfaction at this wonderful club," states Marlene Hammer, who ran the retail aspect of Laurie's pro shop for decades. "Honestly, much of our lives and so many of our friendships are intrinsically connected with these members and this club."

Hammer also spent 13 consecutive summers as the inaugural head professional at Keystone Ranch Golf Club in the Colorado Rockies. Moving the family to a pristine alpine environment at 9,000 feet of elevation to escape the sauna of a south Florida summer proved to be a wonderful mid-career interlude. One of the real beneficiaries of life in Colorado was son Kevin, who honed his formidable golf game at junior events in the intermountain west. "The thing that is really impressive about my father is how many different roles he has played, and how in my opinion he is so exceptional in comparison to many club professionals," states Kevin, a financial advisor and high-level amateur who several years ago was named one of the finest golfers on Wall Street by Golf Digest. The golf gene has been passed to a third generation, as Alexa, the oldest of Kevin and Karen Hammer's three children, is showing great promise on the local high school team.

"You would be hard-pressed to find many others who have set the benchmarks that my dad has. His All-American status at a golf powerhouse like Florida. Winning on the PGA Tour, and ten years later winning the Club Professional's Championship. He is a PGA Master Professional. He held two jobs concurrently, starting both clubs from scratch in Florida and Colorado, which isn't easy, despite the fact that one of the club's is always in the off-season. I'm favorably biased as his son, but by any definition he has had a uniquely successful career."

Another aspect of his success was the Delray Dunes Bethesda Hospital Pro-Am, a major fundraising event started and run by Hammer and his next-door neighbor Murphy for 40 years. They

Laurie and Marlene Hammer

have since passed the organizational reins on to former LPGA Tour stars Beth Daniel and Meg Mallon, who live in the area. But for decades many of the biggest luminaries on the PGA Tour would stop in on a Monday during the Florida swing, and put their skills on display to raise much-needed funds for the local hospital. "We raised in excess of 3.5 million dollars during our tenure," states Hammer with understandable satisfaction. What he leaves unsaid is the millions more raised in private donations by those who learned of the hospital because of their wildly successful annual Pro-Am.

One of the "regulars" who came to the Pro-Am consistently was Dave Stockton. "Laurie and I have been a real Odd Couple over the years," offers the two-time winner of the PGA Championship, among other career highlights. "I went to USC and he went to Florida, we live on opposite coasts, but we have been great friends, and so have our families, for a very long time."

Stockton, who captained the victorious US Ryder Cup team in 1991, continues, "We have shared great times and awful times. We won a team event together on Tour, and my wife, Cathy, was with Marlene when little Cynthia had that tragic accident. Through it all, we have stayed very close. He's a fine player, a wonderful teacher, and a great guy. There are few people I would trust to implement my putting techniques, which really only my sons and I teach. But Laurie is someone who understands golf so completely I would be comfortable with him doing just that. I've often visited him and Marlene in Delray Dunes, and his reputation at the club, and all he accomplished there during that amazing 40-year run, is second to none. He was the first guy in the shop in the morning, and always going above and beyond the call of duty with his members and their guests. When he told me he was retiring, I said what are you going to do with yourself? He's like me, neither of us can sit still!"

"The thing I loved best, and I suppose I miss most, is the constant variety of responsibilities and challenges of being a club professional," concludes Hammer, a member of the South Florida PGA Hall of Fame. "Whether it was teaching a member, working on my own game, playing competitively, taking members to dozens of tournaments around the world including hosting four golf cruises, running an event either for our membership or an outside group, along with Marlene coming up with creative merchandising strategies, running a demo day, taking on a new product line, trying a new promotion, the energy needed and the creativity employed to keep running and growing our large Pro-Am. There was never a dull moment!"

Since his retirement in 2010, Hammer continues to teach golf. He does corporate outings with friends Murphy and Stockton. He has relationships with several clubs in the area where he has a loyal and growing cadre of students at two nearby facilities; High Ridge Country Club, where he was given an honorary membership, and Winston Trails Golf Club. He is often found showcasing his still-formidable skills at the men's game at Quail Ridge Country Club, just across the street from Delray Dunes, where he was also given an honorary membership post-retirement as a heartfelt "thank you" for being such a great neighbor over the decades. The Hammers have traveled extensively and consider it a wonderful education process for his golf life, by playing famous and unusual courses all over the world. Spurred in part by their daughter Julie's career opportunities that have taken her and her husband Judd to live in Sydney, Australia and now London, Laurie and Marlene have visited nearly 60 countries to date, on every continent.

Hammer is hard pressed to find any bad memories of his more than four decades on the job. "Honestly, nothing really stands out." He pauses for a long stretch in reflection, and then murmurs unconvincingly about the fruitless task of trying to appease the occasional member who was perpetually dissatisfied, maybe a slight headache trying to enforce a dress code, or a niggling pace of play issue. All in all, it's not a very impressive list of grievances. "I am lucky to have the positive clearly outweigh the more challenging times, and I thank those members who have been supportive and generous in spirit to Marlene and me over the years."

Think about it: most of us couldn't go 40 days without something truly sticking in our craw; many couldn't last 40 hours, the truly irascible 40 minutes. Yet Laurie Hammer did just that for more than 40 years. It would be a real blessing if we could all develop and nurture such deep contentment in our lives.

CURRENT OR FORMER HEAD GOLF PROFESSIONALS WHO WORKED FOR LAURIE HAMMER INCLUDE:

- Tom Anderson
- Brendon Boyle
- Jason Brown
- Mike Dahlheim
- Ken Everett
- Jeff Hill
- Steve Keiser
- Harvey LaMontagne
- Brad McCallum
- Kevin Perkins
- Regi Starzyk
- Danny Thron
- Frank Vassalotti

Laurie Hammer's tip for fellow golfers:

This move involving the left shoulder will help promote consistently solid ball striking. (Lefties should do the same thing with the right shoulder)

At address make sure your torso has a slight tilt to the right, so your right shoulder is below the left. Be sure to get your weight on the inside of the right foot. Turn the left shoulder down and to the right for a super coil behind the ball. This same move for all shots including short game shots will make it so much easier to approach the ball shallow and level with a more inside-to-out club path. Longer shots at a more consistent trajectory will be the end result.

Laurie Hammer's tip for fellow golf professionals:

In this digital age, with almost everyone using computers, smart phones, and social media, a handwritten note can go a long way. It is important to stay in touch with your members on a personal level. Email is adequate, but whenever possible, take a few minutes to write a handwritten note or card, whether it's a brief overview of a recent golf lesson, a congratulatory note, a condolence card, or whatever the occasion. It takes a bit more effort, but the positive impact it makes with the end recipient is well worth the time it takes and the cost of postage.

MIKE HARMON
Beaufort, South Carolina

Around Secession Golf Club in Beaufort, South Carolina, he's known as "the Old Pro." A sign saying as much marks his designated parking space. But it's a real misnomer: Mike Harmon is still shy of his 60th birthday, and hundreds of his members were born years, if not decades, before he was.

"The name just evolved," Harmon says. "I was only in my early 30s, but that's what they called me."

Mike Harmon---The Old Pro

While the "old" designation is questionable, there's no disputing that Harmon is a pro. It's evident in the way he dresses, the manner in which he interacts with his nationwide cadre of members, the care he takes in running his pro shop, and the way he hits a golf ball.

Maybe the "old" moniker sticks with Harmon because he came on duty at Secession years before the golf course was even built. He's been Director of Golf from the get-go, and was instrumental at recruiting potential members from old-line clubs in the northeast, golfers he refers to as having "high golf IQs," to join the brand-new walking-only, caddie-only national club in the temperate Carolina Lowcountry.

"He was here before there was grass," marvels John Marsh, Secession's general manager since 2004. "It is he more than anyone who took the original vision of the club's founders, the idea of this national club with no carts and mandatory caddies, and made it a reality. It's Mike's charisma, his ability to relate to people, his natural likeability, that convinced hundreds of potential members to join a golf club when no course existed. At the beginning, all they had here was an overgrown island and a bunch of drawings. I've always said Mike could sell ice to Eskimos."

"I call Mike a game-changer. I know of nobody else in this business that has single-handedly made such a large impact and contribution to a facility." So explains his close friend John Farrell, the longtime Director of Golf at the internationally renowned Harbour Town Golf Links on nearby Hilton Head Island. "I've been in the business for about 30 years, have known Mike the entire time, and have never seen anyone better. If there's a better statesman or ambassador for the game, I haven't met him," continues Farrell, who has more than 20 years of tenure at Harbour Town.

"It's a beautiful place, a magnificent walk, always in fine condition, and beyond the golf, it's sitting on that back porch with your buddies post-round, having a drink and enjoying the wonderful view," Harmon says, explaining the reasons Secession has succeeded as a national club.

In the early days, while Secession's course was under construction, Harmon ran events and tournaments for his growing roster of members at other golf courses in the area. At one time, he did duty serving sandwiches and drinks from the caddie shack. Given his own rich history with Secession, the designation "Old Pro" fits Harmon as naturally as the low-slung golf course he oversees fits the marshland and tidal pools of its barrier island home.

"I knew that if this club worked out, that the golf director's job here would be one of the best in the country," Harmon says. He spent two years as the head pro at Moss Creek Plantation, just off of Hilton Head Island, before coming to Secession in 1987. "Not just monetarily, but as far as the environment and membership were concerned. Because we're a national club, our members only come down a few times a year. They can't wait to get here, and it's like having a reunion every week. One of the things I love best is that on many Saturdays I go out and play a few holes with several groups and catch up with them, finding out about their families, work, whatever. I just throw the bag on the shoulder with eight or nine clubs, and play three holes here, six holes there and so on, with at least three or four groups. I love Saturdays, no phones, no e-mail, just golf with great people."

Baseball was Harmon's original stick-and-ball interest, but he ultimately turned down a baseball scholarship at the University of Miami to concentrate on golf at Middle Tennessee State. Harmon received his first set of clubs from his grandfather as a preteen, and began playing at rudimentary 9-hole tracks near his Atlanta home.

"I grew up on these simple, non-irrigated, poorly maintained municipal courses, many of which no longer exist. They've since become public transportation centers and apartment houses. But they gave me an appreciation for firm and fast conditions, because they were brick hard in summer. It was really helpful to my development as a player, especially when I started going overseas," Harmon says.

Harmon has traveled to the UK some 50 times on golf excursions, including an appearance at the 2010 British Senior

Mike Harmon relaxing in front of the Secession clubhouse

Open at Carnoustie. He is a member of the St. Andrews Golf Club, and has nearly as many club pro friends there as he does stateside. "I'm a student of history, love the old feel of the courses and the clubhouses. I love the fact that golf has been played at St. Andrews for hundreds of years before our country was even founded."

He offers a word of caution to those who get caught up in the "once in a lifetime" gestalt that often characterizes those making maiden voyages to the cradle of the game.

"I often travel overseas with our members, and I try and urge them not to drink too much the night before playing one of the best courses in the world. I don't understand why you would want to tie one on before playing Muirfield, The Old Course or places as beautiful as Royal County Down or Old Head. You want to enjoy those rounds to the fullest extent, not merely survive them!"

Secession reflects the sensibility manifested in some of the great traditional clubs overseas. "They keep it simple in the UK, and don't get caught up in extraneous things like fancy food, over-the top service, fountains, marble," Harmon says. "This is one of the reasons golf is problematic in our country, because we make things too complicated. Even at the most elite clubs in the UK, it is simple. You can only get five things to eat, but you have a choice of 35 types of scotch and beer!"

"Lower maintenance standards don't necessarily mean poor conditions, they're just not perfect," continues the Old Pro. "The whole American ideal of a golf course grew out of the pristine, wall-to-wall green of the Augusta National model. While it is one of my very favorites in the world (partly because of the club's founder and my idol, Mr. Bobby Jones) it is hardly the model by which a normal club can function. Very few can afford that type of maintenance budget for their course. If I go somewhere and they tell me how good their wine list and sushi are, I know I'm in the wrong place. A Coke and crackers at the turn is just fine for me!

"It should just be about the golf," Harmon adds. "That's the footprint we have here at Secession. And that's why we've been able to attract the traditional guy who belongs to an old-line club in his home city, who comes down here for the weather, the camaraderie and the simplicity we offer."

There's no simpler word than 'no,' and much as Harmon would prefer to avoid it, using the word is one of the few downsides of the job. "It doesn't happen much but it is never easy," says Harmon with a shrug. "Having to tell people no, their guest cannot use a cart, we don't have a tee time, there isn't a caddy available, whatever. But great golf clubs maintain certain parameters and have the people in place to say 'no.' That is what makes them great. Accommodating everyone almost always comes back to bite you in the butt. Just look at Washington, D.C.!"

Half a lifetime ago, Harmon had a brief dalliance as a Tour pro. "I was slightly in awe of the other players on Tour when I got out there, and that's no way to make a living. My first tournament was the 1980 U.S. Open at Baltusrol. I practically wanted to go in the clubhouse and get autographs. A well-seasoned amateur or pro doesn't think that way."

Harmon played the Tour for three seasons, 1980-1982, and managed a few top 25 finishes. His game is still solid today, as evidenced by multiple PGA Section victories, and by qualifying to compete at the nearby PGA Tour stop at Harbour Town just a few years back.

"A friend of mine was the Director of Golf at Palmetto Dunes on Hilton Head in the early 80s, and he offered me a job for the winter. That's how I ended up in this area."

Tour pro might not have been Harmon's calling, but club pro certainly is. One of his fondest memories at Secession came when the annual Member-Member tournament was renamed The Harmon Cup in his honor. "When the bronze bust that's used for the clubhouse trophy was first unveiled, it brought tears to my eyes," he recalls fondly. "I couldn't speak, and that never happens!"

Above and beyond the affection and admiration of his 700+members, Harmon amasses industry accolades the way Liz Taylor once collected jewelry. He has been honored as Retailer of the Year—not surprising, as he does a tremendous amount of business in a cozy 500-square foot pro shop. He's a recent inductee in the Carolinas PGA Hall of Fame, and only the 41st member in its hundred-year history. Harmon has been honored as the Carolinas PGA Professional of the Year, and has been nominated for National PGA Professional of the Year.

One of his most prestigious honors is the National PGA Bill Strausbaugh Award, presented to a PGA Professional who distinguishes himself by mentoring his fellow PGA Professionals in improving their employment situations. At least ten former Secession golf professionals under Harmon have gone on to run their own businesses.

"Seeing the young men who came in here as assistant professionals learn, develop, and then go on to become head pros elsewhere has been extremely satisfying," Harmon says.

One of those who went furthest in the industry is Franklin Newell—though geographically, he's only a half hour down the road from Harmon, working as General Manager and Director of Golf at the highly-regarded Chechessee Creek Club in Okatie, South Carolina.

"One of the most important lessons he taught me was the importance of member relations," Newell says. "Bill Clinton wishes he could work a room like Mike. When Mike walks into a room he makes it a point to speak to everyone. It's not hard for him, because he is never at a loss for words. He always asks about family and their personal lives. He also constantly stressed to make myself available at all times to play with a group of members and guests, if even just for a few holes. The more you are able to play with them, the better you get to know them and the better they get to know you."

"He has this incredible ability to connect with people of all ages, all ability levels, whether he has known you for years or just met you," concludes GM John Marsh. "It's hard to think of Secession and not think of Mike Harmon. The two are practically synonymous."

John Farrell of Harbour Town deals with the general public at a high-end resort facility, as opposed to private club members and their guests, but theorizes the sensibility is the same. "We are charged with managing people's leisure time, and that's sacred, in some cases more valuable to them than money. Mike gets that, knows people don't come to Secession for a good time, they come for a great time, and he makes it happen. He is so consistent, so dependable and so personable that every time you see him, you think, I'm glad I ran into that guy."

One of the reasons Secession continues to succeed in an increasingly difficult private club environment is the fact that it is such a welcome retreat from the pressures of the "real world." But ironically, one of the most tragic real world events in recent American history gave Harmon and a large percentage of his membership an entirely different perspective on what is truly important. Jeff LeVeen and Stephen Roach were senior executives at Cantor Fitzgerald, and these two well-known and well-liked club members perished in New York City's Twin Towers on 9/11.

"One of the hardest parts of being established in one place for so long is the inevitability of great members passing away," Harmon says thoughtfully. "In my opinion it's an oversight that the PGA program never taught us about that reality. If a pro stays at a club long enough, he will see a great number of his members pass away, and that is always difficult. I miss so many of them, and of course the passing of young men in their primes like Jeff and Steve on 9/11 was particularly difficult, and wrong."

LeVeen and Roach's friends at Secession immediately established the Leveen—Roach Scholarship Fund, which awards grants to college-eligible Beaufort county students who display academic potential, have a love for or relationship to golf, and who demonstrate real financial need. Using donations culled solely from the club's 700 or so members, nearly 200 separate grants totaling well over a million dollars have been awarded since the fund was established late in 2001. In many cases, recipients continued on to graduate schools, found professional and executive positions domestically and internationally, and even became PGA Tour players.

"Most of us will never be remembered after our death like Jeff and Stephen will," says Harmon, who will doubtless be remembered at Secession for as long as the game is played at this lovely club in the Carolina Lowcountry. "Hundreds and hundreds of kids who've benefited will always remember their names."

In the end, Harmon says, "I'm proud I made it out on Tour, but what we've accomplished here is more lasting, both at the club and with the scholarship fund. It gets to the heart of what the game is really all about."

CURRENT OR FORMER HEAD GOLF PROFESSIONALS WHO WORKED FOR MIKE HARMON INCLUDE:

- Bobby Baughn
- Chris Byrd
- David Engram
- Matt Fraser
- Kevin Hodes
- Terry Johnson
- Adrian Jolliffe
- Eric Kennedy
- Franklin Newell
- Bruce Slattery

Mike Harmon's tip for fellow golfers:

For almost 40 years I have swung a weighted stick at home in order to develop and then maintain my golf swing. Even now, as I near 60, it is a part of my daily routine and I believe wholeheartedly that my success as a player, limited as it has been, came solely from this one exercise! I seldom play, almost never hit practice balls, yet when I'm called to play (I often have to search for my clubs) I walk to the tee with my golf muscles in the trim and with a far better mental attitude than if I had done nothing for my game. It's a simple exercise. Just swing the weighted club in slow motion 20 times using the very same swing thoughts you utilize when playing. It only takes two to three minutes (it takes longer to shave), but done religiously each day, you'll soon feel flexibility returning to your swing motion and a muscle memory that helps immensely when you are on the course. *Be careful,* you must do them properly or you'll be adding errors into your swing at the rate of 600 per month! Take your time and do them right. I'd rather see you do three correctly than 20 wrong! I *know* this will help anyone, professional or amateur! The only one this doesn't help is the amateur or professional who has time to hit balls every day, but I know very few of those individuals in my world!

Mike Harmon's tip for fellow golf professionals:

Never forget why you got into the game of golf. You were drawn to this magnificent game because you loved *playing*, and once you fell for the game, you could never see yourself away from the game. But for many professionals, work and family swallow up what little time you have to play or practice, with the result being less time on the course for yourself. Heck, at many clubs, the professional is often taken to task for "playing too much!" Make sure you take some time for yourself, even if it is late in the afternoon. Throw six or eight clubs in a small carry bag and walk a routing of three to five holes. It will re-nourish the soul and take you back to a time when you fell in love with the game of golf!

TOD HECHT
Columbus, Ohio

One could make the argument that Columbus, Ohio is the Manny Pacquiao of golf cities--pound for pound, the finest destination in the game. There are all sorts of great clubs in the area, many of them headed by professionals of exceptional quality. There is Bill Stines at venerable Scioto, the course where Jack Nicklaus learned the game. Larry Dornisch has more than 15 years of tenure at Muirfield Village, the magnificent club and annual PGA Tour stop that Nicklaus conceived and designed after achieving

Tod Hecht on the Monterey Peninsula

his professional fame and fortune. Joe Regner has been of service for over a decade to the members of the Golf Club, a bucolic Pete Dye masterpiece little known outside of central Ohio, but one of the game's classic venues.

However speaking of great fighters like Pacquiao, the most intriguing golf pro in the area, and certainly the most tenacious fighter, is Tod Hecht, formerly of The Lakes Club, who technically is a pro no longer.

Hecht's life hit a massive speed bump in February 2008, and swerved in a direction he never would have considered. During one of his routine off-season workouts he felt a strange 'pop' behind his right eye. He woke up with a severe headache the next day, which was a highly unusual occurrence, and the day after that he suffered a massive stroke at age 47, caused by a dissection (in essence, a small tear) in the left carotid artery. "Whether it was caused by the workout we will never know, but the irony is he had a physical the month before and was pronounced in perfect health," begins his wife, Jan Hensel.

Jan Hensel and Tod Hecht had married a decade earlier in 1998. When first introduced, this prominent Columbus trial lawyer was favorably impressed by the fact that she had met a man who worked harder than she did. "I work at least 50 hours a week, but as the head professional at The Lakes Tod would literally work 70 or 80 hours. It helped our relationship, because I had been single for a dozen years prior, and we were both extremely independent, each with our own busy lives and careers. We had two separate lives that came together."

"The day of his stroke I received a grave phone call. They told me he couldn't speak. When I got to the hospital he couldn't move his right side, and looked absolutely petrified. It was horrifying. For the first 48 hours we didn't know if he would make it. Once he was out of intensive care, he was in the hospital for several weeks. I couldn't work, and was just delegating my cases to my colleagues from Tod's hospital room."

Hensel continues her recollection of the most trying period of her life with uncommon candor. "That first night, in the hospital I did not know whether to pray that Tod lived or died. Not because I had any doubts about whether I wanted him in my life—I did, whatever the future held. But because I just did not know if he would ever be able to accept himself and be happy if he was unable to live a life that revolved around golf—if he could no longer work as a head pro, and if he could no longer play competitively. And I could not bear the thought of Tod being unhappy for the rest of his life."

"Before his stroke, golf was Tod's life," continues the attorney, who has argued cases on several occasions in front of the Ohio Supreme Court. "He had no hobbies. He was a workaholic who loved his work. In 2007, he started taking Sundays off in January and February to spend them with me. We had a hard time figuring out what to do. Throughout our courtship and marriage, the only full days that we had spent together were holidays and vacations."

Hecht, who couldn't really walk or speak at the time, spent more than a month in a rehab hospital. The initial goal was for him to get from his wheelchair into the bathroom unassisted, so he could get back home. Once he got home a stream of therapists worked with him continuously, and his goal then was to be able to get upstairs to use his own shower and sleep in his own bed. "He was bound and determined to get up those stairs, and within a week of being home he did just that," states Hensel.

While at first she was resistant, eventually his wife allowed dozens of different Lakes members to assist her in caring for Tod, so she could get back to her legal duties, which she had more or less ignored for the better part of six months. "An amazing woman and Lakes employee named Terry Moncrief spearheaded the volunteer's efforts. They filled out a calendar themselves, organized it, and we had a rotating group who helped out as much as I needed for several months until we could hire caretakers," continues Hensel.

"Our attitude was, no negativity allowed, no tears, be positive, no speaking in hushed tones. From the moment he was aware of what happened, he never felt sorry for himself or bemoaned his fate. He has worked even harder to recover from the stroke than he ever did as a golf pro, and that's saying something. I have always loved and admired him, but since the stroke my feelings have grown exponentially. Tod has demonstrated more strength of character and courage than I could have imagined from anybody," says his wife, admiringly.

The Lakes community, both the country club and in the surrounding real estate development, banded together and supported the couple in a big way, far beyond the early days of rotating shifts as caregivers. They raised funds reaching the mid-six-figures, with everybody from the bank presidents and the

Tod Hecht and Jan Hensel

businessmen to the gardeners and the grounds crew contributing their hard-earned dollars. Just as importantly, they gave Hecht a renewed sense of purpose as he recovered, to be out amongst all the people he had worked with, and the membership he had served.

"Tod has always been so social, and many stroke victims suffer isolation," explains Hensel. "They don't want to be seen, are embarrassed they cannot speak, or look and act like they once did. The Lakes members embraced Tod with love, and he was happy and willing to accept it. And the money that was raised enabled us to hire a private speech therapist and keep working with a physical therapist long after the insurance money had run out."

Tod Ortlip is a Columbus-area real estate developer who began The Lakes community in 1990, and a close friend of Hecht, or "Hechtor," as he is known in the area. His affection was more of the "tough love" variety, owing to the polio affliction he suffered as a child. "I had to work hard to recover the use of my own right arm because of the polio, and I know that Tod will work until he can regain use of his right arm also. Hard as he worked as our golf professional, now he even works harder."

Hecht began as an assistant pro at The Lakes in 1994, was incredibly popular among the membership, and advanced to the head job several years later. He had more than a decade of tenure as head professional before being waylaid by the stroke in 2008. Ortlip continues, "Tod Hecht was a fixture at the club, admired and loved by pretty much everyone, and did an incredible job. Because we were such a new entity in an established market full of old-line clubs, we always emphasized the service component here, and our efforts were spearheaded by Hecht. Our service is considered second to none, and we owe that sensibility in large part to Tod Hecht's influence. When the stroke occurred out of the blue it cast a pall not only over the entire club, but throughout The Lakes community of 1,500 homes."

Jan Hensel recalls an unforgettable moment that occurred just a few short months prior to Hecht's stroke. "We were on a trip to the Monterey Peninsula the previous autumn. It was one of those intermittently cloudy Carmel days. At one moment during a golf lesson he was taking, just as Tod finished his swing, a beam of sunlight pierced through the clouds and aligned perfectly with Tod's club and posture. On the CD of the lesson, it looks like beautiful Tod, with his beautiful swing, was one with the cosmos."

"We talked a lot, on that trip, about the power of golf in our relationship, even though I am not a golfer," states Hensel, like her husband, a Columbus-area native. "Golf has provided us with opportunities that he and I otherwise never would have had—including spending time in some of the most beautiful places on earth. It had brought us together with many people who have become dear friends. We felt truly lucky with our lot in life."

Despite the struggles, frustrations and setbacks of the last few years, both Hensel and Hecht, who is the father of three adult children from previous marriages, continue to see the glass as half full.

Currently Tod Hecht is a ranger at the golf course he once served as head professional, and is also more deeply involved with the local charity known as Morty's Kids then he ever was when he was logging all of those 12-hour days. While formerly he was involved in long-range strategic planning for the charity, now Hecht is actually teaching at the grassroots level, which helps him as much as his young students. Founded by The Lakes developer Tod Ortlip, and named for a mentor named Bob Morton that he held in great esteem, Morty's Kids is basically a regional version of the First Tee Program. It exposes Columbus-area youth to golf, and provides them with instruction and mentoring. By learning the game's values it increases their odds of making their way successfully into the world.

"Clearly, I did not give Tod enough credit on that dreadful evening," continues Hensel. "Nor did I know that golf—and the relationships that he had formed because of a life devoted to golf—would end up saving his life. The love and support and friendship and encouragement of The Lakes community were truly instrumental in his remarkable recovery. And as he got better, and could no longer work as a golf professional, Morty's Kids has provided his life with meaning and purpose that is so important to him. So in a book highlighting extraordinary golf professionals, Tod's is a story that exemplifies the extraordinary power of a love and connection to the game."

While once he could rope a tee shot 300 yards, now he's only half as long, hitting his 7-wood about 150 yards using his left hand only, control and balance issues necessitating the use of the shorter club. At his best, breaking par, if not a foregone conclusion, was at least a distinct possibility every time this former Southern Ohio Sectional Player of the Year teed it up. Now he is struggling to break 90. His game is a shadow of what it once was, but he is not. "No way am I now where I will eventually be," he says slowly, but earnestly. "I'll continue to improve, but my biggest hurdle is only having about 20% use of my right arm. Someday I'll be taking a full swing with both arms back on the club."

Square-jawed and 6' 4", built like a small forward with a full head of dark hair, now 50-plus but looking maybe 40, the stroke affected Hecht's speech cadence and ability to walk without a limp, but thankfully didn't mar his face, nor sap his inner strength or motivation. "That's life," says the pro, with a slight shrug, speaking emphatically, albeit haltingly. "Your play the hand you are dealt with, and move on as best you can from there."

"One day early on while he was still hospitalized, I spoke to three different doctors," concludes Jan Hensel. "The first two spoke to me, not my husband, and said much the same thing. The damage was so extensive that any type of meaningful recovery was an extreme long shot. The third doctor was the first one who spoke directly to Tod, and not to me. He told him he was a young man, determined, and having been so healthy previously there was no reason to think he couldn't recover 80 or even 90%. Needless to say, we ignored the other two, and chose to believe the third doctor."

The same sentiment is held by thousands of people in and around The Lakes, and throughout greater Columbus, who know and admire Tod Hecht. Like Jan, they chose to believe he would make great strides in his recovery, would always work hard, continue to improve, and someday make it virtually all the way back to where he was before the damaging stroke he suffered in 2008 veered his life in such an unexpected direction.

CURRENT OR FORMER HEAD GOLF PROFESSIONALS WHO WORKED FOR TOD HECHT INCLUDE:

- Luke Bowersock
- Chad Bucci

Tod Hecht's tip for fellow golfers and non-golfers alike:

One of the most important lessons I have always tried to impress upon my students, especially the juniors, is that golf is more than a game; it is a test of character.

It's the only game I know where the player is also the referee; he or she must enforce the rules against him or herself. For that reason, and many others I believe you can learn more about a person during a round of golf than in any other endeavor. How does he react to pressure? How does she respond to adversity? These are the true measure of a golfer, and they are far more important than the numbers recorded on the scorecard.

The stroke I suffered in 2008 has hammered home these lessons about the importance of character, perseverance and a positive outlook. These are the true measures of a person's makeup. Life will throw you curve balls, and there are many things that are out of your control. The one thing that you always have control over, both in golf and in life, is your attitude. I have learned that a positive attitude in the face of adversity will take you far, both in golf, and far beyond the game.

Gary Hobgood
Wilson, North Carolina

Jacks-of-all-trades:

A person who is adept at many different kinds of work.

To understand the tenacious work ethic of Gary Hobgood, the longtime head professional and part owner of Happy Valley Country Club in Wilson, North Carolina, it helps to understand his clientele. Happy Valley is a modestly-priced, semi-private facility, with a token initiation, minimal monthly dues and a daily green fee of about thirty bucks. It's a blue collar club, no collars required, and overalls, t-shirts or denim shorts are OK on the golf course, though men are required to wear shirts. "Women have the option of

Gary Hobgood, grill-master and 2012 Carolinas Section PGA Professional of the Year

wearing shirts or not," quips the pro. "The only coats and ties you might see around here would belong to either cops or IRS agents, and we're not that partial to either of them!"

Besides golf professional and wiseacre, you can also refer to him as a superintendent, chef, salesman, merchandiser and handyman, among other job titles.

"Some might call it being jack-of-all trades. I call it job security," says the 2012 Carolinas PGA Section Professional of the Year. He might not consider himself a trendsetter, but Hobgood's proficiency in so many different areas accurately reflects the contraction dynamic that has enveloped the golf business in the last decade or two.

Less business means less revenue, which means fewer staff members to serve the customers. So pros need to wear more hats, and at facilities where there might have been a Director of Golf, head pro and several assistants, the new economics of the game necessitate that three people do the job formerly allotted to four, or two do the job of three, or in the case of this self-effacing North Carolinian, one guy doing (or capable of doing) the job of pretty much anyone and everyone.

"My first day working on a golf course I was out cutting fairways," recalls Hobgood. "I worked five days on the course, and two days in the shop. My boss emphasized that the golf business was a 24/7 commitment, and even though I was clearing less than $200 a week, I loved what I was doing. I wasn't part of the superintendent's staff, I wasn't part of the professional staff, I was just part of the staff, period."

Hobgood hails from a wide spot in the road named Farmville, North Carolina, just 20-odd miles from Wilson. College was at nearby Campbell University, which he attended on a full golf scholarship. His scoring average was low; his grade point average was high, which is a recipe to become an Academic All-American, a distinctive achievement, and one he remains justifiably proud of to this day. His first job out of school was as an assistant in his hometown, at the Farmville Country Club. It was there, under the tutelage of head professional Tom Braswell, a great mentor and teacher, he began to develop the comprehensive skill set that has served him so well for all these years in his current post.

When he moved over to Happy Valley as the head professional a couple of years later, the mindset was much the same. "My dad retired from two jobs, my mom spent more than 30 years at a local bank, and they instilled my work ethic from the beginning. They both worked hard their whole lives, and I don't know any other way," states the pro, named head professional in 1989, and a partial owner since 2001.

Any given hour of the day, Hobgood might be working the register, giving a lesson, taking a tee time, riding a mower, retrieving a busted golf cart, cooking somebody's lunch, selling a shirt, or even a set of clubs. Often times he's tasked with doing several things at once. He'll take off Mondays, and usually disappears for a week in December with his wife, Cynthia, to celebrate their anniversary. Other than that, at a club that is open 363 days a year (everybody rests on Thanksgiving and Christmas) this fixture of a pro can be found on property more than 300 days annually.

"Whatever it takes, that's what I do. We are a small-budget club, and while we have a solid staff, we aren't exactly overstaffed. So I do what I need to, when I need to, and make sure our operation runs as smoothly as possible."

With so many contrasting duties, it's understandable when an outsider doesn't realize he's dealing with the head professional. "We host a long-running junior tournament every year called the Foyce Jones Invitational, actually named after the pro that preceded me in the job. In fact I played in it myself when I was a kid," continues the pro, now in his late 40s. "A few years back we had to re-sod a green that had died, and I was out there for hours in work boots, shorts and a t-shirt, getting all grimy. A competitor hits his ball onto the green, I pick it up and move it off the new turf, am about to tell him the procedure for play, where to legally drop, and he starts yelling at me for touching his ball. I told him I was the head pro, but he didn't believe me!"

Unlike the volatile young tournament participant, the President of the Carolinas PGA Section has unwavering belief in Hobgood. "Gary is the quintessential blue collar golf professional who truly represents the foundation of the game," explains Chad Newton, head professional at Pinewood Country Club in Asheboro, North Carolina. "Coveralls over cashmere, cooking hot dogs instead of hosting wine and cheese parties, and wearing all hats at his facility make him not only a valuable asset to his club, but the community, and the entire PGA of America. You talk about a pro's pro, he is a friend you can call at anytime, ask a favor, and you know beyond a shadow of a doubt that he will lend a helping hand. Loyalty, honesty, and integrity are the first of many adjectives that come to mind when thinking of my dear friend. I am a better person and professional due to the fact I met Gary my first week in the golf business more than 15 years ago!"

Hobgood, a two-time Merchandiser of the Year in the Carolinas PGA Section, illustrates what a good friend (and businessman) he can be. "My buddy Reid Hill is the head pro at Wilson Country Club, and unlike me, he doesn't stock much in the way of hard goods. He's running his Member-Guest event one year, and a guest is complaining he wanted to buy a set of Callaway clubs prior to the tournament, but there was nothing in the shop."

"Reid calls me, I drop what I'm doing, put the set together, and drive cross town. We put the brand-new clubs in his bag while the guest is having lunch, and he doesn't notice them until

Gary Hobgood, with his wife Cynthia, takes a break from mowing fairways

he gets to the first tee! He wanted clubs, we called his bluff, Reid gave him a bill which he was happy to pay, and we split the profit on the clubs," reminisces Hobgood, who in this case thought customer service trumped the concept of custom fitting, even though technically, the gentleman in question wasn't even his own customer.

Cooking at the club, even for large groups on league nights, is no big deal to the versatile pro, as he does the same thing at home virtually every night of the year. But in front of the stove at home with Cynthia is a far cry from whipping lunch together for patrons at the club in the company of a sales rep. "If one of my reps comes into the shop to show me a new line of equipment or apparel, and I need to get moving, I'll invite them into the kitchen with me. More than once I've been flipping burgers or making French fries while my local rep is showing me the latest line of tees, spikes, irons or golf shoes. I've noticed that concentrating on the two different tasks gets easier the more times you do it!"

David Orr is a renowned teaching professional, and another admirer of this multitasking whirlwind. "Gary epitomizes the phrase, true southern gentleman. It's his demeanor, being so soft spoken, thoughtful, and well- mannered," begins the director of instruction at the PGM (pro golf management) program at nearby Campbell University. When Hobgood was at Campbell the PGM program hadn't yet been instituted, though his age-contemporary Orr would have relished the chance to work with him.

"I've had the good fortune to get to know Gary at a personal level since 1997 and consider him a good friend. He was a strong player in his day at Campbell, and his strong play continues to this day as a frequent competitor in the Carolinas PGA Section events. It's been more than 15 years since we started working together on improving his game and tinkering with his swing. He's quite a player to this day, which is impressive when you consider all the demands on his time."

Hobgood has found that retired military veterans are among the best choices to assist with his 70+ hour-a-week workload. "My dad was an Army vet, and I am predisposed towards the military. The men I hire are among the most honest and reliable people I've met and they are happy to be here. Because they are mature men with settled lives, they aren't looking to move on. In the past I've had young assistant pros that were often talented and hard-working, but the nature of the business is to try and move upward to the next job. We are a straightforward, mid-priced facility, and we had significant turnover as my assistants looked to advance their careers. More power to them, but things are more stable now that I've moved in this other direction."

Hobgood has had other opportunities in golf, but prefers to live in the region he's always known, loves the fact that as a part owner, he benefits directly from all his hard work, and realizes that golfers, courses and pros cross the entire spectrum of the game. "I greatly admire men like Bob Ford and Mike Harmon, among some of the other legendary, very high-profile pros in the business," he states earnestly. "But in the golf world, there's an awful lot more like me then like them. If they are on the Mt. Rushmore of club professionals, I'm happy to be taking tickets at the entrance."

The easier question to ask Hobgood is what is he *incapable* of doing on or around the grounds at Happy Valley. The short answer: Not much. "I'm not a licensed plumber, nor an electrician. But if it can be fixed without having to schedule a service call, we try and fix it ourselves."

One might as well add the title of "swimming pool service man" to an ever-expanding resume. "We drain, sandblast and clean our club's swimming pool every year," reminisces one of the hardest-working pros in the business. "We were trying to save on a service call one time, so I was on the phone with the pool guy, who was trying to explain to me the best way to clean out the pool filter, which is a wide cylinder about five feet high, which looks like a dunk tank you see at a carnival. I climbed right inside it, and while I was attempting to follow his cleaning directions I noticed a few of my co-workers were pretty amused, shaking their heads at what I was attempting to do."

Hobgood chuckles at the memory, acknowledging that by sheer necessity, his organization runs lean, mean, and apparently clean. And at Happy Valley, somebody's got to do the dirty work.

CURRENT OR FORMER HEAD GOLF PROFESSIONALS WHO WORKED FOR GARY HOBGOOD INCLUDE:

- Graham Andrews
- Dwayne Baker
- Lenny Boyette
- Jon Hamilton

Gary Hobgood's tip for fellow golfers:

I see so many golfers go to the range and the first club they pull out is their driver. I would suggest going to the range without your driver and starting with a wedge. Try to create some rhythm and tempo in your swing before going to the first tee. I also get aging members that want that extra 10-15 yards. The hardest thing to tell someone is that it is not going to happen until there is some turn or rotation in their golf swing. I understand that we are all getting older, but get your body to turn as much as it will allow.

On your good days, try shots that are tougher than normal, take a gamble. But on bad days when things aren't going your way, swallow your pride, hit a safer shot and realize every day is not perfect. Chip out sideways if you have to, do your best and enjoy your day.

Gary Hobgood's tip for fellow golf professionals:

I would tell my fellow Golf Professionals to always take the High Road. Always present yourself as a Professional and treat your members and guests accordingly, whatever the situation may be. When you're on the phone taking tee times, ringing up a sale at the register, putting spikes in shoes and re-gripping a club all at the same time, and a member yells at you from across the room, remember to take the High Road.

Know your members sizes and what type of clubs they play and when new merchandise arrives, put it in their hands to hold and see. Our members appreciate the fact that you sometimes know them better than they know themselves. The one thing I try to do is spend time at the driving range. Watch member's swings and offer a tip or a recommendation for a new club to help them. They do come back to see you.

Darrell Kestner
Manhasset, New York

Golf headlines were made in autumn 2012 when a 14 year-old Asian lad qualified for the 2013 Masters. Just the latest evidence that impact players are getting younger, bolder, stronger, longer and more polished, helped in large part by vast experience, even worldliness, unimaginable to the preceding generations.

Winner of the 1996 PGA Professional National Championship

Take for example Darrell Kestner, the highly-regarded head professional at Long Island's Deepdale Golf Club. The West Virginian was 18 years old and in college before he ever saw an 18-hole course. He grew up playing a nine hole, par-32 bandbox in his hometown of Welch, deep in coal mining country. "I suppose I learned how to score on that muni," begins Kestner, who has the unique distinction of playing in major championships in five consecutive decades. "You could drive it up close to the green on the par 4s, and there were extra par 3s, so you really learned to chip, pitch and putt your ball."

In his youth he had also learned pretty quickly that football was not going to be his game, a hard-learned lesson, the irrefutable evidence being three broken shoulders. Luckily the high school football coach, Frank Marino, doubled as the golf coach, and with equal encouragement from his dad Raymond, a car salesman and weekend player himself, Kestner turned his attention to golf. "I was showing more promise as a golfer anyway," begins the three-time Met Section Player of the Year.

Kestner went off to Concord University, in Athens, West Virginia, and the first 18-hole course he encountered was at nearby Pipestem State Park. "I played occasionally in college, though there wasn't a golf team. I began to shoot rounds close to par." His first golf mentor was Vic Sorrell, the head pro at Fincastle Country Club in Bluefield, West Virginia, where he worked a couple of summers during those college years. "The thing about Fincastle was its super-quick, undulating greens, much like I had grown up with. The other notable fact is that it was my first exposure to a Dick Wilson-designed golf course, the man who designed Deepdale," continues the former Met Section Teacher of the Year.

Post-college he went to work at Sugar Mill Country Club, in New Smyrna Beach, Florida, just south of Daytona. It was there the small-town product first got wind of the famed Met Section of New York. "There were some wintering pros there telling me about all the great clubs and the elevated pay rates throughout the area. I had never given it any thought before, but those discussions really piqued my interest."

Talk about starting at the top, Kestner's first exposure to the Met was at the anachronistic and exclusive Fisher's Island Club, technically in New York, but just a short ferry ride from New London, Connecticut. This authentic Seth Raynor design from the 1920s plays firm, fast, and has wonderful natural attributes, not the least of which are gorgeous water views on almost every hole. "I worked one season there for Dave Alvarez, who was new to the position, and through mutual acquaintances hired me as his assistant. It was 1980, my first time really teaching, and working with groups of juniors, and I really started to enjoy that aspect of the business," relates the two-time New York Open champion. Little did he realize he was embarking on a decade-long, 'on again-off again' employment stutter-step throughout the Met Section, so at odds with the long-term stability he has enjoyed at Deepdale for 25 years.

That same year he made the acquaintance of Charlie Robson, the Executive Director of the Metropolitan Section PGA. Robson knows or has met every great pro in the section, and hundreds of others nationwide. "I am familiar with virtually every golf professional profiled within these pages, and have played golf with more than a few," begins Robson, who was still learning the ropes of his position the summer he met Kestner, but has since amassed 40 years of tenure. "In my opinion Darrell is as accomplished and skilled as any of them. But the thing that makes him so unique is what a genuinely nice man he is. He is totally self-effacing, virtually no ego, despite his myriad accomplishments. I've never heard him say a bad word about another person, and I've known his since he came to Fisher's Island nearly 35 years ago."

Kestner surprised himself a bit by earning his PGA Tour card that fall, after the privileged members had departed from Fisher's Island at season's end. But as he recalls a bit ruefully, "I was good enough to get my card and play the Tour in 1981, but unfortunately not good enough to compete with any sort of consistency, so I couldn't hold onto it."

Just a year after his eyes had been opened up to the embarrassment of golf riches throughout the Met, his eyes were opened once again in regards to the skill level and keen focus of his fellow Tour competitors. "I had a great time, and it was so instructive to see the world's best players up close, but my game just wasn't up to speed."

Kestner, ultimately named the Met Section Senior Player of the Year on four separate occasions, explains that precise ball-striking is just one of many attributes that a successful Tour player must possess. "It's also being organized, knowing how to travel, getting the most out of practice sessions, grinding out a decent score when you aren't at your best. I was young, not too sophisticated, and didn't really have a support system. All of that worked against me."

After his "one-and-done," he found an assistant's position at Westchester County's Century Country Club in the town of Purchase, working under Met legend Nelson Long. "Even though he is just a few years older than me, Nelson was a wonderful mentor and great friend. I learned from all of my employers," continues Kestner, "and owing to my unusual circumstances in those early years I had plenty of them. But Nelson was and is a help not just to me, but to any young professional he encountered."

Improbably, Kestner found himself back on Tour the following year. "I guess I was a good enough player to get hot for a week, and earn my card, but over the course of a full season, it just wasn't quite there for me. I didn't have the consistency to survive."

His old job at Century CC no longer available, after his encore year and swan song on the PGA Tour Kestner went to work at Leewood Golf Club in Westchester County. His job afforded him the latitude to compete in the Tournament Players Series, or TPS, an eight-event schedule that was something of a precursor to what eventually became the Nike Tour, Nationwide Tour, Web. com Tour, etc. He was up against fields that included the likes

Kestner is renowned for his teaching ability as much as his playing ability

of future Major champions Ian-Baker Finch, Paul Azinger, Tom Lehman and Lee Janzen. Kestner won the Charlie Pride Golf Fiesta, which was his most significant professional victory he won the 1996 PGA Professional National Championship a dozen years later. But despite his occasional flashes of tournament success, he was starting to see the value and long-term stability of life as a club professional, particularly in the prestigious Met Section. "I realized there was far more to golf than traveling, competing, and being singularly focused on my own game," reasons the five-time winner of the Met PGA Championship.

Kestner's immersion plan continued for another half-dozen years. He spent two years each at Westchester Country Club, then Winged Foot, and finally Sunningdale, working for Bob Watson, Tom Nieporte and Bill Greenleaf, respectively. He also worked winters with Jim McLean and David Glenz doing golf schools across the country during the Met off-season. "Then I finally got the call for my first, and what has turned out to be my only head professional position, at Deepdale."

Looking back on his peripatetic employment situation before he became entrenched on Long Island's Nassau County, Kestner reasons, "there is no right way or wrong way to do it, it's what you make of it. The path I chose was dictated by my sporadic appearances on Tour. My master plan was not to have six different jobs in just over a decade, but that's how it panned out. I benefited from having all these different mentors help shape me into the head professional I eventually became. On the other hand, there's an argument to be made that working at one club for five or ten years allows you to really get established, and develop deep relationships. One way isn't necessarily better or worse than the other."

Kestner's pin-balling days came to abrupt conclusion when Deepdale called in 1989. If one can consider the Met Section a target, for both ambitious pros and the cognoscenti seeking out the game's finest experiences, central Nassau County might well be the bull's-eye. Within 20 minutes of Deepdale's Manhasset location, which is about 30 minutes from midtown Manhattan, are venerable all-world clubs like Garden City, The Creek Club, Piping Rock, Fresh Meadow, and the entire Bethpage State Park golf complex, including the two-time U.S. Open host venue, Bethpage Black.

"I wouldn't hesitate in saying that our immediate area has as many, if not more great and historic golf courses than any area of The Met, which means it compares favorably with any area of the country," states Kestner.

The irony is that his own club, unlike so many of his neighbors, doesn't hail from golf's "Golden Age" of architecture, from the teens and 1920s. Deepdale was born just a few years after their pro, in 1955. A nearby club called Lake Success fell victim to eminent domain, and was razed to make way for the Long Island Expressway. There was no shortage of successful individuals at Lake Success, and a small band of movers, shakers and business titans quickly made plans to build themselves another club a few miles further east, and Deepdale was ready for play as the expressway was being constructed. "I've come full circle," offers the two-time National PGA Senior Club Professional Player of the Year. "The first club I worked at was a Dick Wilson creation, and so is the last."

"Darrell is a great fit at Deepdale," continues Charlie Robson, "and it only makes sense he's been there as long as he has. The club is so discriminating, and its members so accomplished, anything less than a first-rate pro wouldn't jibe. He and his wife Margie make a formidable team. She runs the business aspect of the operation, leaving him the latitude to accommodate his membership completely. He's a great representation of our section, and truly, a great representation of what a PGA Professional should be."

A commonly held belief is that if you can play well at Deepdale, you can play well, period. Ribbon fairways, subterranean bunkering, small and speedy greens are hallmarks of this leafy and secluded property. The membership is limited to begin with, and many members are rarely on property, busy with their business endeavors, traveling, or at another of their clubs. Suffice it to say that course conditioning is impeccable, in large part to the fact that there might be fewer rounds played at Deepdale than any comparable club in the country. The membership rolls are not for public consumption. But considering former dues-payers include Bob Hope, Oleg Cassini and President Eisenhower, the picture is clear regarding the gravitas of the typical member rolling up the clubhouse driveway.

"The club is phenomenal in every way, conditioning on par with Augusta National or Oakmont," continues Kestner, who ought to know. "Working here and having access to this course has helped my own game, helped me gain entrance to 18 majors over the years." Self-deprecating to a fault, he adds, "of course, I've missed the cut 17 times in 18 tries, but I credit my preparations at this club for helping me qualify for all those events to begin with!"

Kestner's greatest competitive triumph came at the 1996 PGA Professional National Championship, when he set a record in victory that stands to this day; 17 under par for the four round event. Summing up his victory succinctly, he offers, "a hot putter can take you a long way in this game, and it's really the great equalizer." He takes equal pride in the fact that his former assistant Matt Dobyns, now the head man at nearby Fresh Meadow, won the same title in 2012, and his eight-shot victory surpassed the record margin long held by the great Sam Snead. "I came close to winning it another time or two, but the field is comprised of hundreds of very athletic, mostly younger professionals from across the country. They can hit it out of sight. I was already in my 40s when I won, and lucky to have won it when I did."

Charlie Robson is quick to dispel the semi-pervasive sour-grapes mindset that Kestner's many on-course successes stem from an all-consuming concentration on his own game. "There have been grumblings for decades that Darrell wins so much because all he does is play and practice. But he is one of the best golf instructors in the world, both with his members, and with PGA Tour professionals. His playing record is practically unparalleled. He has won so much on the club professional level people think he doesn't do anything but work on his own game. This is not the case at all; he gives tons of lessons, and is deeply invested in his membership, doing whatever he can to insure they enjoy their club."

Kestner's playing prowess has earned him the National PGA Senior Player of the Year award in back-to-back years. He's also been awarded the Met Section's Strasbaugh Award, Horton Smith Award, and honored as Teacher of the Year.

Darrell and Margie have been married since shortly before he began at Deepdale. Her golf roots also run deep, her father played on the Wake Forest golf team with Arnold Palmer and the renowned instructor, Jim Flick. Speaking of the latter, who passed away late in 2012, Kestner offers, "Jim became a mentor to me later in my career. And everything he taught me about being a better instructor was dwarfed by what he taught me about being a better person in general."

He goes on to point out the irony that around the Met, Nelson Long, his old boss at Century CC, is known as "Uncle Nel," due to his mentoring ways. However he is literally Uncle Nel to Margie, one of her blood relations. "Margie working my inside operation has worked out wonderfully, because it frees me up to spend time with my members, take care of other business, give lessons and devote time to my own game," concludes Kestner.

Good enough. It's a telling phrase for the pro to use, describing his playing abilities during that hectic stretch when he was an on-again, off-again Tour player. Good enough to hitch his wagon to that unique traveling circus, not quite good enough to stay for long.

However in the decades since, he's proven that he's the right man at ultra-posh Deepdale. And if you are good enough to last for 25-or-more years working for a membership as discriminating and accomplished as theirs, you are also good enough for pretty much any club job that exists.

CURRENT OR FORMER HEAD GOLF PROFESSIONALS WHO WORKED FOR DARRELL KESTNER INCLUDE:

- Michael Breed
- Matt Dobyns
- Jeff Gschwind
- Jim Morris
- Brendan Reilly
- Dwight Segall
- Jeff Stephens

Darrell Kestner's tip for fellow golfers:

We may not all be able to swing like Tiger Woods, but we should at least be able to address the ball like he does. But since we all don't have a coach or video camera the mirror is the next best thing to give us feedback. By watching yourself in the mirror you can work on your address and posture, so you can at least imitate a great golfer at address. Do mirror work as your practice in developing a better setup and remember that this is the first step in developing a better and more reliable swing.

Darrell Kestner's tip for fellow golf professionals:

Surround yourself with great people. Nelson Long, my mentor and the National Bill Strausbaugh award winner, said this is the key to success as a club professional. You cannot be everywhere or do everything yourself. Whether you need help in teaching, playing, merchandising, or public relations, if you have great individuals around you, they can make you look like a star!

Charlie King
Greensboro, Georgia

How did Charlie King end up as a renowned golf instructor, and popular golf instruction book author? It can be distilled down to seven words of frustration, words he must have muttered time and again when he was trying to overcome a late start to the game, and turn himself into a competitive player: *There's got to be a better way.*

Charlie King's frustration as a golf student molded him into a preeminent teacher

Spending most of his sporting youth on the basketball courts and baseball diamonds in his hometown of Decatur, Tennessee, meant that King never swung a club in anger until he was 19. "I went out on a lark with some friends at Tennessee Tech," begins the longtime pro. "Like any first-timer, it was mostly awful, but I hit a shot or two which intrigued me. That's all it took for me to get the golf bug, and to get hooked."

The first couple of years were self-taught trial-and-error, emphasis on error, as King battled a terrible slice, and all sorts of beginner's maladies. Then, an epiphany on the intramural field. "One of my buddies on the golf team showed me how to hit a draw by concentrating on the inside corner of the golf ball and rolling my forearms after impact. It immediately added 10 yards to my irons, and 25 yards to my drives. I dropped ten shots from my game in a couple of months, and towards the end of college I could shoot in the mid 70s. That little lesson, casual as it was, opened my eyes to how amazingly effective golf instruction could be," recalls King, since 2006 the Director of Instruction at Reynolds Plantation, an expansive and impressive golf, boating and real estate community hard by the shores of Lake Oconee, in central Georgia, about 90 minutes east of Atlanta.

It's remarkable how a potentially mundane decision, choosing one fork in the road over the other without much forethought, can catapult a life into a previously unseen direction. In this case, it was a college senior, in search of an 'easy A,' who on a lark decided to enroll in an elective class that he might have easily forgone. King had fallen in love with golf, was on hand to see Larry Mize's sudden-death chip-in to win the 1987 Masters, and shortly thereafter, in a Business Administration class at Tennessee Tech, the professor tasked each of the students to write down their ultimate goal in life. Charlie King impulsively wrote, 'Win the Masters.' However unlike the freewheeling, big-swinging Bubba Watson, the unlikely 2012 Masters champ, famous for never having a formal golf lesson in his life, King immediately sought professional help to get his burgeoning game Augusta-worthy.

That summer after graduation he took a job working golf course maintenance at a club in Chattanooga, and booked a lesson with a teacher of great renown, whose students included prominent amateurs, even a Tour pro or two. "He watched me hit balls for awhile, then immediately started to make these wholesale changes," recalls King, still exasperated more than 25 years after the fact. "He had me dramatically widen my stance, lose all knee flex, take my head off the ball, and employ a one-piece takeaway. And this was just for starters. If I questioned him, he would say, 'have you ever seen Sam Snead? Have you ever seen Ben Hogan?' The implication was that there was only one way to do it right, and his method was superior to anyone else's method. I didn't know enough about golf instruction to question the man at the time."

His game suffered as he diligently attempted to implement these profound changes in the succeeding weeks, and when he questioned the methods being taught, was abruptly told, 'I don't teach quitters, so quit if you don't like what I'm doing.' King didn't quit golf; he just quit the dogmatic instructor.

Further experimentation with other instructors recommended to him lead to further frustrations. Feeling like a Guinea Pig, as succeeding teachers used what King deemed the Baskin-Robbins approach, their swing philosophies and teaching techniques varying with the monthly arrival of the latest major golf publication. Then there was an interlude with another name-brand instructor, whose attitude could best be described as indifferent, if not downright standoffish. "He seemed to just be going through the motions, as if he had bigger fish to fry. He never asked me my long-term goals, never suggested any drills, and never even asked me if I wanted to book a second lesson! Throughout this period of instructor experimentation, I never heard a word about the short game. There was no addressing my inability to play to my potential in tournaments, never a word about club-fitting, flexibility or fitness."

All these experiences took place in the late 80s and early 90s, as King was getting his footing in the business, and attempting to play mini-tours. With mediocre results in golf's bush leagues, competing in the Masters, never mind his original goal of winning a green jacket, became as far away and unreachable as the summit

Charlie King uses a skills-based teaching philosophy to help students improve

of Everest. But a more attainable goal took its place: Becoming a teacher that could systematically help all golfers, not by using the method technique, or 'one-size-fits-all,' which can be beneficial to those with the right body type, but will be less than ideal for everyone else. Instead he became a skill-based teacher, working with an individual's particular strengths and weaknesses, their unique physicality, to help them improve. "The eight years I spent teaching aspiring club pros to teach the game at the Golf Academy of the South were wonderful," explains the father of two teenagers. "When my playing career stalled, I realized the best way to serve the game, and tap into my natural affinity to help others, was by teaching them to teach, so nobody would have to experience the level of frustration I did when I was seeking to seriously improve my game."

"Skills teaching in golf is analogous to learning to swim," explains King. "When you first get in the water you take things one step at a time. First you learn to dunk your head, then float, then kick your legs, then arm motion, then breathing during the stroke. You put it together in the shallow end before you go to the deep end. In golf, we learn the pre-swing, which is grip, stance, posture, etc. Then impact, which is striking the ball solidly, face angle and face control, body motion, consistent width in the swing, then eventually rhythm and tempo of the swing. You put it all together, just like when you learn to swim in a methodical way, and you can effectively improve an individual's golf game rapidly and permanently."

"The World Golf Hall of Fame is full of players with distinctly individual swings," explains King, who was tapped in 2003 as one of GOLF Magazine's Top 100 Teachers. "A good teacher can work with a player who is more upright, or lower to the ground, or has a unique swing like a Jim Furyk or Lee Trevino, and help them improve."

King's first book came out in the year 2000. Self-published and based in large measure on his former frustrations in learning the game, "You're Not Lifting Your Head!" was a story-and-lesson-series rolled into one, and with more than 13,000 copies sold, this slim paperback was a surprise hit. "I wrote the book because I wanted to tell the story about how frustrating learning the game can be if you don't approach it the right way," says King.

A more ambitious publishing venture came some years later, when King co-authored a combination instructional book and work book, called "Golf's Red Zone Challenge," along with fellow instructor Rob Akins. In football the "red zone" is the 20-yard line and in, and while there are plenty of teams that can move the ball up and down between the 20s, it's getting in the end zone that counts. King designates golf's 'red zone' as 100 yards and in, and using the football analogy, it matters not a whit if a player can whistle drives prodigious distances and hit crisp approach shots straight as a string. To play better golf one must get the ball in the hole effectively, which means chipping, pitching, sand play and putting are paramount, and regularly turning three shots into two will ultimately take five or even eight shots off the final scorecard tally. That's the emphasis of the Red Zone Challenge, where six specific short-game drills systematically help players get the ball in the cup quicker than they could previously.

"Our research shows that those who methodically follow the 12-week program we outline will improve as much as 75% in their short game skills," continues King, who once served as Director of Instruction at PGA National in Orlando. "We format the Red Zone Challenge into a casual competition among resort or corporate guests at Reynolds Plantation, and my hope is to someday take the skills challenge nationwide, in the hopes of motivating thousands of golfers to sharpen their short games in this enjoyable contest format. My vision is to someday see this as ubiquitous and well known as the Oldsmobile Scramble."

Dr. Rick Jensen is a well-known sports psychologist who has worked with more than 50 Tour pros on the PGA, LPGA and Champions Tours. "I have known Charlie since he was playing the mini-tours. He's impressive as a teacher in numerous ways, but overall I would say that the best attribute he has is his understanding that playing good golf goes far beyond perfecting the golf swing. He is far beyond the traditional 'fault and fixes' type of instructor," explains the Ph.D, whose clients have won more than 200 times on their respective tours, and more than 30 combined Majors. "He is a great skills teacher, with a holistic approach to the game, almost like a coach as opposed to just an instructor. He helps his students hit the ball better, control the ball, and manage their game more effectively. He works with everyday golfers as opposed to Tour pros, so his profile is lower than it should be. In my opinion there are very few golf instructors that are as skillful as Charlie."

King's short-game kingdom at Reynolds Plantation is in close proximity to The Taylor-Made Kingdom, one of the most technologically advanced club-fitting operations in existence. Close at hand is the marquee Oconee Golf Course, (one of seven on property) three minutes away is the posh Ritz-Carlton hotel, and his ever-changing roster of students includes a steady stream of club members, some highly skilled and others still learning, hotel guests, instruction-and-equipment junkies, and corporate visitors. Although he might be best known for his short game prowess he estimates that half the time he is tasked with teaching the full swing.

When the weather becomes stifling in central Georgia, King heads to the superb Maroon Creek Club, in Aspen, Colorado. "It is an amazing facility, one of the finest private clubs in the nation, and for all of its wintertime acclaim, many people think Aspen is even more delightful in summer."

Another bonus: King shares teaching duties at Maroon Creek with the venerable Craig Shankland, one of the best-known and most highly-regarded instructors in the world. "Craig was a mentor to me 20-plus years ago when I was just finding my way as a teacher," explains King. "Now we find ourselves working together in this mountain paradise every summer, and I feel as though my career has come full circle."

King's most recent publishing venture is a 60-page electronic book called "The New Rules of Golf Instruction," which is geared for both teachers and students. Topics include fitness, mental coaching, effective practice techniques, and the benefits of club fitting and video analysis. "I would have liked to have a resource like this all those years ago when I was seeking proper instruction," concludes King.

"Golf is still on a downward trend, and one of the main reasons is the game's difficulty. If I can teach my students how to significantly lower their scores by improving their short game, and also teach my fellow instructors how to teach golf more effectively, then I feel I am doing my part to help this great game I love."

Charlie King has influenced approximately 800 students to excel in careers as teachers and golf professionals in the eight years he spent at the Golf Academy of the South from 1992 to 2000. The teachers include Nancy Harvey at Dana Rader Golf Academy, Matt Wilkes at Mike Bender Academy and Rob Bowser at Reynolds Golf Academy. The pros and executives include Tony Chanci at Billy Casper Golf and J.C Patino at Summit Golf in Panama. He continues to influence teachers through his New Rules golf Coach Certification program and as part of the PGA of America faculty for the Professional Golf Management program.

Charlie King's tip for fellow golfers:

To master bunker play you must master taking divots – about 8 inches long, shallow and right between your feet. A great drill is to keep the ball out of the equation until you develop a consistent divot. So draw a line in the sand perpendicular to your feet. Put that line in the middle or maybe just a little bit in front of your stance. Take a swing and get the divot to start about 4 inches behind the line and end about 4 inches past the line – about an

8-inch divot and if it's a 7-inch divot, make it 3½ on both sides. And watch the sand fly and then do it again.

Swing on a circle tilted over a good swing plane but don't adjust and swing out to in; only if you see the ball going to the right of the target should you line up a significant amount or any amount to the left. But the key is to become the master of the divot. Once you've got that consistent divot, bunker shots become much easier.

Charlie King's tip for fellow golf professionals:

When I was growing up in the '70s, there were 3 channels on television. Then in the '80s came Fox so there were four. When cable television arrived it became hundreds of channels. Now we have You Tube, so there are hundreds of thousands.

I started posting videos to You Tube in 2008 and You Tube calls your videos a channel. I didn't get the significance of that until a couple of years later when I realize it truly is your very own TV channel. If you build an audience that is looking for your next "show," you can build a group of followers for the lowest cost in history.

My advice is to create your channel to meet the wants and needs of the marketplace. All of us can get our message out now for our instruction or our golf course. No Excuses.

Jim Langley
Carmel, California

Universal admiration. It's a noble-but-unattainable goal, akin to making 18 consecutive birdies and shooting 54 in the U.S. Open. Who among us can claim universal admiration? It's a short list, certainly, names like Mother Theresa, Nelson Mandela, John Glenn and heroic pilot "Sully" Sullenberger come to mind, though human nature being what it is, they doubtless have a smattering of detractors themselves.

Even without the use of his right arm, Jim Langley's golf swing is impressive

In the golf world, particularly in the insular and cloistered world of the finest private clubs, Jim Langley probably comes as close as anyone else. This former Tour player served as head professional at the incomparable Cypress Point Club for 34 years, winning armies of friends and admirers along what turned out to be a rocky journey.

Universal admiration might be too bold a statement. But those who are indifferent or negatively inclined towards Langley are akin to those who come to the oceanfront 16th tee at Cypress Point, one of the most famous and exhilarating par-3s in all of golf, with it's pounding surf and green jutting precariously across an intimidating chasm of sea-foam, and aren't immediately awestruck. In other words, one in a million.

Langley retired in 2006, and is modest to the point that he isn't quite comfortable talking about himself. Luckily he has no shortage of allies happy to do so for him. "I don't know anyone in any field who is more respected than Jim Langley, he is the best there is," offers his great friend Ken Venturi, who was named both the PGA Tour Player of the Year and the Sports Illustrated Sportsman of the Year concurrently in 1964, the year he captured the U.S. Open. "He's a credit to the game of golf. I literally cannot think of anybody I have ever known who is or was a better golf professional than Jim."

After working as his assistant pro for about six years, Casey Reamer succeeded Jim Langley as the Cypress Point head professional upon his retirement. "He is one of the nicest, kindest, gentlest people on earth, and due to his deep faith, there's a light about him that most people don't possess," explains Reamer. "This position has allowed me to meet and spend time with lots of wonderful people, but Mr. Langley is in a class by himself, he walks a different line than anybody else I've ever met. Anyone who knows him well would say the same thing. There are plenty of golf pros who can teach you how to be a great professional; how to give effective lessons, become a savvy merchandiser and become adept at member relations. Jim Langley can do all that, but his teachings go far beyond that. He can teach you how to be a better person, a better husband, father and friend."

However Langley cannot teach you to become a natural athlete as he was, that unique skill set of neurons, hand-eye coordination and fast-twitch muscle fiber the province of a chosen few. He began playing golf left-handed, mirroring his right-handed dad, who was a member of the Salinas Country Club, not even 20 miles inland from the Monterey Peninsula. He was a decent player, but when he switched to his natural right side as a teen, his game took off. But golf was just another game at which the 6'4" Langley (rhymes with gangly) excelled. He was recruited to play tight end at Stanford, but instead opted to play basketball at Cal. His decision to stick to the hardwood resulted in a national championship, as the Cal Bears first beat Oscar Robertson's Cincinnati Bearcats in the semifinals, and then defeated the Jerry West-lead West Virginia Mountaineers 71-70 in the 1959 NCAA Championship Game.

Langley played little, but still caught the eye of knockout cheerleader Louetta Vienop, and they were married less than a year after their college graduation. "I hadn't really noticed Jim before that," explains the Napa, California native. "But the cheerleaders voted for 'Best Legs' on the basketball team, and he won in a landslide! And when a sorority sister of mine from his hometown of Salinas who knew him in high school told me what a great guy he was, and a perfect gentleman, I started to pay attention!"

After a stint in the Marines, Langley went to work as a salesman for International Paper, with no plans to make a living in the golf business. But as his recreational play became stronger, and some local tournament wins came his way, he began to take the game more seriously. "A fraternity brother of his who was also a friend from Salinas sponsored his efforts to get on Tour," recalls Louetta, mother of their four sons. In the first professional event he ever entered, he got his PGA Tour card right on the number at Qualifying School.

In those days of Monday qualifying, Langley was a 'rabbit' along with a hundred other hopefuls, driving to each Tour stop trying to make the field. After three years of middling results, he heeded the advice of PGA Tour star and fellow Californian Dave Stockton, and began to gravitate towards golf instruction. He spent about six months teaching in Westlake Village, north of Los Angeles. But feeling homesick for Northern California, and wanting to get closer to both of their families, the Langley family headed back to Salinas. The aspiring pro found what he hoped would be temporary work packing lettuce crates at an agricultural concern. On a whim he submitted a resume to Cypress Point, knowing full well that their head professional, Henry Puget, had served the membership for more than 40 years. But within a couple of months Puget retired, and the club president famously said to the shocked Langley, "we're going to take a chance on you."

"It was astonishing to me that my dad, with five years of so-so results on Tour, and a short stint as a teaching pro, with virtually no experience as a club professional, and filling lettuce crates to make ends meet at the time, took over at Cypress Point," begins his son Brennon. "But in 1971, that is exactly what happened. Some pros that land top jobs have this incredible reputation preceding them. My dad had virtually no reputation. But he grew into the job, grew in stature over the decades, and became an icon in this business. It's a wonderful and amazing story."

Brad, Brett, Brennon and Bryan, spread throughout their 40s, are the Langley Boys. Only youngest brother Bryan has chosen to eschew the "family business." His older siblings include a golf course superintendent, a teaching professional, and Brennon, formerly a pro and now a Cypress Point caddie.

The third of Jim and Lou's sons considers himself a good luck charm. The day Brennon was born in April of 1969 was the day his dad had his best finish on the PGA Tour, second place behind Dale Douglass in South Carolina's Azalea Open. "How cool is it that the

Jim and Lou Langley with their four sons

PGA Tour Qualifying Tournament was his first pro event? Never a day on a mini-tour or satellite tour. Even as the collegiate golfers we became, and with dad nearing 50, neither Brett nor I could ever quite get the best of him on the course."

Brennon recalls somberly how his dad's life went seriously off-course on a fateful autumn day in 1987, a decade into his Cypress Point tenure, when he was victimized in a horrific car collision. "He was helping to push a disabled vehicle off of Highway 101 near San Jose when a sun-blinded driver entering the on-ramp hit him at accelerating speed." Reports indicated Langley was thrown 40 feet. He broke both legs, numerous ribs, punctured his lung, and most permanently, suffered serious arm and shoulder damage, rendering his right arm virtually unusable from that day forward.

"He was in the hospital for well over a month. When he first regained consciousness he was mostly concerned about the club and the members, and how they were getting along in his absence," marvels Brennon.

Langley's spirit remained intact, buoyed by the support of the membership, the staff, his many friends, his whole family. Among his numerous well-wishers was Ben Hogan, himself all too familiar with devastating car wrecks. He was bolstered by his deep Catholic faith, and his recovery was aided by his fitness level and natural athleticism.

"I think he's the most inspirational man I've ever met," concludes his third-born son. "He's so warm-hearted and giving, despite the challenges he's faced. He's candid, and when he asks someone 'how are you?' He is really listening and reacting to their answer, it's not just a greeting. He is completely invested in the lives of his sons and grandchildren. A club pro's life is so hectic, but he was at every sporting event he could get to, and if not at work, was home with my mother and his sons. The auto accident was a real misfortune, but I've always maintained he's a better putter one-handed then when he had both hands on the club!"

Ken Venturi has been friends with Langley for so long he cannot specifically recall when they met. "All I can tell you he is one of my very best friends in the world, and he served as best man in my wedding to Kathleen. He's one of the main reasons I've always enjoyed visiting Cypress Point, and the accident that robbed him of the use of his right arm was an all-time tragedy."

The former US Open champion recalls the wisdom of his father, whose livelihood was selling nets and other supplies to fisherman on the California coast. "Dad used to say that excuses were the crutches of the untalented, and I never heard Jim say a single word about that accident, or make any type of excuse. He's always been upbeat, always positive."

"I was very close to Byron Nelson," continues Venturi, who spent 35 years as a color commentator for CBS golf broadcasts before retiring in 2002. "He really helped me with my game, but never charged me for his time and expertise. When I asked him how I could every repay him for all he did for me, he said, 'be good to the game, and give back.' That's the exact path that Jim Langley has chosen, despite his setbacks. He is the epitome of Byron's philosophy; he's a credit to the game, and always gives back."

His successor Casey Reamer, who took over Langley's job on January 1st, 2006, continues in the same vein. "Jim led by example. The car wreck cost him the use of his arm, and doubtless left him with other injuries that never fully healed, yet he never complained about that, or about anything. It makes it kind of tough for anyone on the staff to mutter about feeling under the weather, or tendonitis affecting their golf game, or having too much on their plate. Occasionally he would say, 'you have to give what you have.' And that would refer to anything; time, attention, money, even the clothes on your back."

"I never knew him before the accident, but he had a reputation as an excellent player," continues Reamer, who hails from Morro Bay, near San Luis Obispo, several hours south of the Monterey Peninsula. "Even swinging with just his left arm across his body, he could shoot in the low 80s at courses like Cypress Point and Bandon Dunes. He was an excellent chipper, a great bunker player, and at his height, the way he would coil, with a straight left arm and the club way above his shoulder, it's really something to behold. It was like a one-armed Tour-caliber swing."

However there was never a Tour-caliber ego on display. "Jim would caution us to practice humility," states Reamer, who spent five years at Pebble Beach before first coming to Cypress Point as an assistant in 1999. "He stressed that the club was bigger than all of us, Cypress Point comes first. Everyone needs to be grateful to be a part of something so special, and from the locker room attendants to the caddies, even the members themselves, seems to understand that. He would stress that we are all privileged to work here, be a part of this incredible place, and that trumps everything else."

How influential has this humble servant of golf been? The Langley is a charity tournament that was initiated about five years ago by the Northern California Section of the PGA. The event is held on iconic courses like Pebble Beach and Spyglass Hill, and exists to raise funds for a wide range of worthwhile organizations like Folds of Honor, the American Heart Association, and dozens of local causes. "Some years ago we gathered a group of luminaries from our area, including Jim Langley, to discuss initiating a major charitable golf tournament," explains Nancy Maul, the Managing Director of the NCPGA Foundation, which oversees The Langley. "It was decided that because he epitomized what it means to give back to the community, the best name for our new event would be The Langley. He reluctantly agreed to it, only because the rest of us insisted it would be the best way for us to raise the most funds. It seems every year when we have our tournament review Jim is quick to point out that he would support a name change! But that won't happen because The Langley is here to stay."

The event's namesake not only helps immeasurably in fundraising, he also helps get some of the game's brightest stars to lend their support. The first five legends honored at The Langley were Arnold Palmer, Ken Venturi, Tom Watson, Johnny Miller and Jack Nicklaus. All five Hall-of-Fame members made their way to the event, and gave generously of their time with all the attendees. Adds Maul, "Because Jim has been such a wonderful ambassador for golf, and given so much to the game, anyone we approach as a potential honoree will make every effort to be there in person, and so far everyone has."

Jim Langley and Casey Reamer overlooking the famed 16th hole
at Cypress Point

Ken Venturi has often recounted a wonderful lesson imparted by his father regarding humility, so germane in this discussion of Jim Langley. "I remember one time at the family dinner table after I had won the San Francisco City Championship. I was going on and on about my greatness, I was running out of accolades for myself," recalls the 14-time PGA Tour winner. "When I finally finished crowing, my dad says to me, 'are you through son? Let me tell you this: When you are as good as you are, you can tell everybody. But when you get really good, they'll tell you!' Obviously that message has stuck with me my whole life, and in that same vein, I am thrilled to speak so highly about my great friend Jim Langley. He's never been one to talk about himself, what he's accomplished, and what he's overcome. But I'm here to tell you I have never met a finer person in all of golf than he."

History tells us that when Ted Williams retired, Carl Yastrzemski followed him not only as the Red Sox next leftfielder, but also eventually as a Triple Crown winner, and a member of the Baseball Hall of Fame. Of course, not one in five thousand NBA fans could tell you that when Michael Jordan first retired from the Chicago Bulls, his replacement in the lineup was a nondescript journeyman named Pete Myers.

Time will eventually tell us whether Casey Reamer's Cypress Point legacy will be more like a Yastrzemski or a Myers. But he knows how privileged he is to have such an exalted and coveted position, particularly at such a young age. "I plan on staying here as long as they will have me."

Even if he exhibits the same longevity, Reamer is resigned to the fact he will be hard pressed to fill the same shoes as his legendary predecessor. "Jim set the bar sky-high," concludes Reamer. "No one can do what he did, or be who he was. I can only try and be as great and as humble and as giving a man as he is, but it's an impossible task. Not just for me, but for anybody."

One last fact about this much-venerated professional. Upon his retirement, the club he had served so faithfully provided him with an honorary membership. Gestures like this are not uncommon. Club boards will oftentimes extend themselves in this manner to a long-serving professional upon the completion of their duties.

However Cypress Point had only provided one such honorary membership prior to Langley's in its long and distinguished history. That was bestowed upon the nation's 34th president, Dwight D Eisenhower. Just another telling example illustrating what a special man Jim Langley is, why he belongs in such ultra-exclusive company.

Jim Langley's tip for fellow golfers:

When you need a high, soft shot around the green, keep the backswing shorter and accelerate through the shot. A longer backswing tends to make you slow down through impact and will lead to more missed shots. A shorter short tends to require a shorter swing with a more aggressive follow-through.

Jim Langley's tip for fellow golf professionals:

In regards to merchandising, be wary of this year's 'hot driver,' or 'indispensable putter,' and be careful regarding the quantity you pre-order of these particular clubs. There are lots of very good drivers and solid putters manufactured each year. Tendencies and new technology are different from one company to the next. Some brands will always remain popular despite the current trends, so don't get stuck with merchandise that might quickly become obsolete, and negatively impact your bottom line.

John McNeely
Banner Elk, North Carolina

Virtually every golf professional, no matter how beloved, long-tenured and admired they might be, is an employee. Their realm might be as prestigious as the Palace of Versailles, as exclusive as Camp David, but they are nevertheless subject to the whims and fancies of the members and the board. The chance of abrupt dismissal, the furtive and hasty exit through the kitchen door, though remote, is always a possibility.

John McNeely (left) with Diamond Creek co-founder Wayne Huizenga.

Not so for the enterprising John McNeely. After a long and distinguished career, his crowning achievement was forging an alliance with billionaire Wayne Huizenga. Together, and as equal partners, they built one of the most amazing private golf clubs most folks have never gotten wind of: Diamond Creek, in the Western North Carolina mountain hamlet of Banner Elk.

McNeely's story does not have quite as many twists and turns as the infamous highways and Blue Ridge byways snaking through the region he now calls home, from Boone to Blowing Rock, from

Asheville to Linville and points beyond. But even though the road atlas indicates that from his modest beginnings in Statesville, North Carolina, to his majestic fiefdom in Banner Elk is less than a hundred miles, it has been far from a straight line from point A to point B.

John McNeely's basketball prowess earned him a full scholarship to North Carolina State, where he shared the hardwood with the legendary David Thompson and Tom Burleson, two of the greatest collegiate players of all time. A balky back and the prospect of limited playing time going forward made him reassess his options a few years later. At the urging of his younger brother Gary, then a scholarship golfer at the University of Tennessee, he took up golf in earnest, and transferred to East Tennessee State. In leaving his Wolfpack teammates McNeely missed out on the undefeated 1973 season and the national championship that followed, but despite whatever disappointment he felt, he was laying the groundwork for the rich career in golf that was soon to evolve.

"I wasn't going to hold up physically playing Division I basketball, and when I got the chance to play golf for Hal Morrison at East Tennessee State, I took it." Coach Morrison was renowned for taking kids who weren't recruited by golf powerhouses like Georgia, Florida, Wake Forest and Houston, and molding them into fine players regardless. After sitting out a season due to the transfer, McNeely found a place on the squad, and eventually as captain helped the team to a pair of Top 10 finishes in the NCAA Tournament.

A major break: Late in his college career, he had a convincing match-play victory over a fellow competitor named Don Edwards in the North and South, one of the most prestigious amateur tournaments in the nation. "I remember the encouragement I got during the summer tournament circuit from Coach Jesse

Haddock at Wake Forest," recalls McNeely. "It was wonderful how supportive he was to all the competitors, not just his own guys."

The vanquished Edwards was the reigning club champion at Winged Foot Golf Club, outside of New York City. He suggested McNeely would be well served meeting and perhaps working for the legendary Claude Harmon, their vaunted club professional who won the 1948 Masters, the last club professional to ever win a Major. The idea gained further traction due to the fact that a gentleman named Pat O'Hara, the father of one of McNeely's golf teammates, J.P. O'Hara, was the lawyer for the New York Giants and a respected and influential member of Winged Foot himself.

"I met Mr. Harmon for a lunch interview at a Manhattan restaurant, but we weren't alone," recalls McNeely, smiling at the memory. "He had brought along Howard Cosell and Frank Gifford to chaperone!" Harmon had set up the 'ambush' to see how his potential new assistant, who grew up very modestly in a small Carolina town, could handle himself around people of influence. "My dad was a truck driver and a milkman," continues McNeely. "I wasn't used to eating in fancy places, or dealing with celebrities, but I managed to make it through lunch without embarrassing myself."

However he almost didn't make it through his next test. Harmon insisted his assistants be fine players, the only way to get any lesson revenue from the discriminating clientele at Winged Foot. McNeely was following in the footsteps of former assistants like Dave Marr, Mike Souchak and Jackie Burke, who eventually won about 35 times combined on the PGA Tour, including three Majors. When the newcomer made the turn in 40 nervous strokes during his initial round with members, Harmon cautioned him a one-way bus ticket back to Statesville was looming. McNeely rallied and returned in 31, shooting under par for the day, and kept his job.

He wintered in Palm Springs, working as an assistant at the famed Thunderbird Country Club, along with Dick Harmon, one of his boss's four sons. "Now there are a hundred courses in the desert," explains McNeely, "but back then there might have been ten, and Thunderbird was preeminent." The club's membership was incredibly powerful and influential, including men like John Mulcahy, the owner of Waterville Golf Links in Ireland, tire magnate Leonard Firestone, and former president Gerald Ford.

Claude Harmon retired a few years later, and urged McNeely to work for his son Dick, who had recently been named the head pro at River Oaks Country Club in Houston. "River Oaks is the most prominent club in Houston, among the best in all of Texas, and has an excellent national reputation due to its elite membership and classic Donald Ross golf course," offers McNeely. Three years later, as he was turning 30, he was offered his first head job, and took over at Annandale Golf Club in Madison, Mississippi.

One of the indelible memories of his time at Annandale was his exhibition match with the course designer, the greatest golfer who ever lived. The fact that McNeely was a shot better than Jack Nicklaus, who won his unprecedented 18th Major championship a year later, at the 1986 Masters, was secondary. "I was fortunate to shoot 71, and Jack shot 72. But what really stays with me is how he was so kind to my dad, who had recently suffered a stroke. Jack was walking next to and chatting with my dad, who was confined to a golf cart, hole after hole. That's why he will always be a hero to me."

An interested observer that day was Bruce Davidson, the first assistant professional McNeely had hired at Annandale. They had met initially when Davidson was visiting River Oaks several years earlier as a member of the Scottish Boys team touring the

US. "John has been like a big brother to me since we first met. Like all younger brothers do with their older siblings, I've idolized him for nearly 35 years. He's always been a better player and teacher than I have, but trying my hardest to be just like him meant that I became better at both myself," begins Davidson, who, after leaving his club job to begin a stint playing competitively on the European Tour, eventually became the Director of Golf at River Oaks, where he first met McNeely the assistant pro in 1979.

Davidson and his teammates originally came to the States at the behest of Jackie Burke, who after leaving Winged Foot founded Champions Golf Club in Houston with three-time Masters champion Jimmy Demaret. "Even though Mr. Harmon has been gone about 25 years, his 'circle of influence' remains strong," marvels McNeely. "I only worked for him for a short time, but golf aside, he helped me in so many ways, teaching me how to conduct myself and deal with the elite, helping me to smooth out the rough edges, so to speak. For example, I ended up traveling to Africa with his son Dick, and giving lessons to the King of Morocco! Not exactly an everyday experience."

Neither is a day at Diamond Creek. Nobody stumbles upon the club by accident; you need to know what you are looking for to find it. The entrance sign is the size of a rural mailbox, and it's at fire hydrant height. The short driveway leads to a foliage-framed wrought-iron gate, and beyond and around the first bend in the road is a hundred foot natural waterfall cascading down a rock wall. It's an unforgettable first impression.

More than a dozen years before that innocuous wrought-iron gate was installed, McNeely began to get the impression that the mountain region of western North Carolina would be well served with a different type of golf club. After seven years at his inaugural

Jack Nicklaus flanked by Wayne Huizenga and John McNeely

Mississippi job, McNeely then spent 13 years at Grandfather Golf and Country Club in Linville, where he saw firsthand how the region explodes in popularity come summertime. Not hard to understand, because when the thermometer is pushing triple digits in Atlanta, Charlotte, Nashville and throughout Florida, it's usually 20 or more degrees cooler at elevation.

The hectic nature of a short season, in combination with droves of avid golfers and a full tournament slate meant that the area's six or eight private courses were often crowded. Many people felt they had to join a second club so they could play when they wanted to, and these additional memberships almost always required a real estate purchase. "I came to the realization that a golf-only club, featuring caddies, with no tee times, few tournaments and with a minimal real estate component, would be a welcome addition to the area," explains McNeely.

Years before McNeely started scouting the surrounding area for suitable land for his vision, where he eventually found a thousand acre parcel that was a former sheep ranch, and long before he approached acclaimed architect and fellow North Carolinian Tom Fazio to build his dream course, he started to become close to Wayne Huizenga, who was a member at Grandfather.

Huizenga, whose high-profile holdings have included the Florida Marlins, Miami Dolphins, Waste Management Inc. and the Blockbuster Video Chain, was building a full-service country club in Palm City, Florida called The Floridian. He wanted McNeely to spearhead the golf operation. The new club featured a Gary Player-designed championship course, eventually a 55,000 square foot clubhouse, full staff, expansive wine cellar, on-site cottages, a helipad, even a marina. The only thing missing were members.

"It was literally a private club, just for Wayne and his wife Marti, their family, friends and guests," states McNeely, who spent 15 winter seasons as the club's director of golf. "Eventually Wayne and Marti would send out letters inviting certain friends to become 'honorary members' for the year, which afforded them privileges at the club, but no dues or initiation. The honoraries would pay for their food and drink, cottage lodgings and their guest fees, but otherwise Wayne underwrote the entire operation himself. It was this amazing Santa Claus quality of his, and he paid all the operating expenses, which were nearly eight figures annually." One can only imagine that in certain circles, the annual 'honorary member' letter from the Huizengas was as hotly anticipated as an invitation from Augusta National to play the Masters.

McNeely and his close friend Bruce Davidson had introduced Houston business magnate and Diamond Creek member Jim Crane to Wayne Huizenga. This introduction eventually led Crane, a scratch golfer, to purchase The Floridian from the billionaire in 2010. The course has since been renovated by Tom Fazio, and the infrastructure expanded and revamped, including a brand-new Butch Harmon Golf School on property. The club is currently building a membership roster in the traditional fashion. Crane subsequently purchased his hometown Houston Astros, and was quoted as saying, "owning a Major League team and a first-rate golf club were two things that I never thought I would be able to accomplish. But I was able to pull it together and I am very happy about it."

Speaking of happy, as McNeely was laying the groundwork for Diamond Creek, he was thankful that Huizenga expressed an interest in taking part in the project. He understood the vision, saw the niche his pro wanted to fill, and came in as the financial partner. "I knew dozens of individuals who seemed interested in becoming members, and things were moving forward, but it would have been a huge risk to take the project on alone. It took about four years from conception to completion, from 1999 to 2003, when we opened the golf course and the clubhouse concurrently," continues McNeely. "In retrospect it was a huge relief when Wayne provided the financial stability to make Diamond Creek a reality. It was that much easier because we had been working together for years, knew each other's strengths, and were on the same wavelength when it came to understanding what a fine private golf club should be."

"John and I have enjoyed many great times together through golf, trips all over the world, with friends old and new," adds Wayne Huizenga. "Also at The Floridian, through development and construction, with an invitational membership concept that was unlike any other. Teaming up to build Diamond Creek and watch friends enjoy both Florida and North Carolina, has also been something special."

The 30,000 square foot lodge-style clubhouse at Diamond Creek is one of the game's most unique and welcoming. Bark siding, dark wood, hundreds of framed photographs, stocked bookshelves, rustic chandeliers, stone patios, multiple fireplaces and million dollar mountain views are all hallmarks of one of the most inviting golf-oriented habitats to be found anywhere. "From course conditioning to the dining experience to the clubhouse ambience, we strive for consistent excellence, not perfection, in all aspects of our operation," states McNeely.

Late in 2012 a new majority owner came into the picture. Dan Friedkin, a longtime member of Diamond Creek and the chairman of The Friedkin Group, took an interest in acquiring the club, planning to add even further polish to this little-known gem. In addition to his work as owner of Houston-based Gulf States Toyota, Friedkin is an avid golfer and accomplished aerobatic pilot who actively flies and restores a variety of vintage fighter aircraft. The club's new majority owner is planning on piloting Diamond Creek to even greater levels of success while taking pains to protect its natural aesthetic beauty amidst majestic surroundings. "Dan is sure to be a wonderful steward of this remarkable property, and it pleases me greatly that our club is in such good hands going forward," states McNeely. "My great friend Bruce Davidson has also become part of our Diamond Creek ownership group, and we are elated to have the expertise he will bring to the table."

Earlier in his golf career, when he was playing a bit more competitively, the Diamond Creek visionary gained entry to some scattered events on the PGA Tour with so-so results, although he profited greatly at one tournament in particular. "I caught a flier lie in Hattiesburg one time, and airmailed my approach shot practically into the grandstands behind the green," he recalls with a shake of the head. "A young woman, attending her first golf event, admonished me for almost braining her. I apologized for my inaccuracy, we got to talking, and the long and the short of it is Sharon and I have been married for more than 25 years! She was instrumental regarding the look and feel of our Diamond Creek clubhouse, which most members and visitors feel is one of the real highlights of our operation. In fact, Tom Fazio calls it one of his favorite buildings in golf."

Even though he is now past 60, the pro's golf skills are not exactly dissipating into the ether. He still breaks par with regularity, and every so often goes far lower than that. Not long ago during a casual round, in the company of good friend and Diamond Creek member Bob McNair, owner of the NFL'S Houston Texans, McNeely holed out twice from the fairway within an hour's time, first for double eagle and then for eagle. It was two exquisite swings, five holes apart, the end result five under par. The news went viral in the clubhouse, and upon his return one of his longtime members, a former Wake Forest golfer named Bill Argabrite who knew him way back when, claimed in mock dismay, "here it is 40 years later and you are still getting lucky!"

McNeely considered his career arc. He thought of Coach Hal Morrison at East Tennessee State taking him under wing, a man who loved the game so much and was held in such high regard by his players that when he passed, many of them gathered at Diamond Creek to scatter his ashes to the wind. He reflected on the tough-love tutelage and real-life lessons administered by Claude Harmon, and his son Dick. He considered his relationship with Bill Greene, who advocated on his behalf last-minute when the search committee at Grandfather Golf and Country Club had officially declared the recruitment process for their new head professional closed. He thought fondly of his decades-long relationship with his best friend and fellow professional Bruce Davidson. Obviously he thought of his long and fruitful partnership with the golf-mad billionaire. He laughed, and nodded along with everybody else. He couldn't disagree.

CURRENT OR FORMER HEAD GOLF PROFESSIONALS WHO WORKED FOR JOHN MCNEELY INCLUDE:

- Brian Allabastro
- Mike Brooks
- Dan Capozzi
- David Cowger
- Bruce Davidson
- Ray Davis
- Joe Devaney
- Matt Frazier
- Nathan Groce
- Joe Humston
- Kevin Hodes
- Reid Johnson
- Dale Kahlden
- Todd Killian
- Cliff Mann
- Mike Mann
- Marina Marselli
- Ken McDonald
- Michael Meredith
- Mike Mola
- Oliver Peacock
- Brendan Reilly
- Scott Schmidt
- Adam Shanks

- Kellie Stenzel
- Matt Swarts
- Kurt Thompson
- Winston Trivley

John McNeely's tip for fellow golfers:

I'm not going to offer any instructional technique. Instead, an overall thought that virtually all golfers could benefit by. Remember that life is short, this is a great game, and be sure to savor the time you spend with friends both old and new. Take pleasure not only in being with them on the golf course, but also in the post-round drink you share with your foursome. Enjoy the great times that golf provides for those of us who love it. And lastly, when you contemplate a risky shot, also consider how easy or tough it will be to make your recovery.

John McNeely's tip for fellow golf professionals:

I encourage the members of my staff to be ladies and gentlemen every day they come to work. Very few have enough talent to make it out on Tour, but good manners and attentive service are within reach of everyone. I emphasize that this might be their last chance to leave a lasting impression. I encourage all members of our entire team—the golf professionals, maintenance crew, food and beverage personnel and housekeeping staff---to be the first to say good morning with a nod or a smile. Everyone enjoys and appreciates the small things.

Jerry Mowlds
Portland, Oregon

Don Zimmer is legendary in baseball circles for never having earned an honest dollar outside of the game. Every paycheck he ever drew was due to his playing career in both the minor and major leagues, as a coach, a manager, and now in his dotage, a team advisor.

Jerry Mowlds has followed a "Zimmeresque" path in golf. Other than pocket change earned berry-picking in his boyhood, he has been a caddie, tournament player and golf professional for

Jerry Mowlds---the 1984 PGA Professional of the Year

some 60 years. "I've never gotten wealthy from the game," begins the longtime director of instruction at Pumpkin Ridge Golf Club outside of Portland, Oregon. "But I've never been on the welfare rolls, either. I've loved golf since I was a kid, and am thankful I've been able to earn a reasonable living in this wonderful game."

However if his career path was a round of golf, the Montana native has been forced on several occasions to play shots from deep rough, uphill and into the wind. As his narrative unfolds, it's plain to see there have been more than a few obstacles placed in his path.

Originally from Great Falls, Montana, Jerry Mowlds moved to Oregon prior to his tenth birthday. It wasn't too many years later he began caddying at Royal Oaks Country Club in Vancouver, Washington, just across the Oregon state line, which is where he came to the attention of head professional Harry Clow, who eventually gave him his first job as an assistant pro. He had hopes of attending the noted golf power University of Houston, but lack of funds kept him at home. Unfortunately the University of Portland discontinued both the golf and tennis programs simultaneously after his sophomore year, and already a married father at age 19, he declared himself a professional golfer. Shortly thereafter he won his first pro event, but the paycheck wasn't as easy to procure as the victory.

"Back then they had a six-month 'cooling off' period when you turned professional," recalls the former Oregon Open winner. It was a way to insure that you were serious about being a professional, because there was no such thing as the PAT, or playing ability test at that time. So basically they invited me to participate in the event, with no intention of paying me if I won. I made four birdies in the final five holes to win the Oregon Assistant's Championship, but all I got was a pat on the back!"

Shortly thereafter he went to work at Riverside Golf and Country Club in Portland, under Eddie Hogan, one of the most respected professionals in the northwest. "At my first job at Royal Oaks I had the latitude to work on my game daily, but Riverside was a different story. Between giving lessons and shop duty, I needed to learn how to maximize my limited practice time, and still keep my game sharp." His game stayed sharp enough that club members funded his attempt to make it on the PGA Tour. He played his way into the final group in the final round at the 1967 Phoenix Open, getting paired with eventual champion Julius Boros, and ultimately finishing fourth.

His boss Hogan was known as a fine but volatile player, hard on himself, so consequently he didn't win as much as he might have. He had a reputation as a great teacher, but lacked patience when students couldn't grasp concepts quickly, so consequently Mowlds was brought in to nurture slow-learning students, which is when he really began to find both his stride and his ultimate calling as a teacher.

Where Hogan truly excelled was as a merchandiser. "In those days there were no massive golf discount stores, no Edwin Watts, or anything like that," recalls Mowlds, who played in two US Opens and a PGA Championship. "The green grass, on-site pro shop was the main avenue for golfers to obtain equipment and apparel, and Eddie would stock upwards of a thousand pairs of golf shoes in his inventory."

Eddie Hogan was only in his late 50s when he suffered an untimely death in the autumn of 1968, drowning in a tributary of the Columbia River during a duck hunting excursion. Hogan was alone at the time of this mysterious boating accident, and his unexpected passing cast a pall over not only the Portland golf community, but throughout Oregon. Named the co-head professional along with the other assistant pro at Riverside, it was only a year or so later that Mowlds realized the shop wasn't big enough for both of them. So he struck out on his own, purchasing and refurbishing a driving range in Vancouver, Washington.

At the time of his purchase, the PGA of America had just recently consented to allow their members to forgo working at an actual golf course, and instead own or lease a driving range. But they refused to allow apprentices to work there, which was counterintuitive to providing a full range of employment opportunities, and giving these apprentices much-needed experience.

"The PGA has always been a very conservative organization, and at that time in particular it was slow to change, and it took awhile for me to convince them that apprentices could fulfill the duties of a golf professional, yet not be employed as a golf course per se," continues Mowlds, a former winner of the Northwest PGA Championship. "It was ludicrous that they would refuse to allow them the chance to work and teach at driving ranges. It was about this time I became active in my local chapter politically, and remained so for many years forward, as chapter president, then section president, and eventually serving in a national capacity."

The PGA fracas wasn't the only storm that Mowlds had to weather at his ill-fated driving range. His nascent business bore the brunt of one of the only documented tornadoes to ever touch down near Portland. In April 1972 the most damaging west coast tornado in over a century ripped his business to shreds, scattering debris, shredding containment nets, and practically reducing the pro shop-snack bar to rubble. "I was at a Pro-Am 300 miles south of Portland, had driven the green of a par-4, and was looking over a 20-foot eagle putt," recalls the six-time winner of the Oregon PGA Championship. "An official came out, told me I had an emergency call, and before the line went dead my wife simply told me to get back home, the building had been blown over." In the pre-cell phone era, with no local news reports, Mowlds and his Portland-area colleagues had no choice but to make tracks back home post-haste.

That eagle putt was never stroked, unlike the insurance company, which at least stroked a check for some of the value of the now-destroyed business. "The only way to realize any insurance compensation was to rebuild, so in essence I had to buy the range twice." Several years after reopening he was offered the head job at Columbia Edgewater CC, and after running his range for a year

Mowlds has been one of the Northwest's preeminent teachers for some 50 years

or two while maintaining his head professional duties, he sold the range in the middle 70s.

His stint at Columbia Edgewater Country Club in Portland lasted for 17 years, and it was no small point of pride when he named the 1984 PGA Professional of the Year in the midst of his tenure. The club also received a shout-out from Golf Digest, which tabbed it as having one of the lowest aggregate handicaps amongst the membership in the entire nation. "Not only did a large percentage of the membership maintain single-digit handicaps," recounts Mowlds, who was also named Professional of the Year in the Pacific Northwest on four separate occasions, "but we had dozens and dozens of players who were three handicaps or better. The running joke was that our club championship was the most prestigious and hard-to-win title in Oregon!"

"I grew up in Seattle, and Jerry was well-known as one of the great players, teachers and club professionals in the northwest," offers Jim McLean, one of the game's most highly-regarded instructors. "He's about ten years my senior, and was a real role model for me. He was always one of the top guns, and someone I looked up to." Before launching his well-known golf schools at Miami's Doral Resort and in Palm Springs, McLean was the head professional at some of the most prominent clubs in the Met section of New York, including Quaker Ridge and Sleepy Hollow.

"I truly don't think I would have advanced as far as I did if I didn't see firsthand how Jerry operated, and how innovative he was," continues McLean, a PGA Master Professional and the 1994 PGA National Teacher of the Year. "It was the way he ran his clinics, his pro shop merchandising, his marketing techniques, his member interactions, everything. To me he's on the same level as icons like Jackie Burke at Champions in Houston, or Claude Harmon at Winged Foot. He is the consummate golf pro, a one-in-five-thousand type of guy, which is why he was my lead instructor for so many years at my school in Palm Springs, you just don't find gems like that very often."

Speaking of gems, Mowlds became the first director of golf at Pumpkin Ridge, with its indelible USGA imprimatur, when the facility opened in 1992. This charmed club was the host venue when Tiger Woods won his unprecedented third consecutive US Amateur in 1996, as he stormed back from five down to beat Steve Scott. The very next year 30,000 partisan fans were in her corner, but even the cheering throngs couldn't quite get Nancy Lopez the US Women's Open crown that eluded her for her entire career. She settled for second place behind England's Alison Nicholas. Mowlds was front and center at these events, but after five years in the top position, when a management change necessitated that he become predominantly a coat-and-tie administrator and back-office bureaucrat, he chose to move towards instruction exclusively, which was his true passion. He's been the director of instruction ever since.

"Some club memberships are very instruction-oriented, and others aren't. Columbia Edgewater has a membership that loves and seeks out instruction, which is probably why there are so many strong players. Pumpkin Ridge, wonderful as it is, with its two fine courses, memorable history and impeccable service, just isn't wired the same way. The lesson-taking culture isn't strong, despite the fact we have plenty of beginners, and many golfers who could dramatically improve their games. It's just another challenge to face, and overcome. I love it though, and will stay until retirement, although some people like to joke I'm already past retirement," laughs the 70-something Oregon legend.

I've had bumps in the road like everybody else," concludes the PGA National Hall of Fame member. "But the pitfalls and setbacks I've encountered don't change the fact I'm very satisfied with the trajectory of my career. I wish things had gone differently at certain times, but I wouldn't change anything. I've had a fulfilling life as a golf professional, and wouldn't have wanted to do anything else."

CURRENT OR FORMER HEAD GOLF PROFESSIONALS WHO WORKED FOR JERRY MOWLDS INCLUDE:

- Terry Anderson
- Scott Basse
- Les Blakley
- Randy Chang
- Chuck DaSilva

- Andy Heinley
- Dan Hixson
- Scott Larson
- Garth Mattson
- Jeff McRae
- Wayne Moberg
- JD Mowlds
- John Mulliken
- Todd O'Neal
- John Thorsnes
- Bruce Wattenburger
- Todd Young

Jerry Mowlds' tip for fellow golfers:

The short game is where you either waste strokes or save them. Many hit the ball well enough to shoot good scores but are foiled because of seldom getting "up and down." I have taught a more forgiving chipping method for many years, with one ball position, one size swing, one swing speed and the same landing zone relative to the edge of the green. The only variable is the club you chip with.

I recommend a "putting style" with the set up like a conventional putting set up except the ball is played inside of the back foot instead of inside the front foot. The chosen club is held near vertical, the heel of the club is not touching the ground, the face is held very square, even to the point of looking slightly closed, the body is bent over from the hips, the arms are both bent evenly and the stroke as in a long putt, long and smooth with no "hit" at impact. It's a sweep, land the ball within the first six feet of the greens edge and allow for the natural roll.

With the same speed and length of stroke, the ball will roll a predicable distance every-time. I have found that there is 12 feet of roll difference between normal lofted clubs; for instance, a nine iron will roll 30' after landing, an eight iron, 42' and so forth. These are averages on a normal green that is fairly flat, so read the green to make allowances for uphill downhill, faster or firmer or softer greens. This make the long chip, say 70 feet or so, much simpler, a five iron rolls 78' after landing. Do not fall into the trap of trying to make the lower lofted irons get up into the air, let them be very low shots, the lower the better. Keep the shaft leaning forward at impact, think of sweeping the floor, keeping the dust from flying.

Jerry Mowlds' tip for fellow golf professionals:

The business today is much different then when I started more than 50 years ago. Back then most facilities in the northwest were equity clubs, or privately owned daily fee or semi-private courses. Nowadays privately owned or single-facility operations are in the minority.

Corporate ownership means more bottom line focus than ever before. A successful golf professional today has to keep his or her eye squarely focused on the bottom line, while at the same time keeping members or regular customers happy with the operation, and the way they are treated.

The dilemma is that one concept can make the other one difficult. Financial decisions need to be made that often won't please the clientele. Today's pro must have a regular presence at their facility, be visible to their members and customers, often on the first tee during busy periods, and available for discussions and conversations. Some things cannot be left to assistants, as people like talking to the boss. But the pro needs to answer to upper management and/or board of governors in regards to keeping costs in line and profits up, which is far from easy in today's climate.

In some ways the game of golf has been taken out of the golf business, which makes it tough for some to adjust. One of our great advantages as golf professionals is our teaching acumen; we must use it to grow the game, and develop lasting relationships with our clients and customers.

Jim Mrva
Rochester, New York

When traveling golfers consider their favorite destinations, it's a predictable list: Myrtle Beach, Scottsdale, Greater Orlando, Rochester, the Monterey Peninsula, maybe Coastal Oregon or the Alabama Golf Trail.

Did someone mention Rochester? As in upstate New York, not far from Canada, between Buffalo and Syracuse, on the shores of frigid Lake Ontario? Virtually no one would deem the third-largest city in

Jim Mrva – 2010 PGA Professional of the Year

New York as a golf hotbed, but the truth is that the interest level is high, and the roots run deep.

Some of that has to do with the legacy of native son and stylish dandy Walter Hagen, winner of eleven Major championships, who almost single-handedly brought needed luster to the phrase "professional golfer," which was just as much insult as occupational description before he came of age in the 1920s. "The Haig" was born in 1892, three years before the Country Club of Rochester came to fruition, and the man and the club were intertwined almost from the get-go. Hagen began caddying there at age seven, eventually became their assistant pro, and apparently impressed the membership enough that when he captured the 1914 U.S. Open he was on his way to ultimately being named their head professional. Famed golf course architect Robert Trent Jones, 14 years younger than Hagen, also spent time in the CCR caddie yard.

The town also embraces the women's game. The local LPGA Tour stop, now known as the Wegmans LPGA Championship, contested at the prestigious Locust Hill CC, is consistently one of the two or three best-attended events on that Tour, and has been for the 35 years of its existence.

While there are nearly 50 courses in sum total in and around the city, much of the attention is focused on what some refer to as "The Big Eight," an octet of highly-regarded private clubs that all hail from golf's 'Golden Age' of architecture in the teens and 20s. The aforementioned CCR is the oldest, Oak Hill, one of very few clubs to host the U.S. Open, U.S. Senior Open, U.S. Amateur, the Ryder Cup and PGA Championship, is easily the best-known.

Monroe Golf Club, a fine Donald Ross design, is another leading light, and their longtime Head Professional Jim Mrva one of the most highly regarded pros not only in Rochester or the region, but nationally. Look no further than his designation as National PGA Professional of the Year, the greatest accolade in the business, which he was awarded in 2010. Unassuming to a fault, Mrva murmurs, "they have to give it to somebody," but random selection had nothing to do with it. To quote the old Smith-Barney TV commercial, he got that award the old-fashioned way--he earned it.

Of course, earning his way is nothing new to Jim "buy a vowel" Mrva, the son of a Czechoslovakian immigrant who labored intensely in the tannery section of a shoe factory to earn a modest living. The irony is that Jim's dad Frank Mrva, known as Max, who sailed to Ellis Island as a penniless child, with his name pinned to his coat, ended up living a bit of a "white shoe" life, despite the fact he was sweating while stretching leather in the factory doing piecework. The work was demanding, the quota relentless. But when the daily bread had been earned, there was time most every afternoon to get to the golf course, where he would play and practice with dozens of like-minded buddies, factory workers all.

"Immigrants who otherwise couldn't speak a word of English were taught to say 'which way E-J?' when they arrived in America," begins the 60-something Mrva, born in Endicott, New York, about 170 miles south of Rochester. "The Endicott-Johnson Shoe Factory was one of the world's largest, and they offered good benefits, health insurance, and subsidized housing for their employees. So there were thousands of eastern European laborers who made their way to Endicott to build their lives in America."

Many of them also made their way to the company golf course, which was built for both the workers and executives. If the name En-Joie golf club rings a bell, it's because it was home to the PGA Tour's BC Open for 35 years. But decades before the course was home to the pros it was home to the proletariat, and Max Mrva, who became an excellent golfer in his own right, even winning the club championship several times, raised his family in a modest tract home just two blocks from the club.

"I was crazy about golf from the get-go," continues the Western New York PGA Hall of Fame member. "Lots of kids in the neighborhood were. Many of our dads were physically strong from the factory work and strong players also. They lived simple lives. There wasn't much travel, or lots of 'extras' around the house. Our vacations were always local, maybe up to Lake George in the car for a few days. But they ate heartily, played hard, and could really play golf. And that was just the way we grew up."

Mrva grew up caddying and playing, eventually working in the golf shop for longtime head professional Bill Dennis. He was a good player locally, and ended up at New Jersey's Rutgers University, captaining the golf team his senior season. He came back to Endicott post-college with a journalism degree, "not qualified to do much of anything," chuckles the pro. He eventually became a carpet installer with his father, who had given up factory work. He broke into the golf business unexpectedly, the beneficiary of a "local boy makes good" scenario, but the local boy wasn't Jim Mrva. Instead it was the En-Joie assistant pro, Richie Karl, who won the B.C. Open in 1974, making him the last club pro to date to actually win on the PGA Tour.

The unexpected win sent Karl off to chase additional riches on Tour, and a sweater-folding vacancy in Bill Dennis' golf shop. He tapped Mrva to be his new assistant, and the young husband and father saw opportunity and a rediscovered ambition in the green grass that was conspicuously absent from a world of carpet tacks and deep-pile.

"I had shagged balls for Bill's students during their lessons as a kid," recalls the former Western New York PGA section president. "And it always intrigued me how he would interview the student about their game, their strengths and weaknesses before they began hitting balls. That stuck with me when I went to work for him as an adult, and really helped my teaching."

Some informal teaching precipitated his next big break. "There was a little Italian guy named Nemo D'Agostino who drove a bulldozer around En Joie from time to time, because course renovations were always ongoing. He would jump off the 'dozer when he saw me, and always ask for advice with his swing or grip, and we became quite friendly," recounts the PGA Master Professional. "Turns out he owned the construction company, was a person of influence at his club in Utica, chairman of the greens committee, and some years later when the head professional at Yahnundasis Golf Club retired, Nemo recommended me for the job!"

Out of the blue, and with no prior experience at either a private club or as a head pro, Mrva was handed the reins at a classic old club dating from 1897, a little-known gem designed by Walter Travis, the three-time U.S. Amateur Champion. "I spent four fabulous years there after working as an assistant at En Joie for the previous five. We were very content, and could have stayed there for far longer, but then Monroe Golf Club contacted me."

Two main reasons lured Mrva the 130 miles due west. The first was the reputation of Rochester as a private golf Mecca, with its wide array of clubs. The second was that Monroe's infrastructure was larger, offering more of a support staff, with additional assistants and shop personnel, the better for the up-and-coming pro to improve and increase his service level, and perform his duties more effectively. "I began my duties in 1983, Susie and I raised our three kids in Rochester, and it's been a pleasure to serve the Monroe membership these past 30 years."

Craig Harmon, another National PGA Professional of the Year, who already had a decade of service under his belt at nearby Oak Hill before Mrva came to town, has nothing but high praise for his friend and colleague. "It goes without saying that Jim is a great golf professional. But more importantly, he is a great human being. He

Mrva never realized he was soon to be featured in a book with nearly the same name

has such zest for his job, is constantly trying to improve and gives anything and everything he can to his members and their guests. He makes time for everyone, which is a difficult chore in a business like ours."

Harmon, 40 years the head man at Oak Hill, and the son of legendary Winged Foot professional and former Masters Champion Claude Harmon, continues. "My father was the consummate golf professional. I feel Jim is cut from the same mold. I consider that high praise, and not a compliment I offer to very many others in this business."

Upon relocating to Rochester, Mrva was amazed to learn about the Twilight League, which is an interclub competition between many of the Big Eight clubs that has been going on for more than 75 years. "All these clubs have survived, even thrived, through economic ups and downs, with major employers leaving the area, through wartime, through various levels of interest in the game." His home club is also home to the prestigious Monroe Invitational, a leading amateur event also past its 75th birthday. Past champions include Jeff Sluman, Dustin Johnson, Chris DiMarco and DJ Trahan, all of whom went onto win multiple PGA Tour titles.

Besides the plethora of PGA sectional awards he's amassed, from merchandising to mentoring to community service, it was Mrva's interest in charitable pursuits that brought him to the attention of the PGA of America, and ultimately to the high honor bestowed upon him in 2010. He has long been a Big Brother in that eponymous organization, and served on the Board of the First Tee of Rochester since the beginning. "We hosted an outing for disadvantaged kids at a local college golf course when the PGA Championship came to Oak Hill in 2003, which precipitated the founding of our local First Tee organization. We then did something similar five years later when the Senior PGA Championship came to town."

Speaking of his award, he recalls with amazement how a hundred Monroe members flew to Orlando for the ceremony, along with 40 family members and dozens of former assistants. But despite his successes, he always models himself after the example of local golf legend Sam Urzetta, the 1950 U.S. Amateur champion, who then spent 37 years as the Country Club of Rochester's head professional. "Sam, who was a mentor to me and to numerous other pros in the area for years, was honored with the Country Club of Rochester's Thistle Award, which has only been bestowed three times since its inception," recounts

Mrva, with awe. "His acceptance speech was 20 minutes long, and he never said the word 'I.' He only looked to give credit to others, and downplayed his own achievements and legacy. That's who I try to emulate."

In 40 years in the business Mrva has only made three stops, at En Joie, Yahnundasis and Monroe, and describes the membership at each club in similar fashion: "They have all been wonderful people, treated my family and I like their own, and couldn't have been nicer to me or my staff." His across-the-board commendations seem curious. It's a well-known fact that one of the wearisome attributes of a golf pro's job is dealing with certain members, patrons or guests that can be challenging, if not demanding, if not downright difficult. How to explain this four-decade rainbow ride of brotherly love?

"I think it's the whole of upstate New York," reasons the sliver-haired pro in conclusion. "When people think of New York they usually think of the city. But upstate is comprised of small towns, agriculturally oriented, factories, shipping businesses and blue collar jobs. People have to work very hard up here. Those who become successful enough to join these nice clubs don't look down or pull rank on those who serve them, because they remember their own roots."

So does Jim Mrva. His unconventional journey from factory background to factoring so significantly in the golf business is an immigrant tale well worth recounting, as unique and ambitious as America itself.

CURRENT OR FORMER HEAD PROFESSIONALS WHO WORKED FOR JIM MRVA INCLUDE:

- Rob Agresti
- Scott Bates
- Dave Champagne
- Bob DiBerardinis
- Bryce Finnman
- Brady Foore
- Mike George
- John Harmon
- Theron Harvey
- Jon Hoecker
- Mike Hulbert
- Jim Kane
- Jeff Kiddie
- Sean Lalley
- Greg Mulhern
- Debbie Murphy
- Matt Pittsley
- Jeff Pulli
- Kevin Regan
- Eric Schomske
- Jim Scott
- Charley Winn
- Tom Yeager

Jim Mrva's tip for fellow golfers:

When I first learned to play the game we were taught to pitch and play sand shots with our hands ahead of the ball. If we happened to chunk it, we were told to put our hands even more forward. This position creates a very steep angle of attack into the shot and requires a precise hit on the ball. If your club lands even slightly behind the ball, you will hit a fat shot on soft turf or the club will bounce into the ball on firm ground.

Practice sliding your wedge along the ground rather than hitting down into the ball. Imagine a wide motion back and through versus a narrow up and down swing. Setting the wrists too quickly on the backswing contributes to a very steep angle. Mimic the backswing of Steve Stricker who uses very little wrists in his backswing combined with a gentle body rotation on his follow through.

A good drill to help with this is to lay three tees on the ground back to back pointing in the direction of the shot. Practice brushing the tees sending all three tees forward and down the fairway. Brush the grass instead of taking a divot.

Jim Mrva's tip for fellow golf professionals:

As I was leaving En-Joie Golf Club in Endicott, New York to go to my first Head Professional position at the Yahnundasis Golf Club in Utica, New York my boss, Bill Dennis, GM/Golf Professional said one thing to me:

"Treat everyone you meet like family and you'll never go wrong. Treat members, employees, salesmen and fellow Golf Professionals as you would like your father, mother, sister and brothers to be treated. Treat everyone as equally as you can. Show everyone respect and compassion no matter what their stature or importance."

Bill was an incredible guy who was the Golf Professional at En-Joie Golf Club from 1962-2000. En-Joie Golf Club was built and run by the Endicott-Johnson Shoe Corporation from 1929 to 1961. The company encouraged all of its employees from management right down through factory workers to play golf. When the company fell on hard times the course was given to the village of Endicott in 1961. The new membership included factory workers, doctors, lawyers, businessmen and golfers from every walk of life. The club operation was overseen by the Mayor, Village Trustees and a Golf Commission. Bill was a very special man. He treated all of these varied people equally. He was a man of honor and integrity.

Other than my father, I learned more from Bill than anyone else in my career. Whatever good fortune in golf has come my way I owe to what Bill Dennis taught me all those many years ago. To this day I encourage my assistant professionals and fellow employees to follow this simple rule.

Fred Muller
Frankfort, Michigan

L ove affair. There are no better words to describe Fred Muller's relationship with the glorious Crystal Downs Country Club in northern Michigan, where he has faithfully served as head professional for nearly 40 years. It's been more than a half century since he initially stepped on the property as an interloping teen, befriended the pro, and played the magnificent Alister MacKenzie design for the first time.

Fred Muller hard at work

It wasn't long thereafter that he put aside boyhood ambitions like professional athlete, or even more sensible career paths like English professor. He instead began dreaming of working at this little-known golf Nirvana, tucked amidst imposing hardwoods, peppered with wild fescue grasses, with long range views of both Crystal Lake and mighty Lake Michigan beyond. 15 years after first conceiving of this life by the lake, finding a career in the game he loved, Muller in fact took the reins. He's been there ever since.

"It's one of the finest creations of arguably the greatest architect of all time, working on a beautiful piece of property, at the height of his creative powers, with his construction foreman being Perry Maxwell, who later went on to great acclaim himself as a course architect," enthuses Muller, now in his mid 60s. "The classic clubhouse sits on a 250-foot sand dune overlooking Crystal Lake, with the golf course itself tumbling down the hill away from the property's apex."

Acclaimed golf course architect Tom Doak has been singing its praises for decades, and is so fond of the layout he became a member himself. "When I first visited, Crystal Downs was off the radar of the top-100 lists, and as the designated tour guide for the course, Fred Muller was clearly interested in the opinion of anyone who'd played enough golf around the nation to assess how the course stacked up. We became friends for life when I offered my opinion that it was in the same class as the best courses in America."

The course was the brainchild of Standard Oil executive Walkley Ewing, who wanted to build a golf course and summer getaway near Lake Michigan in the village of Frankfort. While the original 1927 course routing was nondescript, Mackenzie worked his magic and completely revamped the golf course. Now northern Michigan is one of the best-known and most-visited summertime golf destinations, with hundreds of courses, anchored by large resorts such as Treetops and Boyne Mountain. But when Crystal Downs came to fruition more than 85 years ago, some four hours from Detroit and well over five hours from Chicago, it was the lone outpost of its kind.

Barely 6,500 yards long, its serene setting, amazing roller-coaster greens, quartet of short-but-strategic (under 360 yards) par-4 holes, abounding fescue and dramatic bunkering combine in a seamless way that makes the golf course an unforgettable experience. When Fred Muller first saw it as a 14-year old in 1962 he was immediately smitten. "My parents had rented a cottage for a week on Crystal Lake that summer," recalls the Michigan native. "I was getting interested in golf, made my way over there, and Johnny Vaughn, who was the pro, somehow took a liking to me. I played over there a couple of times in the early evening with him that week, and we stayed in touch."

Muller eventually headed south to play golf at Georgia State, where he became acquainted with the great Bobby Jones when he took his first job as an assistant professional at the posh Capital City Club in Atlanta after graduation. All the while he was in occasional contact with Vaughn back in Michigan. "Whenever I was back at home I would try and pay a visit. We probably played together a few dozen times over the years, and he helped me with my game."

More importantly, he helped him with his career. When Vaughn planned his retirement several years in advance, he strongly recommended Muller as his replacement. The protégé was cast into a uniquely desirable circumstance, where his first head pro job was in the offing, but still a couple years away. He figured if his 'dream job' was soon to be a long-term reality, he better get some head pro experience. So after nearly a decade down south, both in school and at Capital City, he headed back to Michigan.

The difference between Capital City Club, which would occasionally feature a ten-piece orchestra to entertain the Atlanta aristocracy during lunch, and counted three former British Amateur Champions on the membership rolls, (Jones, Charlie Yates and Harvie Ward) and his new club near blue-collar Flint, Michigan, was a chasm that made the Grand Canyon seem like a crack in the sidewalk.

Davison Country Club was thriving in the mid 70s, the auto plants and body shops going full bore, and the club would fill up with third-shift factory employees just off work at dawn, who according to their pro at that time, "would ingest beer intravenously so they could gesture with their hands at the bar!" It was just two short years, they knew his position had an expiration date on the day he began, but the membership was so fond of Muller they presented him with a plaque featuring every member's name and $3,000 cash the day he left. "It was an amazing and unexpected bonus," recalls the pro, "kind of an unofficial severance package, all in folding money. What was just as great is they decided to promote my assistant pro, Mike Minto, to the head job, and he's been there ever since."

The cash windfall was useful, because there wasn't much money to be made at Crystal Downs is those early years. Muller was single at the time, and spent his seven month off-season playing tournaments, for a while in Australia, and then in South America, where he found himself in the final group on the final day of the Brazilian Open no less than three different times. While that exotic crown proved elusive, he did capture the Michigan Open, and was a six-time champion of the northern Michigan PGA Section. "I never made much money playing, but because back then my income at the club was also pretty sparse, the tournament winnings were a nice supplement, percentage-wise!"

Muller describes the Crystal Downs membership that he has served so faithfully as a very low-key, but highly accomplished group. Hailing predominantly from greater Chicago, St. Louis, Detroit, Cincinnati, and Indianapolis, most members have been around the club and Crystal Lake for generations. Despite the fact that many are captains of industry or highly-skilled and sought-after professionals, the club has a low-key vibe, nothing ostentatious or grandiose about it or its members.

Fred Muller (bottom left) with his Crystal Downs staff and caddie corps

Tom Doak, who has built some of the world's most stunning courses in the last dozen-or-more years, credits his long-time pro with giving his design career a jump start. "When I first ventured to northern Michigan to visit Crystal Downs some thirty summers ago, Fred Muller already seemed like he would be the professional there for the rest of his life," offers the creator of 'must-play' courses like Oregon's Pacific Dunes and New Zealand's Cape Kidnappers. "He was the epitome of the old-school club pros I met in those days, a fine golfer with a great sense of humor and a better short game. He played practically every evening, and wasn't likely to be beaten on his home track, even by visiting Tour pros."

"Not long after my second visit to the club," continues Doak, "and before I became a member, another local pro called Fred and asked his advice on finding an architect for a new public course in

Traverse City, which is about 40 miles to the east. That was how I wound up with my first solo design job. He did the same for my colleague and fellow architect Mike DeVries a few years afterward. When Fred Muller talks, about golf, anyway, people listen!"

"Our members not only have a tremendous loyalty to the club, but an affinity to Crystal Lake and Frankfort also," continues Muller. "There have been deep lifelong friendships forged here, marriages have resulted, and the whole club has a close-knit feel that is highly unusual."

The club itself might be close-knit, but such is not always the case between the year-round population and the seasonal visitors. To help reduce friction between the two populaces, Muller began inviting any fulltime resident of Benzie County out to play its crown jewel at season's end. "I came to this area from 150 miles away, so I have a good sense of the dichotomy that exists. More than a decade ago we began having the locals out one day in October, and to say it's been a popular program would be a vast understatement," continues the Grand Rapids-raised pro. "The tee sheet is filled from dawn until dusk, we feed them while they are here, and they treat the course with meticulous care. The end result is that the locals, who might have been either indignant or at least apathetic about Crystal Downs' existence, now see this gem as a source of civic pride, and something they've become invested in on a personal level. It's lots of work because in late season we are down to a skeleton staff, but its become an invaluable tool for us, and a day that everyone greatly enjoys."

Muller also finds enjoyment in the club's resurrected caddie program which he brought back from dormancy in the year 2000. The advent of golf carts meant that caddies went extinct in the 1960s, but the pro brought them back. He recruited, trained and retained a group of some 20 core caddies, several of whom have gone onto become Evans Scholars, which have greatly mitigated the expense of their college educations. "It's always bittersweet when they leave," continues Muller, who held onto one former co-worker by marrying her. Kay is the club's former tennis pro, and mother of their two children. "I know it's inevitable, but I hate to lose my employees; caddies, assistant pros, golf shop personnel, despite the great pride I take in seeing them move upward and onward. Mentoring them and teaching them the business brings us close together, and when they leave it's always tough to see them go."

What he would really like to see go is the unreasonable expectations of golfers everywhere as they pine for a blemish-free golf environment. "The game is too perfect, too manicured. Golf would still be great for virtually everyone if conditioning was 90% of what it is. The problem is that last 10%, trying to put every last blade of grass in place, costs a fortune!"

In a golf world where the typical head professional changes jobs about as regularly as we hold a presidential election, it's enlightening to hear the philosophy of a man who took his 'lifetime position' in the same year that Gerald Ford gave way to Jimmy Carter in the White House. "It has to be a great fit," concludes Muller, "there has to be a comfort level between the pro and his fellow employees and bosses on the administrative side, and a kinship between the pro and the membership. I never left because I love the area, think this club is absolutely outstanding, the membership is phenomenal, and I've felt the same way since I first saw it 50-plus years ago. From my office window I can see the golf course, Crystal Lake, and Lake Michigan beyond that. It's amazing, and I can honestly say that there has never been a day when I didn't feel like coming to work in all the years I've been here."

CURRENT OR FORMER HEAD GOLF PROFESSIONALS WHO WORKED FOR FRED MULLER INCLUDE:

- Jim Boyle
- Jeff Drimel
- Bob Fossum
- Marc Gilmore
- Dave Hall
- J.D. Kittleson
- Dave Layman
- Dave Mabry
- John Miles
- Mike Minto
- Tom Patterson
- Paulo Rocha
- Matt Sayad
- Mark Styles

Fred Muller's tip for fellow golfers:

I've had quite a bit of success putting, both personally and in teaching the concepts of putting. Most golfers make a big effort to have a perfect line for their putts, but think that proper pace is simply going to happen. They are wrong, and often during the ensuing stroke they question pace and everything goes wrong. They speed-up or decelerate, jerk or jab.

Over my long career at Crystal Downs, which have some of the most difficult greens in the nation, I've developed a method to determine "pace" during the approach to the putt. Briefly, too many players make needless and thoughtless practice strokes before each putt. It is the final practice stroke that counts, and is the one that will be repeated due to short term muscle memory for the actual stroke. So bottom line is to make sure your final practice stroke is very thoughtful and repeatable before actually putting.

One other word of wisdom: Never putt a putt within two feet. The most popular theory is that one should not take "gimmies" during daily play because it leaves one unprepared for a putt that truly is important. I suggest if you never putt, you never miss and thus you'll be very positive under pressure. I say this tongue in cheek but the pace stuff is important.

Fred Muller's tip for fellow golf professionals:

The PGA like many professional organizations requires periodic recertification of its membership. Members receive recertification points for attending meetings, seminars, and CPR lessons etc.

Many years ago I was attending just such a seminar. The topic was "How to hire an assistant." The presenters suggested that the three most important criteria for hiring are that the applicant must be computer literate, loyal to the PGA, and be able to pee into a jar without showing signs of drug use.

I stood, was recognized, and noted that my three criteria were entirely different. I want employees who have a strong command of the English language, an outstanding sense of humor, and a passion for the game of golf. They shrugged, and there you have it.

Phil Owenby
Richmond, Virginia

More than 20 million copies of the book <u>Don't Sweat the Small Stuff</u> have been sold since it debuted in 1996. But it's a safe bet Phil Owenby never rushed out to his local Barnes & Noble.

Owenby, the Director of Operations at the superb Kinloch Golf Club in Richmond, Virginia, is far too cool (and congenial) a customer to actually perspire. But he does conspire, along with an incredibly friendly and accommodating staff, to provide

Phil Owenby leaves no stone unturned

both an attention to detail and service element to members and their guests that is almost unparalleled. For Phil Owenby, nothing is too small, incidental or trivial to escape his notice.

That's just one of the reasons he was noticed decades ago by Vinny Giles, who might be the most prominent amateur golfer this country has produced in more than 80 years, since Bobby Jones completed the Grand Slam and retired in 1930. The Kinloch principal won the 1972 US Amateur, the 1975 British Amateur, competed on four Walker Cup teams, and captained another.

He then captured the US Senior Amateur in 2009, and the 37 years between USGA victories is a record that will likely never be equaled.

While his competitive record is enduring, so is this venerable golf club he helped establish in the rolling countryside of pastoral Goochland County, which has been winning raves for its conditioning and impeccable customer service since its debut in 2001.

Giles' spent his career as a sports agent, and the high-profile golfers he has represented include Major champions such as Davis Love III, Justin Leonard, Lanny Wadkins, Tom Kite, Ernie Els, Beth Daniel and Meg Mallon. Owing to his professional background, it's easy to understand his agent's analogy. "I have been fortunate to visit and play at many of the great golf clubs both in the US and overseas," states Giles, who won the Virginia Open and the Virginia Amateur a total of ten times in combination. "I can honestly say I wouldn't trade Phil Owenby for any other club professional of my acquaintance. If this was the NFL, I would have given up my star player and additional draft picks to land him! I've known him for more than 40 years, he used to be the head pro at the course where I grew up playing in Lynchburg, Virginia, and there was never a choice about who we wanted running our golf operation at Kinloch."

Originally from Charlottesville, Virginia, young Phil was still in grade school when his family moved to Raleigh, North Carolina. His dad and uncle decided to partner in a new golf venture called Wildwood Country Club. "My dad was a banker, my uncle Ralph Lang was a golf pro, and they went into business together, my dad taking over club operations," begins Owenby. First exposed to the game at age six, moving to Raleigh at age nine, thanks to the ministrations of Uncle Ralph, a scratch player by age 12. Maybe more importantly, in all the countless hours he spent at the club, the youngster began to get a feel for what it was like to run an entire golf operation, from the office to the dining room to the driving range, an early and informal education that would pay huge dividends down the road.

A strong high school player, he won a golf scholarship to North Carolina State, but tangling with future PGA Tour stars over at Wake Forest like Jay Haas and Curtis Strange made him realize his future was in the clubs, not with the clubs.

Despite the dozen-plus years he spent in Tarheel territory, Owenby's future career was slated to play out exclusively in his Old Virginia Home. After his 1976 college graduation he began back in his hometown of Charlottesville as an assistant pro at Farmington Country Club. Three years later he nabbed his first head pro job at age 24, at Hunting Hills Country Club in Roanoke. Then it was off to Boonsboro Country Club in Lynchburg, where he first came to the attention of distinguished member Vinny Giles, about a dozen years his senior, who took on a mentoring role. Seeing the young pro's potential, and his desire to improve as an instructor, Giles introduced him to acclaimed teaching professionals like Davis Love Jr., Bob Toski and Peter Kostis, among others.

Four years later he took over at Roanoke Country Club, where he spent a dozen productive years before being tapped by Giles to spearhead the operations at their shiny new club outside of Richmond, a post Owenby, not yet 60 years old, has no intention of relinquishing until his retirement sometime well down the road.

"Roanoke CC was where I really started to find my stride as a golf professional," explains Owenby. "My previous job in Lynchburg had 300—400 families, but back in Roanoke for a second time it was more like 600-700 families. Because I had grown up in a family golf operation where we ran everything, I attempted to do the same thing."

It wasn't just the work ethic and natural acumen that eventually paved his way to Richmond. It was the fact that virtually all of Kinloch's key players were aware of and impressed with his demeanor and intelligence. Course architect Lester George was doing renovation work at Roanoke CC, and had regular interaction with Owenby. A highly regarded golf professional and entrepreneur named Charlie Staples owned a nearby golf course called Countryside, one of many courses he owned nationwide, and he ended up as one of Kinloch's original managing partners. Even the original landowner where Kinloch was created, C.B. Robertson, who served as another founding member, knew of Owenby, owing to the fact that his college roommate was president of Roanoke CC. "Many people helped me get to where I am today, and helped us get Kinloch to a certain level," admits the unassuming pro. "Charlie Staples was certainly one of the most essential, his familiarity with club operations and knowledge about starting a golf club from scratch were indispensable."

Owenby commenced work at Kinloch in January of 2000, and the course opened in spring in 2001. Acclimating to life in Richmond, meeting founding and potential members, setting up accounts with vendors, hiring staff, all while working from a modest trailer, as the handsome, dark wood clubhouse didn't open until autumn of 2002. "Wearing all the hats I do is probably the most pleasing aspect of the job, and being involved with the culture of this club from the beginning. "Whether it's hiring, food and beverage, recruiting, marketing, membership, golf, administration, and other aspects of our operation, I enjoy working with our terrific team in all areas."

He also enjoys summing up the Kinloch experience thusly: Southern hospitality. It's as good a two-word phrase as any to succinctly describe the graciousness that imbues the club. At Kinloch, employees tend to act, not react, and the little touches they provide make a massive impact. If a valet notices a member's car has less than a quarter tank, unbidden, he'll gas it up at the corner filling station, the fuel charge then reflected on the member's monthly statement. If a guest staying at one of the club cottages prefers a hypo-allergenic pillow, a staffer will make a quick run to the local department store. If a guest orders a refill of the same beverage post-round, it's made note of, and the next time he visits the barman will pour him the same libation in advance.

Because of the Giles influence, Kinloch is a competition-oriented club, with dozens of excellent players on the membership rolls. But it's also a business club, an entertainment-oriented club, single-memberships only, no family memberships, virtually all men, which is why the service element is such a vital component to the entire operation.

"The expectation levels of our members and their guests keep the adrenaline flowing. There's always something to improve, and we can never stand pat, or rest on our laurels around here," continues Owenby. "We are in this together, and from the caddie master to the chef, the locker room manager to our golf staff, we try to identify and hire enthusiastic, proactive individuals who can anticipate and deliver the type of service that's expected once you come through our gate."

There have been comparisons made between Kinloch and Augusta National, due in some part because of the stellar amateur careers of their respective founders. They are both wonderful clubs in flawless condition, and an invitation to play either venue is coveted. But the National has the Masters, and thus the mystique and history that cannot be replicated. "Nothing in our lifetimes can approach what has transpired at Augusta over all the decades," states Giles, who was invited to play in the Masters on nine separate occasions. "I'm just pleased that some folks even mention us in the same breath. It's quite a complement for a club that's barely a dozen years old."

According to Giles, one of Owenby's few faults is that he works too much. "I think he's on property 14 hours a day at the least. He's absolutely tireless, but to be honest I think he overdoes it, and I bet his wife would agree with me." Giles adds that Owenby is a classic example of the iron fist in a velvet glove. "He's a stickler for detail, the most service-oriented person I have ever seen in my life, in any field, leaves no stone unturned, and holds his staff to extremely strict standards. The best compliment we receive is from first-time visitors who say that after 20 minutes on property they feel like they are members. Phil is the nicest guy in the world, but if you miss a trick, or somehow slack off in some capacity, you will quickly find that he's not the nicest guy in the world! That said, he has a very loyal staff, and they think the world of him."

"We have a wonderful golf course, Lester George did a fantastic job in designing it, but Kinloch is just as much about the people," states Owenby. "It's about excellence, commitment and dedication. It's about treating people above and beyond what they have come to expect, it's about reaching and surpassing high goals that we set for ourselves."

Initially speaking, the goals were more modest. Kinloch was conceived as an upscale daily fee course (perhaps a $50 or $75 green fee in Richmond) but when Giles walked the property after it was cleared he realized that the setting and ambience were so

Phil Owenby with mentor and acclaimed amateur champion Vinny Giles

special that the course needed to be more than a daily-use facility. "I approached C.B. Robertson, suggested we turn it into a private golf club with a national membership component, and even though it didn't make the same sense from a financial perspective, he agreed, and that was the direction we chose."

"We originally thought our national memberships would be a fairly small group. But of our 500 or so members, only slightly more than half are local," explains Giles. "Part of that is the business community in Richmond has contracted, but another part is that the club's reputation has grown quickly. We are a second club for most of our national members, and the golf course, the staff, and Phil Owenby himself are a large part of why we have enjoyed this popularity from those who live outside the area."

"Besides the complete faith I have in him and the respect I have for his abilities, Phil was the obvious choice because we both figured this would be his last job in the business," concludes Vinny Giles, now the club's honorary chairman. "I dislike change, I prefer continuity, and I didn't want to hire a pro that was going to use our club as a stepping stone to another job he might have deemed better." An ironic concept, because in part due to Phil Owenby's renowned attention to detail, there are few golf jobs better than at Kinloch.

"The 'to-do' list around here never goes away," concludes the driven pro, who continues to fret (if not exactly sweat) about the small stuff. "No matter how much we do, there's always something else. The list might get shorter for awhile, but it never disappears completely, there are always additions."

One might think this admission would come with a heavy sigh, or at least a shrug of the shoulders, this Sisyphean list confronting him each and every day. But it's the opposite—the pro offers a smile of satisfaction as he makes the pronouncement. His 'to-do' list is his lifeblood, his raison d'être for coming to work every morning, and Phil Owenby wouldn't have it any other way.

CURRENT OR FORMER HEAD GOLF PROFESSIONALS WHO WORKED FOR PHIL OWENBY INCLUDE:

- Mark Fry
- Greg Guman
- Jonathan Ireland
- Josh Points
- Patrick Seither
- Andrew Shuck

Phil Owenby's tip for fellow golfers:

If you struggle to bring your practice game to the golf course itself, I suggest going out for your regular practice session and allot 90 minutes for a 9-hole Captain's Choice round with two golf balls. If your handicap is greater than 10 and/or you are attempting to gain more confidence with your game on the course, play two ball Captain Choice selecting the BEST shot after each play. This method will allow you to score at your potential and give you the most confidence in your game. It also promotes you swinging more freely and being more aggressive around and on the greens. With two chances for each shot you will notice a more fluid and target approach to each shot. Try to play this 9-hole practice session alone to give you a better potential for concentration and focus on your game. Along with the benefit of hitting the shots on the course with various types of terrain and surfaces (fairway, rough, bunkers) versus the practice tee, you will also have the added opportunity to work on course management, shot strategy, trajectories and distance control.

For the more skilled players I suggest the same two ball Captain's Choice, but selecting the WORST ball after each play. This method is a challenging format as it requires each shot to be played with positive focus based on result. We find too many shots are hit on the practice tee without regard for the next shot to be played. The variation of playing the WORST of the two balls in this Captain's Choice practice game demands more concentration on target, strategy and course management.

I have found this type of practice to be very beneficial along with a great amount of fun for my fellow golfers. We all will find more time to practice if it is enjoyable and improves our scores!

Phil Owenby's tip for fellow golf professionals:

There are many attributes that characterize a successful professional in the golf industry. One of those that I believe is the most valuable is ANTICIPATION. This is a quality that allows the individual and team to provide a level of hospitality and service that will be a level above. Anticipating the wants and needs of your clientele, your teammates and your governance will provide the added ingredient to insure success. It involves being conscientious and ahead of schedule with various aspects of your services. Each club or course has the basic necessities of operating the business. View each aspect of these fundamental procedures and impress on every fellow staff member the importance of always having your doors open, staff in place, facilities clean and product ready BEFORE the clientele is expected to arrive. Their expectation is the fuel for our anticipation. We must be thinking ahead and be prepared to provide a level of service and presentation that will exceed their expectation. The anticipation of expectation will give us the benefit of preparing ahead of time and providing a positive experience, which will insure a return visit and support of our operations.

Anticipation is a core value for our operations that is expected from each of us associated with the club. It comes in many forms and can be applied to every staff position in the operation. I challenge each of us to communicate with every staff member on our teams to offer three to five items of anticipation that will improve service, efficiency, relationships and exceed expectations of clientele and/ or fellow staff members. It improves the accuracy and efficiency of responsibilities while offering a more concentrated and comprehensive level of hospitality for our members and guests. I have found that people notice the little things that are completed for them without having to ask for the service. Anticipation in any and every area of our businesses is the quality that will distinguish the operations and elevate the stature of our staff members. Make it a priority to anticipate the wants and needs of your customers along with your fellow staff members and you will experience a positive growth in your operations.

Tony Pancake
Carmel, Indiana

The majority of golf professionals go from little-known club to lesser-known club, and the closest they get to a high-profile golf event is walking the grounds, or watching on TV.

Not so with Indiana native Tony Pancake. His distinctive name is matched by an equally distinctive career, having held the top job at several of the best-known and most highly regarded clubs in the nation. He has also been host pro at important golf events some half-a-dozen times,

Tony Pancake—back home in Indiana

more than a career's worth, all the more impressive considering the man is just past 50.

One needn't possess the deductive reasoning powers of the Inspector General to see the correlation between Pancake's impressive resume and his early exposure to an impressive lineup of teaching professionals. Despite being an all-state golfer in high school, he was lightly recruited heading to college, mostly in the Midwest, but chose Alabama. "I was determined to go to the warmest-weather school that offered me a scholarship," begins the Director of Golf at Crooked Stick, outside of Indianapolis. "I wanted to be able to work on my game year round."

Working on his game quickly became working in the game. After two years on the golf team, the undergrad went to work for the esteemed teaching professional Hank Johnson at North River Golf and Country Club in Tuscaloosa. "I was basically a 'go-fer' at the Golf Digest Schools that were occasionally held at the club, and I watched and learned from teaching luminaries like Bob Toski, Jim Flick, Peter Kostis, Jack Lumpkin and Davis Love Jr.," continues Pancake, who is quick to admit he might have learned just as much outside the classroom than inside of it as he pursued his accounting degree.

Lumpkin took a liking to the aspiring pro and shortly after his graduation, hired him as an assistant at the Elk River Club in the mountains of western North Carolina. In these early years he also worked as a teaching pro in Cleveland for a bit, spent a winter season in Vero Beach, and eventually out at Troon Country Club in Scottsdale, which had the added benefit of keeping him close to his fiancé (now his wife and mother of their four children) Libby Akers, who was a finalist in the US Girls Junior Amateur in 1980, and a scholarship golfer at ASU. "I give lots of credit to Scott Davenport, who I worked for in both Alabama and Florida, for really mentoring me. He taught me as much or more about being a successful golf professional as anyone else I've met or worked with."

Pancake was just 24 when he was hired for his first head professional's position, at Valhalla Golf Club in Louisville, Kentucky. "I had good references from some of the big name professionals who had taken me under their wing, and I guess they liked the fact my hometown was just an hour or so north, across the Indiana state line." Worried about his youthful appearance, "I looked about 16 at the time," he recalls, Pancake thought about wearing spectacles to make him look older during the interview, but decided he would sink or swim with his usual contact lenses. He swam.

In the nine years he spent at Valhalla, he was host pro at the 1996 PGA Championship, in which Mark Brooks bested Kentuckian Kenny Perry in a playoff. "It had been nearly 45 years since Kentucky hosted a Major, and I concentrated on making sure the players, fans and my own members had a great time and were well taken care of that week."

After a single-year dalliance as head professional at Hurstbourne Country Club, a 27-hole facility cross-town from Valhalla, Pancake was tapped for another big job, at prestigious Baltimore Country Club, a Top 100 facility featuring 36 holes of golf including an A.W. Tillinghast classic from the 1920s. "We had three small kids at the time and wanted to stay in Louisville, but I couldn't resist the opportunity to work at such a highly-regarded club."

Baltimore CC had 3,000 total members, 800 of them golf members. "I always study the membership directory when I begin a new job, to accelerate my familiarity with the members," explains Pancake, whose career in Baltimore spanned six years; three years as head professional, and then an additional three as Director of Golf. "But in this case, I might as well have been trying to memorize the phone book! I noticed there were about 75 different Miller's in the directory. When I first met all the members at an introductory meeting in 1998, I said, 'it'll take me some time to learn everyone's name, but I figure if I call you Mr. Miller I'll be right about 10% of the time!"

The Baltimore years were fruitful and rewarding for the pro and his entire family, but the perfect opportunity was still to come.

Pancake's longtime friend and home state mentor Jim Ferriell was edging close to retirement after spending nearly 30 years as the head professional at Crooked Stick, one of Hall-of-Fame architect Pete Dye's most compelling and renowned creations. Crooked Stick is where then-unknown John Daly burst onto the golf scene by winning the 1991 PGA Championship, and it is the club where Pete and his wife Alice make their summertime home. "It was a chance for Libby and me to get back to our families, and to work in a more intimate setting of just 225 members. We were eager for the opportunity."

However the Crooked Stick brass didn't quite match the pro's enthusiasm. In all of his previous job interviews, the smooth-as-batter Pancake was either offered the position that very day, or could sense he was the leading candidate. Not so for this most-coveted job, they had him back six separate times before offering the position. He explains the unique approach that made him the 'can't-miss-kid' three different times before Crooked Stick made him sweat.

"I think it's a combination of preparation, conversation skills, and being able to personalize my presentation so it related to the needs of the Committee," offers the pro. "In my experience, most candidates use handouts during interviews—tournament formats, pictures of scoreboards, their resume, things of this nature. I wanted the attention to be on me, not on any ancillary material I brought along and passed out to the committee. I also made the point of learning a bit about the committee members beforehand, and where their specific interests lay. If there was a mother who had kids playing I would emphasize to her the junior program I would develop. If there was a low-handicap member I would emphasize the competitive events I would plan. If there were beginning golfers on the committee I would tell them specifically

Tony Pancake flanked by Peyton Manning and Jim Nantz

about the clinics and introductory basics I had implemented in previous positions."

"My feeling was that if I got the job, and someone asked me a pointed question on a Thursday afternoon, I wouldn't have a handout to give them, I would need to answer their question at that moment. By replicating the same environment in my interviews, I showed them what I was capable of in a more transparent manner, and I've been fortunate that things have worked out."

Until Indianapolis. What turned out to be his 'final interview' was "the most nerve-wracking round of golf I ever played," recalls Pancake. He was paired in the prestigious Dye Cup with Boyd Hovde, who was representative of the type of passionate, sophisticated, and in many cases, talented golfer that calls

Crooked Stick their home club. Hovde is a former Indiana Amateur champion, a member of the Indiana Golf Hall of Fame, and the club champion many times over. Also in their foursome was the tournament's namesake, renowned course architect Pete Dye, himself a former Indiana Amateur Champion, and Mickey Powell, a former president of the PGA. Pancake sensed that his Hoosier status, self-assured manner and engaging personality could only take him so far. Crooked Stick wanted a real stick as head pro, and when he managed to shoot a round near par that afternoon, the job was finally his.

It's not a job he plans on leaving. Though he's had four head professional positions in a career of 25-plus years, he's not looking for a fifth. "We are Midwesterners by birth, we love Indianapolis, and this wonderful club. Crooked Stick was created nearly a half-century ago, and I am involved in long-range planning for the next half century," continues Pancake, who is also the manager of club operations in addition to being the director of golf. "The members want and expect a first-class golf experience and that is my passion, delivering it not only on special occasions, but every day. I hope to stay here for the duration of my career."

Most football fans would have assumed that iconic Colts quarterback Peyton Manning would have also spent the duration of his career in Indianapolis. But he maintains fond memories of his longtime Crooked Stick membership and his good friend. "Tony Pancake is the ultimate professional," begins the four-time NFL MVP, considered in most circles to be the ultimate professional himself. "I have been fortunate to have played some great courses around the country, and one thing that is obvious is the immense respect and admiration that each hosting pro has had for Tony. I have seen his hard work and dedication firsthand at Crooked Stick, and he is a great role model for the assistant professionals at the club," continues the current Denver Broncos quarterback and former Super Bowl champion, himself a role model for young quarterbacks everywhere. "I have taken lessons, taken golf trips and have played many a round with him at The Stick, and have always enjoyed our time together. I appreciate his work and I value his friendship."

Some of the national championships Pancake has been involved with at Crooked Stick include the Solheim Cup, the US Women's Amateur, the US Senior Open, and the PGA Tour's BMW Championship. "They have all been exciting in their own way, but probably the most fun was the 2005 Solheim Cup, albeit nerve-wracking at the same time."

Though he has many fields of expertise, nowhere on his resume does it say audio technician. So even though it was not his fault that the public address system wasn't functioning as he was introducing the first set of team pairings on the first tee the first morning of the competition, he was still in the firing line. "It was live on Golf Channel," recalls Pancake with a sigh. "The first tee was buzzing with noise because there were thousands of people on hand. Because the PA wasn't working, almost no one could hear me announce the first match, but I couldn't stop and wait, because the cameras were rolling."

American team captain Nancy Lopez, always a default choice for one of the world's nicest people, was "pretty direct," recalls the pro, when she told him to get the system fixed before the second set of pairings was due on the tee several minutes later.

Because he prides himself on preparation, because he's a stickler for detail, Pancake had no problem with the tongue-twisting nature of some of the names on that European Solheim Cup Team. Learning a dozen foreign names was a far easier task then memorizing the 800 golf members at Baltimore CC in short order, so despite the inherent pronunciation pitfalls of players like Gwladys Nocera, Ludivine Kreutz and Maria Hjorth, once his PA system was up and running he introduced them as easily as he might have introduced the Pointer Sisters—Ruth, Anita and June.

"Some names are easier than others, to pronounce, and remember," concludes Tony Pancake. "My last name, which is of German extraction, caused me plenty of grief when I was young. But in regards to my career it's been a benefit. Kids love it, adults will always remember it, and I'm thankful to my wife Libby for taking it!"

The name was given to him. But what of the work ethic, ambition, intelligence and people skills that have taken him to the heights of his profession? Those he came to all on his own.

CURRENT OR FORMER HEAD GOLF PROFESSIONALS WHO WORKED FOR TONY PANCAKE INCLUDE:

- Ryan Alvino
- Marty Bauer
- Tim Bolton
- Kevin Cloud
- Aaron Crooks
- Justin Defont
- Jason Diaz
- Mike Finney
- Jeff Hamady
- Brian Hughes

- Bill Hull
- Kyle Miller
- Chad O'Dell
- Ted Pogorelc
- Bill Pollert
- Keith Reese
- Chuck Schuyler
- Andy Scrivner
- Brett Smith
- Ron Snider
- Mark Tanner
- Bud Taylor
- Chad Vaughn
- Bob Wampler
- Patrick White

Tony Pancake's tip for fellow golfers:

Improving the short game is the key to lower scoring, so here's an effective practice regimen to do just that. First, dedicate approximately 50% of your practice time to the short game area, which I consider shots inside 30 yards. The four shots that you need to learn to execute include putting, chipping (low trajectory), pitching (high trajectory) and bunker shots. I encourage you to learn the fundamentals of each shot either through reading or taking a clinic and/or private lesson.

Take 20 minutes during a practice session getting the ball "up and down" similar to what you face on the golf course. Take one ball and drop it from where you want to play, select a hole on the green, play the shot and then putt it into the cup. Par is 2 on every hole.

Your "Short Course" should include a short putt (inside 10 feet), long putt (over 30 feet), short chip, long chip, short pitch, long pitch, short bunker shot and long bunker shot. You can use any of your wedges depending on the trajectory and roll the shot requires. Par for the 8 holes is 16. There is pressure involved since you are playing for score and you only get one chance at each shot, and you will quickly find out which area of your short game needs work – putting, chipping, pitching or bunker play. You can then spend more time working on the fundamentals of that particular shot before playing your "short course" again. As your short game improves you can design a tougher "short course" and include more uneven lies, shots from the rough, buried lies in bunkers, etc.

Tony Pancake's tip for fellow golf professionals:

I was fortunate to work for and with some great golf professionals early in my career and the common thread I noticed was their ability to anticipate the needs of the membership. Most golf professionals are excellent at solving problems but the superstars are those who see potential problems before they occur. This ability to "anticipate" is not as difficult as you would expect. Just imagine yourself in your customer's shoes and "anticipate" what they are thinking, what their expectations are and what would make their experience extra special. You'll be amazed at the ideas you will come up with to exceed the expectations of your members, guests and customers and make them feel extra special.

Scott Puailoa
Santa Barbara, California

Scott Puailoa has never needed to burnish his resume. He's only worked at one club his entire adult life. But should he ever decide to test the employment waters elsewhere imagine the puzzlement his CV might cause after the GM had conducted a face-to-face interview:

- Additional Language Skills: Samoan
- Special Talents: Samoan Fire Knife

Scott Puailoa with Ben Hogan

This highly regarded golf professional has the map of Ireland's County Clare, (his mother's ancestry) not Samoa, writ across his face. But the fact is that Puailoa (pronounced Pooh-Eye-Low-Ah) has a deep affinity for and with his father's people. The twin tenets of respect for all people, and deep affection for one's extended family, both of which are endemic to this unique island culture, go a long way in explaining his ongoing success as the longtime head professional at the Valley Club of Montecito, one of the greatest west coast clubs that most folks have never even heard of.

Puailoa, just past 60, explains that his grand-dad is full Samoan, and offers with a chuckle, "I'm the only Irish-Samoan golf professional I know of, on the west coast, anyway!

In the last several decades there has been a noticeable burst of exotic, multi-syllable, vowel-centric names that have become prominent in football:

Pacific Islanders like Mosi Tatupu, his son Lofa Tatupu, Edwin Mulitalo, Junior Seau and Troy Polamalu all found or continue to have success in the NFL. Though he ultimately chose golf as his profession, Puailoa was a standout on the football field himself, due in no small part to the ministrations of his father, Satini, who coached him at Santa Barbara's San Marcos High.

The coach's son was a star quarterback and defensive back, even at 5'9" and 200 pounds. After a couple of standout years at Santa Barbara Community College, where he was an All-State Western Conference player in both football and golf and MVP of both teams, he became the first Samoan to earn a scholarship in both football and golf at the University of the Pacific, a Division I school in Stockton, California. "Despite the success I was having on the football field, I started to concentrate more heavily on golf, figuring that offered better prospects for the future."

His golf interest initially stemmed from his dad, who worked at the local municipal course on the weekends, supplementing his income from high school teaching and coaching. "I grew up around the course, and started playing junior tournaments. I was very active in the Southern California Junior Golf Association from ages 12 to 17, and managed to win a few events along the way," explains the pro.

Lee Mikles has known Puailoa since both boys were playing junior golf together in the late '60s. Mikles played collegiate golf at Arizona State and then on the PGA Tour for three years before embarking on a successful Wall Street career.

"Scott was one of the most incredible three-sport athletes this region has ever seen," states Mikles, who wasn't at all surprised when his longtime friend was inducted into the Santa Barbara Sports Hall of Fame. He was inducted not only for his decades-long service to the Valley Club, but also due to the fact that during his high school years he was an All-Channel League selection in football, basketball and golf and the San Marcos Male Athlete of the Year in 1972. "I will also say he is far more competitive than 99% of the players I knew on Tour," continues Mikles. "But despite his competitive streak Scott is the same mild-mannered, kind-hearted guy I have known for 45 years, although he is taller, broader and with far less hair!"

Upon his college graduation in 1977, Puailoa went back to his high school alma mater in Santa Barbara, and began coaching football alongside his dad. He remained on the staff for 20 years in total, eventually working alongside his brother, Satini III, who had taken over the program once their dad retired.

That same year he was also hired as an assistant pro at the prestigious Valley Club, a longtime fixture on numerous worldwide Top 100 lists. He made a single attempt at PGA Tour Qualifying School, and was readying for an encore. But the head pro, a short-timer at the club, resigned. Puailoa was asked to replace him, and the decision was sealed. He has been there ever since, for more than 35 years a fixture at this wonderful, yet little-known classic.

"This is a real throwback club, it has the look and feel of some great eastern clubs, partially because some of the original members came from back east," reasons the Pasadena-born pro. It's a 1929 Alister MacKenzie design in a bucolic parkland setting, with distant ocean views on half-a-dozen holes. The course routing is out-

and-back like a traditional links, the tenth hole being the furthest point from the clubhouse. "It's a small, intimate membership, very close-knit, and we only do about 18,000 rounds annually, not many, considering the year-round climate is so ideal." He describes Santa Barbara as a coastal desert, and the meager 13 inches of annual rainfall comes predominantly from January through March. "Bottom line is the weather is beautiful basically all year long."

Lee Mikles adds, "Our club opened less than a year after Cypress Point opened, and in many ways it's 'the club that time forgot.' People of notoriety wouldn't be comfortable here, and our membership wouldn't be comfortable with them. We are two hours from Hollywood, but are as anti-Hollywood as you can imagine. The course is intimate, almost anachronistic, at 6,600 yards in length. It won't be modernized, or lengthened appreciably, because we don't hold outside events. But the bunkers and greens were redone to MacKenzie's initial specifications a few years ago, and this return to the original roots is pleasing to our membership."

It is better known in California, but with an ankle-high profile nationally, Valley Club is considered in much the same breath as the aforementioned Cypress Point, Olympic Club, San Francisco Golf Club, Riviera and L.A. North as among the finest handful of private venues in the state. "It's somewhat intentional," relates Puailoa. "Our members have always wanted to keep this place quiet, and well under the radar. We have no high profile events and very few outside events in general. It's a member's club, first and last."

Speaking of which, the first and last woman that Scott ever looked at is his wife Darci. She's not a golfer herself, but is the niece of a former PGA Tour player and answer to an excellent trivia question. Who is the only player to make his solitary PGA Tour victory the U.S. Open? That would be Uncle Orville, AKA Orville

Scott and Darci Puailoa

Moody, "The Sarge," who captured the 1969 Open for his only Tour win. Darci and Scott are high school sweethearts that have been married since his college days. They have two daughters and seven grandchildren, ranging in age from high school to grade school.

Moody made a splash on the Champions Tour, with 11 victories, but his nephew-by-marriage never got the chance. "I made several attempts to qualify for the Champions Tour a decade back," recall Puailoa. "But my focus changed when my dad got sick, I began to concentrate on his comfort and health, and have since decided that the competition aspect of my golf game is no longer important."

He has always maintained his interest in coaching football, even traveling to American Samoa with perennial All-Pro Troy Polamalu, the star safety for the Pittsburgh Steelers, to conduct clinics as recently as 2011. But as his golf career gained traction Puailoa turned his inner fire towards golf, and the flame he carries for the lifetime game and his chosen profession still burn hot.

"Scott still has the same zest for golf today as he did in junior high school," continues Mikles, winner of the prestigious and exclusive Horatio Alger Award, given to only ten high-achieving individuals annually. "He is a great promoter of golf, his enthusiasm extends to all his members, and his encouraging attitude affects everyone at the club. It doesn't matter if he is with the 90-year old member who can only play four or five holes, the rank beginners, the low handicap players or the juniors. His main concern is that everyone has a good time," explains Mikles, a Valley Club member himself for more than a dozen years.

"This sounds odd, but in 35-plus years I've never really felt like I was coming to work," states Puailoa. "I have a passion for the game, for this beautiful facility, and for the wonderful, golf-loving membership that has embraced me. Every day we are talking about, working on and thinking about golf. I'm fortunate to make a living within this realm, I couldn't ask for more."

He supplements that living, just a tiny bit, as a member of a Polynesian Review, including grass skirts, sarongs, aloha shirts, island music, Samoan dancing and fire effects. "I'm too old for some of the more dramatic parts of the show that I used to be involved with," admits Puailoa, who may look like the club's bouncer, but these days is actually the band's bass player.

He comes by the performance gene naturally. He grandfather emigrated from Samoa in 1924 and was an original member of the Screen Actor's Guild, working under the name Chief Satini. The band is named Aiga, pronounced "eye-en-ga," which is the Samoan word for family. In this case it's truth in advertising, because the band members, which vary depending on the gig between eight and 15 individuals, include Puailoa's wife, brother, sister-in-law, cousin, and various kids and grandkids.

"We get plenty of questions because none of us look very Samoan. People see me speak Samoan with other family members, and they probably think I'm either adopted or a linguist!"

Over the years Aiga has performed at the Valley Club nearly a dozen times. "The membership used to get such a kick out of it, especially my participation," he recalls with a smile. "Think about it: How often do you see a golf professional performing or entertaining people in some manner, particularly at their own club?"

A great part of his longevity has to do with his deep embrace of his father's culture. Samoans emphasize respect and love for one's parents, family, elders, and all those you encounter. "In Samoa, large, extended families make up entire villages," states the former PGA Professional of the Year, Merchandiser of the Year and President of the Northern Chapter of the Southern California Section. "I feel the same way about the membership at the Valley Club. To me it's like an extended family, and the club is like their second home, which is why I sincerely welcome everyone when I see them."

Just don't get on his bad side. "If I'm cornered in a dark alley, there is no one I would rather have by my side than Scott, yet he is a gentle soul," concludes Mikles, now the CEO of a chemical company. "I am a huge fan of his, but then again, I don't know anybody at the Valley Club who isn't!"

Puailoa is as constant and steadfast a presence as the rhythmic waves breaking at the city's famed Goleta Beach. He explains his loyalty and longevity, his aversion to profound change or upheaval very simply. "When I am fortunate enough to find something that works wonderfully for me," concludes the smiling pro, referring to Santa Barbara itself, his wife Darci, and the Valley Club, "I can't imagine doing any better, so I'm not inclined to let it go!"

CURRENT OR FORMER HEAD GOLF PROFESSIONALS WHO WORKED FOR SCOTT PUAILOA INCLUDE:

- Eric Barnes
- Tom Gocke
- Fred Shoemaker

Scott Puailoa's tip for fellow golfers:

If we look at team sports, we will recognize the importance of quality practice. Can we incorporate that same concept into our golf practice? I believe so. One aspect of quality practice is contingency or simulated practice. Allow yourself to get into the imaginative mind by practicing game situations. Peak performance can be achieved by executing the learned process through pre and post shot routines, not mechanical thoughts.

Scott Puailoa's tip for fellow golf professionals:

As a golf professional, I believe there are three things that separate us as PGA Professionals. Number one is who you are as a person. You have character, integrity and kindness along with a passion and love for the game and the people who play it. Two, you have a respectable game, and you compete in tournament golf when you can. Three, you have an in depth knowledge of the game and can teach it to others. Let's remember why we got into the profession.

Dana Rader
Charlotte, North Carolina

Dana Rader's golf school is at the Ballantyne Resort

Have an attitude of gratitude. It's a saying that's become popular in recent years; you can find it on t-shirts or greeting cards in New Age bookstores and curio shops that stock incense, massage oils and healing crystals.

It's not that Dana Rader isn't grateful for all her successes, the fact that she's recognized throughout the industry for her entrepreneurial skills and teaching acumen. She is equally thankful she's been able to teach and influence hundreds of thousands of golfers over the years, helping them get more enjoyment out of the game she loves. But her mantra might be better described: Have an attitude of latitude.

It is the latitude her parents afforded her in her youth, to try different things, sometimes failing in the effort. It's the latitude she so desperately craved early in her career when she felt pigeon-holed, as she was trying to find her place in the golf business. It's the latitude she continually gives her loyal cadre of instructors, many of whom have stayed at the Dana Rader Golf School since the day the doors opened, through boom times and bust.

"My parents, Jean and Vernon, gave my brother and me plenty of rope, but cautioned us not to hang ourselves! Dad was an avid golfer, an entrepreneur and a former POW in World War II, so I suppose he valued freedom and independence more than most," begins Rader, consistently honored as one of the game's finest instructors by all the major golf publications.

"He told us, 'you are free to try what you like, and do what you want within limits. We will trust you until you prove otherwise. But don't waste your dime and call me from jail, because if you go that far, I'm not going to help you!' As a kid I was riding motorcycles, as a teenager I drove solo to Myrtle Beach; these were activities and experiences way outside the norm for that time and place."

Originally from Morganton, North Carolina, just an hour-and-change from where she has long since established herself in Charlotte, Rader has cut an imposing figure since her youth. A shade below six feet tall since her early teens, she developed into a solid basketball player who never showed much interest in golf despite her dad's encouragement.

The 'aha' moment occurred when a high school friend marveled at her natural swing after cajoling her onto the course out of summertime boredom. She quickly became obsessed with the game, reading every book she could find, both biographical and instructional, and started practicing diligently. In a habit that has never abated, she began keeping meticulous and voluminous notes: number of balls hit, shot shapes, shot results, even atmospheric conditions.

Rader quickly became a force on the local golf scene, then as she got closer to scratch, on the statewide scene, and in combination with her already formidable basketball skills, went off to Pfeiffer University to play hoops and join the men's golf team. She had a tremendous advantage in her development as a golfer because her home club Mimosa Hills offered her a pair of amazing mentors: Joe Cheves and Billy Joe Patton. The former was the club's head professional for 30 years, and enshrined in the Guinness Book of World Records. Not only did he better his age more than a thousand times, amazingly he shot 64 at age 81, and then shot 70 a few years later at age 87, and the 17 stroke differential between his age and score was one for the record books. The latter was best known for almost winning the 1954 Masters as an amateur, played on five Walker Cup teams, and captained another. In tandem, they accelerated Rader's interest in, understanding of, and love for the game.

"Joe was very polished and professional. Billy Joe was more flamboyant and countrified. The combination of their guidance, along with my dad's, who was a low handicapper himself, really helped me along," relates Rader, who eventually was able to shoot 70 from any set of tees at Mimosa Hills—women's, men's, or championship.

Post-college Rader took a job as an assistant pro at renowned Myers Park, one of Charlotte's distinguished private clubs. She felt constrained by her shop duties, and despite the membership's financial support as she made a run at the LPGA Tour, she was despondent and disillusioned after her failure to secure playing privileges. "I didn't pick up a club for nearly a year, other than to demonstrate the grip during lessons," recounts Rader.

"There was a time when I seriously considered leaving the game to go into telemarketing," recalls the LPGA Master Professional. "I was making a pittance at Myers Park, and my telemarketing salary would have tripled my golf earnings. But I realized that golf was what I thought about in the morning when I woke up, and before

I went to sleep, and I couldn't give that up. I feel the same passion for it today, and continue to think the game is a great revealer of character, discipline and tenacity. The game teaches you that you won't get your way in life all the time, or even much of the time. And that's about as important a lesson as a person can learn."

After two years mainly on cash register duty, the fledgling pro left Myers Park for nearby Raintree Country Club, where there was a bit more responsibility in terms of running tournaments, facilitating group outings, and generally interacting with a less homogenous crowd then previously. "It was an improvement, but honestly my first five years in the business weren't ideal. It was a real challenge for me, looking for my niche."

Her next job, at River Hills Country Club, across the state line in Lake Wylie, South Carolina, was more to her liking. "I became the teaching professional there, worked my own end of the range, and started to develop autonomy as I became more established." Five years later, much to the chagrin of the South Carolina membership that had grown so fond of her, Rader returned to Raintree, her reputation as an instructor continuing to grow. "My second stint there was seven years long, and was far more productive and fulfilling then when I was there initially," continues the former LPGA Teaching Professional of the Year. "It was all instruction based, no more answering the phone or grunt work. About five years into the position, the Raintree brass allowed me to rename the operation the Dana Rader Golf School."

Rader, the author of a popular instruction book called <u>Rock Solid Golf,</u> looks back in retrospect. "I didn't realize until after the fact what it was I was searching for. It was the same independence and latitude afforded me back when I was young, under my parent's roof."

Dana Rader demonstrating a fine point to members of her golf school staff

It was a natural shift for the golf coach to move into public speaking, her platform emphasizing that inspiring, motivating and encouraging people, no matter what the particular endeavor, would yield positive results. A restaurateur hosting a gathering where Rader spoke was impacted to the point where he signed up for her golf school, and thereafter, made a point of introducing her to a local developer named Smokey Bissell, who was developing what would soon become Charlotte's only in-town golf resort, the Ballantyne Hotel.

"Mr. Bissell was looking to add an instructional component to his resort and golf course operation. I got in for a last-minute interview, and had to postpone or otherwise rearrange more than 20 scheduled golf lessons that day to make my appointment," recalls Rader, shaking her head at the memory. "He had about 80 applications to run a golf academy, but my proposal was the only one with a business plan, and I was fortunate to be awarded the opportunity."

Her golf academy opened in 1997 at the west end of the driving range, preceding the actual opening of the golf course itself. Rader began with four full-time instructors, eventually increased that number to eight, and currently has about 15 total employees including support staff in this million-dollar enterprise.

One of her longtime admirers is LPGA legend Nancy Lopez, who has watched Rader's business grow through the years. "I have known Dana for a long time, and have worked with her numerous times in Charlotte with my work for the March of Dimes. She is very classy, and you can see right away what a strong businessperson she is. She is very bright, has a great personality, people like her and gravitate towards her. She has a serious side of course, but also a fun-loving side, and people just naturally like her, which isn't an attribute that everybody has," explains the Hall of Fame member, who has that very same attribute in abundance.

Rader's venture flourished owing to the booming business climate in Charlotte. The upscale hotel was consistently booking incentive groups and corporate outings, and what better way to recreate after meetings and seminars than by taking a golf lesson or clinic prior to heading out on the course? In excess of 15,000 students would come through the door on an annual basis, and familiarize themselves with Rader's three basic tenets to improvement—physical, mental and emotional. "First we evaluate any physical limitations, injuries and flexibility issues. Then we observe ball control from different target lines with different clubs. In order to help with the mental and emotional aspects of the game we must understand what is happening with the mechanical aspects."

"Second is the mental aspect. We have to empower them with a belief that they can make changes in their swing, and teach them how to take the mechanics on the course by providing a productive and effective pre and post shot routine. The most important factor that creates success for our students is a practice program that mirrors their play. This helps with their mental game so that they are better prepared to play the game. They have to hit shots in practice on the range and on the course with a quiet mind. We try to get them to clear the chatter out of their head so they can perform. This takes a lot of practice and mental discipline."

"Lastly is the emotional aspect, helping them with performance anxiety. We listen to their thoughts and feelings and help them through the change process and through the ups and downs of the game. This emotional aspect is vitally important. The game of golf is very personal and students need to have coaches that care and understand their fear and doubt."

There was fear and doubt throughout the city when the financial crisis rocked banking-centric Charlotte in 2008, and the flush times turned fallow. "Our revenues dwindled significantly, and this place occasionally looked like a ghost town. I could barely grasp what I was seeing," sighs Rader. "I went to the banks for assistance in meeting payroll, everyone cut down their hours, and we persevered."

"As an entrepreneur I consider it imperative that I create jobs for people. I love team-building, and have been so fortunate to attract and keep great employees," continues the former Charlotte Business Woman of the Year. "And once things stabilized a bit, and our revenues began to return closer to the levels were accustomed to, I continued to operate with my long-time philosophy of allowing my instructors and support team the latitude to do their jobs with few constraints, no micro-managing or interference needed."

One of the reasons the golf school remains such a viable entity is because of its namesake's prominent media profile. Skill, smarts and tenacity aside, sometime a media profile increases due to a potent combination of empathy and serendipity. "A member of my foursome was a complete beginner, shaking like a leaf, at Pebble Beach some years ago," recalls Rader, who was taking part in an LPGA Summit at the time. "At the expense of my own game, I really got into helping her that round, stance, swing, everything, and she was so grateful for the guidance. Wouldn't you know it, inside of a few months she left her reporting job at a Dallas newspaper, and was named the editor of Golf for Women Magazine!"

A regular instructional presence in the now-defunct magazine, along with ongoing contributions to the other mainstream publications, keeps her at the forefront of her profession, and the telephone ringing. Despite her myriad other administrative duties, "the boss" teaches upward of 30 hours a week herself in the high season every spring and fall.

Continues Lopez, who won nearly 50 times on the LPGA Tour, including three Major championships, "I respect Dana, and think she's very trustworthy. If I had a secret to tell I know I could count on her to keep it! You can also tell how much she loves golf. I've watched her teach, and she manages to maintain the enthusiasm of someone giving their first lesson. That gusto in combination with her knowledge and professionalism makes her an amazing teacher. The ladies love her, they can tell how sincere she is in her love of golf, and her desire to get them enthused about the game. Dana is the type of person that when you haven't seen her for awhile, and then see her heading your way, you are really excited to say hello and catch up. That to me is a wonderful complement."

"Much as I adore golf, and have devoted my career to helping others get more enjoyment from the game, I never wanted to be pigeonholed as just a golf professional," concludes Rader, recently named one of Charlotte's 50 most influential businesswomen.

"To be engaged in my community, to provide jobs and careers for deserving, talented individuals, and to be recognized by others as a competent businessperson in a town that is so business-oriented, those are accomplishments and accolades that will make me proud for the duration of my career. I am indebted to all my mentors, colleagues, and the various role models who have helped me along my career path. I'm thankful my reputation isn't just as a fine golf professional, but as a fine professional, period."

Dana Rader's tip for fellow golfers:

There are lots of teaching methodologies and it can be confusing. My best advice to all golfers is a simple one. There are many roads to take to learn the game but you must pick one and stay on it. Golf is about skill development and every time you change teachers, methods or use the latest fad tips you under-develop your skill. Golf must be learned like anything else and that is with the proper skill progression and not with a "try this, try that" mentality. Find a good teacher and stay on task with developing your skills and you will have a lot more fun.

Dana Rader's tip for fellow golf professionals:

One thing that is very critical is choosing the right work environment. There are three core decisions you must know before you step in to an environment that could be toxic. First, know your core values so you will know if you and the culture have similar values. Second, is the leader learning? You want to be under a leader that is growing and getting better, not complacent and behind on current trends in the industry. Thirdly, how will you grow and what can you expect from leadership to help you grow and develop to be the best you can be?

Rick Rhoads
San Francisco, California

Everyone knows that good things come in small packages. Resilient things come in small packages also. Look no further than Rick Rhoads, for more than 35 years the head professional at the magnificent, yet little-known San Francisco Golf Club.

Rick Rhoads (left) with his friend and fellow PGA Tour competitor Gary Player

The Los Angeles native battled through family tragedy, personal obstacles, a six-year military commitment and serious health issues to carve out a hard-fought seven-year career on the PGA Tour in the late '60s and '70s before settling in to the only club job he has ever had or ever will hold.

"When I was on the Tour," begins the soft-spoken Rhoads, now in his late 60s, "there was only one guy my height, but Rod Curl outweighed me by 50 pounds!" Yes, athletes are bigger and stronger than ever. But even back then a 5' 6", 130-pounder inside the ropes was more likely to be the standard-bearer than a tournament competitor. Rhoads had to work extra hard just to keep up with the more physically imposing competition. It's no surprise he gravitated towards Gary Player, admiring the bantamweight South African's grit, determination and single-minded pursuit of excellence.

"Rick and I both knew that as smaller players, we had to make up for our stature with passion and hard work," relates Player, a nine-time Major champion and Grand Slam winner. "I always enjoyed playing with Rick, not only because he is a great guy, but partially because he was one of the few men smaller than me!"

The Rhoads family had migrated from St. Louis when Rick's granddad Harrison was awarded the first-ever Chevy dealership (then known as an 'agency') in Beverly Hills in 1926. Rick's dad Hank, a non-nonsense Stanford grad and World War II bomber pilot, eventually took over the Chevy agency, and it remained a family business until 1960.

Rick's older brothers were fine athletes, both high school quarterbacks, "but I was the runt of the family," admits the longtime pro. "I played all the sports when I was younger, but I turned to golf in my teenage years when competing in team sports became more problematic." The family had a membership at the renowned Los Angeles Country Club, where Rick worked on his game incessantly.

His mother Elaine, who he describes as "the glue of the family," had a heart attack and died at age 42 when Rick was a sophomore and a member of the golf team at the University of Southern California. "It was hard on all of us, but especially my little sister Lorraine, who was still at home." Lorraine had won the California Girls Junior Golf Championship back-to-back before her mother's untimely passing, but then lost interest in the game. "My dad enticed her back when she was 16 by offering her a car if she lowered her handicap to a four. She did so, collected the bounty, and unlike me, gave up the game for good." (An aside: Her interest in golf was renewed later in life by her son, Roger Tambellini, a three-time winner on the Web.com Tour, who has also played in nearly 80 events on the PGA Tour.)

Rick's father, a taskmaster, wanted him to become a part-time student, and come to work for him in a new business venture. He resisted, saying, "I told my dad I thought I could make All-American." He went to his golf coach, Stan Wood, and asked if he could get a tuition scholarship to complete his education. Wood provided the financial assistance and Rick's motivation and determination jumped to a new level. He made All American that year and again his senior year.

Oldest brother Ron preceded Rick at USC, playing #2 on the golf team behind Dave Stockton. He spent about 15 years in total as the head professional at Riviera and Sherwood Country Clubs, but was felled by a fatal heart attack in his early 60s. Middle brother Roger matriculated at Stanford, like his dad. "We all wanted to make our own way in the world, and my two brothers and sister always backed me all the way." The irony is that in adulthood, all three of Rhoads' sons followed him into the golf business.

Harrison Rhoads, Rick's grandfather, was a member of the famed Thunderbird Club in Palm Springs, where Rick impressed their legendary professional Claude Harmon by winning the Palm Springs Invitational as a college sophomore. "At the time it was the most prestigious event in the state other than the California Amateur," relates the two-time Northern California PGA Teacher of the Year. "When I graduated USC in 1967, Mr. Harmon had an opening on his Winged Foot staff for a 'teaching-playing professional', and I was fortunate to be selected."

Rhoads was following in the footsteps of predecessors like Mike Souchak, Jackie Burke and Dave Marr, and living back east for the first time in his life, his employment situation was curious, to say the least. To sum it up as a MasterCard commercial: Salary: Zero. Benefits: Priceless.

It was eight straight months of having breakfast and lunch virtually every day with his boss, the former Masters champion, and whoever his guests might have been, like inaugural Masters champ Craig Wood, or the Silver Scot himself, Tommy Armour. It was keeping all lesson revenue, having every afternoon to work on his game, playing rounds with influential Winged Foot members, and be instructed and mentored by Mr. Harmon. It was consistently having high finishes in tournaments like the Met Open, Westchester Open and various pro-am events, and cashing checks regularly. "For a job with no base salary, I did very well."

The 'no salary' phenomenon was something he needed to get used to, because the following season he was on the PGA Tour, the ultimate meritocracy. "Mr. Harmon set up his son Butch and me in beautiful high-rise apartments down on Worth Avenue in Palm Beach, and I was one of the 20 players who made it through Qualifying School and onto the PGA Tour. Butch made it the following year."

Rick's PGA Tour 'honeymoon' was short-lived, as he received his draft notice in July 1968 while competing in the Western Open. "There were no deferments, or reserve units available, everyone was heading to Vietnam."

Luckily for the rookie, Al Geiberger, who in 1977 became the first man to shoot 59 on the PGA Tour, and who was another prominent member of the USC golf family, set him up a golf date with an influential general. The military man was so impressed with Rhoads' abilities that he found him a place in the National Guard in Santa Monica. "It was a tremendous break, but unfortunately it didn't absolve me of having to go through basic training at Fort Ord."

It wasn't just the six-month forced hiatus that came while he was playing just well enough to retain his card going forward. It was also the fact that the commitment necessitated four-week breaks for additional reserve training in the summertime, including plenty of additional air travel from his home near Sacramento down to the training facility in Santa Monica. It disrupted the schedule that he needed to keep himself, both practice-wise and from a physical fitness standpoint, in a competitive mode.

"Don't misunderstand; I was proud to serve my country, and extremely thankful that I never had to go to the Asian jungle to fight," continues Rhoads. "But it just so happens my military service coincided pretty much exactly with my playing career. And the added travel and obligations took precious time away from the goal of improving and climbing on the money list."

Trying to measure the life of a modern Tour pro with a journeyman in the 1960s and early 1970s is like looking back at a daguerreotype. When Rhoads was struggling tooth and nail to make a living on Tour, private jet travel was for the President (or maybe Arnold Palmer.) There was no caravan of courtesy cars, no five figure checks for fortieth place finishes, no all-day daycare, or cooking classes or shopping sprees for the wives. But compared to basic training, the reservist sorely missed life on Tour, peripatetic and uncertain as it was. "Tournament golf on that level is highly competitive, and was often a struggle. But I loved every moment, because being out there with the best players in the world afforded me the opportunity to learn and improve."

Another setback: Running to stay in shape, he was bit by an unleashed dog, as a precaution endured 14 rabies shots over the course of two weeks, and when he suffered a bout of internal bleeding shortly thereafter, the doctors discovered polycystic kidneys. "They monitored my health carefully from that day forward," explains Rhoads, who eventually underwent a kidney transplant at age 60. "All my boys volunteered for the transplant, but Kevin proved to be the best match. Owing to the proliferation of the cysts, by the time I had surgery my kidneys weighed ten times as much as they should have."

Rhoads won the Venezuelan Open in 1967, his only professional victory, but despite some decent finishes and late afternoon weekend pairings, was never able to grab the brass ring (or winner's check) in the States.

At a dinner he never forgot, an unexpected admission from one of his idols regarding the rigors of tournament competition surprised the young pro, giving him a different perspective of the Tour life. Rhoads' dining companion had everything the struggling pro aspired to. An exempt player, a winner on Tour, a Major champion, Ryder Cup player, with numerous endorsements. "I was shocked when he said, 'winning is so tough, it's almost not worth it.' He was a guy who knew how to hold a 54-hold lead, tough as nails. He said that there are 20,000 people lining the fairways waiting for you to screw up, and 10 million more watching on TV. All the guys in the hunt are playing looser than you, because they aren't in the lead, or the spotlight. He said it gets so bad you can barely swallow."

"All those years I was working so hard to get where he was, and when he told me how brutal it was once you got there. Although it shocked me to hear this admission, I still thought the PGA Tour was where I wanted to be."

Rick Rhoads and his three sons---golf professionals all

For the second time in his career, Rhoads benefited from fantastic timing. The first was when Claude Harmon hired him at Winged Foot with the ink still drying on his college diploma. Nearly a decade later, thanks to a connection through a member of the club's Board, he became aware of a pending opportunity at San Francisco Golf Club in 1976. "Joan and I had two boys. They were getting to be school age, and I'm not setting the PGA Tour on fire." He told the powers-that-be he would drop out of the Los Angeles Open to come up and interview. But Sandy Tatum, the famed amateur who won the NCAA Individual golf title while at Stanford, head of the club's search committee and eventual president of the USGA, told him to wait until the event's conclusion. Rhoads' enthusiasm for the opportunity, combined with his resume, personality and work ethic, won him the position he holds to this very day.

"It's not the type of job that ever really becomes available, but my predecessor wanted to get back to his hometown of Santa Rosa, about an hour north of San Francisco, which paved the way for me." He sums up a career closing in on 40 years with four simple words: "I'm a lucky guy."

"This is a small, understated, extremely private club, just a few miles from the city, but on a beautiful piece of forested land, with a sandy soil base that makes for great golf. The weather is conducive for golf almost all year long. We have a great membership that loves the game and its traditions. The club was formed in 1895, and A.W. Tillinghast designed the course at its current location in the 1920s."

"Rick Rhoads is an extraordinary head pro and is a wonderful asset to the San Francisco Golf Club," offers Gary Player. "Rick is full of experience from his time on Tour, and is an outstanding teacher. I've known him for more than 45 years, and can say his greatest qualities are his enormous character and kindness. He loves and cares about his members, and is a genuine man. As one of the oldest clubs in the west, I feel that San Francisco Golf Club has won the lottery with Rick."

In notable contrast to nearby Olympic Club, the five-time host site of the US Open, with its multiple courses, numerous membership categories and sizable roster of members. The sprawling clubhouse at Olympic, not even a mile away, is visible from the first tee at San Francisco Golf Club. But it is a literal truth when Rhoads comments, "we can see them, but they cannot see us."

In the current golf climate, it is unlikely that Rick and Joan's three boys will ever build a single club legacy like their dad. But they are all Class 'A' Professionals, and making their mark at some of the most prestigious venues in the game. Curtis is the oldest and is just across the way, an assistant pro at Olympic Club. Kevin, a Master Professional and recent father of twin girls, does triple duty 3,000 miles to the east. He is the teaching professional at The Country Club, in Brookline, Massachusetts, and also coaches both the men's and women's teams at Harvard. Youngest son Ryan is currently an assistant pro at the posh Monterey Peninsula Country Club, about 120 miles south of San Francisco, in Pebble Beach.

Their dad doesn't lose sleep over the future employment possibilities for his boys, or the precarious nature of the profession. Though well aware that major contraction in the golf industry has closed hundreds of courses, and made good club jobs much harder to come by and keep. "Despite how the game has diminished in certain ways in the last 20 or so years, there will always be great clubs, and there will always be stable clubs. There will always be a need and market for first-class professionals."

So concludes the silver-haired Rick Rhoads, as first-class as they come, himself the essence of stability for nearly four decades at the wonderful -beyond-words San Francisco Golf Club.

CURRENT OR FORMER HEAD GOLF PROFESSIONALS WHO WORKED FOR RICK RHOADS INCLUDE:

- Kevin Bresnahan
- Nick Diamond
- Scott Farr

Rick Rhoads' tip for fellow golfers:

Here is a formula for success when hitting a standard sand shot. Get in a bunker about 10 yards from the flag stick. Draw a line 2 or 3 inches behind the golf ball, perpendicular to the target. Draw a second line 6-8 inches after the ball. Aim your body slightly left of the hole. Open the face of your sand wedge to the right of the hole to create more loft and bounce. Practice with only two thoughts in mind. First, have your club head enter the sand near the first line and exit near the second line. Second, use loose wrists to slap the sand so that sand flies out of the bunker. Concentrate on hitting the sand, not the ball. We want to go under the ball about an inch. You will hear the club slap the sand if you do this correctly. Practice a bit, and then can then walk into a bunker calmly and with confidence.

Rick Rhoads' tip for fellow golf professionals:

Although you might have acquired a great deal of knowledge about the golf swing, I would like to suggest two things that you should apply to your arsenal of information.

The first is to figure out the best way to organize your information and the second is to simplify all of that knowledge to make it clearer and more understandable for both you and your students. We have all been in a state of confusion both as teachers and students, but it does not have to be that way.

I had the good fortune to play on the PGA Tour for a number of years which afforded me the opportunity to learn at the highest level. I learned that the better players were better at the basic fundamentals. They knew and applied these basics better and more simply. They were also able to isolate and correct problems more quickly. Deane Beman, a tournament winner, and later the PGA Tour commissioner, told me at the time that I needed to truly observe the best players. They are the models, closely observe what they do and observe their ball flight.

Bill Safrin
Hamilton, Massachusetts

Contrary to popular belief, particularly among his younger charges, Bill Safrin was *not* the host pro the last time the U.S. Open was conducted at the delightfully anachronistic, curiously named Myopia Hunt Club, on Boston's North Shore. That final of the four U.S. Opens held there

Bill and Kathy Safrin with their children

was contested more than a century past, in 1908. Safrin hasn't been there quite that long, it just seems that way.

There are many atypical twists to this Pennsylvanian's tale. It's the rare golf pro who spends time in the Ivy League, was raised in a single-parent household *by his father* in the 1950s, or whose pro shop once served double duty as his bedroom. But despite these unusual circumstances, here's what truly sets Safrin apart: His long, fruitful association with one of the coolest, most revered, littlest-known, peculiar-but-prestigious private golf clubs this nation has ever produced: Myopia Hunt Club.

Founded in 1875 by the four sons of the mayor of Boston, the Prince Brothers were Harvard baseball players who were nearsighted and wore glasses. With equal parts whimsy and accuracy, the named their sporting association the Myopia Club, with baseball and sailing among the club's primary activities. But with hunting becoming increasingly popular, the club needed far more acreage than the suburban Boston town of Winchester could offer. So they relocated some 30 miles north of the city to the current site amidst the pastoral farmlands of Hamilton, Massachusetts, and in 1882 renamed themselves the Myopia Hunt Club.

Now more than 130 years later, it still feels as though one arrives to the first tee via time machine. This eccentric gem of a golf course features blind shots, bizarre hills, tawny, waving fescues, narrow footpaths, gargantuan par-3s and single-file fairways. It's no surprise that the three highest 72-hole scores that actually won the U.S. Open took place at Myopia.

The classic New England clapboard-style clubhouse was originally a farmhouse, dating from 1772, built by a Revolutionary War colonel named Abraham Dodge. Also on property is Gibney Field, the oldest active polo field in America. The club's brick maintenance building is one of the original "court tennis" (sometimes referred to as "real tennis" or "royal tennis") buildings in America. Suffice it to say that the rare combination of antiquity, pedigree and quality make the Myopia Hunt Club an entity unto itself.

Bill Safrin and his bride Kathy rolled down the club's long, rough-hewn driveway in the spring of 1980. It was his first day on the job, the first day of the spring season, and the first time the pro had ever laid eyes on the place.

"I had attempted to visit the club prior to my interview in downtown Boston a month or so earlier," recalls Safrin, like the club's original founders, an Ivy League baseball player, in his case at the University of Pennsylvania. "The traffic on Route 128 was snarled, and I realized I had to turn around if I was going to be on time for the interview downtown. So I never saw the club until the day I took over."

It's just as well. Perhaps the daunting prospect of all the work needed to get his new fiefdom up to snuff might have scared him away. Except that hard work has never scared the Philadelphia native.

"I was always self-supporting," explains the soft-spoken pro. "My mother was never in the picture, and my dad, who worked as a professional fundraiser, didn't make much money. So my siblings and I learned early on that we would need to work hard and earn our own way for whatever we wanted in life. Growing up without a mother wasn't ideal, but it taught me independence, and I've been making my own way since boyhood. Due to necessity I had to develop a very strong work ethic from a young age."

Enrolled at the Wharton School of Business, he realized partway through his undergraduate work he wanted to pursue a career in sports. His education interrupted by the Vietnam War, Safrin became a medic during his military service, and when he eventually continued his education he graduated from Temple University in Philadelphia. "My dad had moved to Dallas for a time, which is where I was stationed temporarily as a medic. He belonged to a 54-hole golf facility called Brookhaven, and when I was in my early 20s I started playing almost every day, as much as possible. Within a few months I had worked my way down to a 3-handicap. It was then I decided to focus on a career in golf."

Eventually back in Philly, Safrin worked full time in a machine shop as he completed his undergraduate work. With his diploma in hand he decided to get into the golf business, and used the same technique that has served Fuller Brush salesmen for generations—he went door-to-door. "I had no PGA accreditation, but was hungry to get in the business, and would have worked for just room and board, no salary, if necessary." His future, which would prove to be in the world of very private, very high-class clubs, was portended from the get-go. His first job was at Gulph Mills Golf Club, considered at the time to have a membership consisting of the crème de la crème of Philadelphia High Society. "The head pro was Willie Scholl, who became my first mentor in golf," recalls Safrin. "He asked me what my salary requirements were, and I told them I had none, I just wanted a job. He told me I sounded perfect!"

After learning the ropes during his first full season, he spent that winter watching the shop, (and unbeknownst to the membership, sleeping on the pro shop floor to save rent) while his boss repaired to Florida to play mini-tours. But the second winter he went to work at another bastion of the aristocracy, the Gasparilla Inn Golf Club, south of Sarasota, Florida. "It was the Gulf Coast equivalent of Palm Beach, but not as showy or as formal," recalls Safrin. "In Boca Grande, where Gasparilla was located, the people were just as wealthy and powerful, but it was low-key, the atmosphere was more relaxed."

Gasparilla and Gulph Mills had plenty of commonality, and it was here that the fledgling pro first heard of Myopia Hunt Club, which also had a fair amount of representation at this western Florida enclave. "It was there I got my first taste of the incredible power of networking," offers Safrin. "I got the Florida job because my boss in Philadelphia recommended me to his friend Bob Kinard, the head pro at Gasparilla. I also quickly realized that I would never have had the exposure to the types of successful, connected and powerful people I was meeting in both Philly and Florida if I hadn't gotten into the golf business."

Over four years at Gulph Mills and two winter seasons at Gasparilla, the up-and-coming pro learned that while discriminating memberships such as these might not warm up to the 'new guy' right away, over time and with a first-rate performance, a mutual trust and affection will eventually develop between the professional and the club members.

Bob Kinard turned down an offer to become Myopia's head professional, in part because he had little interest in building a junior program from scratch. Although he cautioned his young assistant that Myopia would consider him 'tainted' because he worked for the man who spurned their offer, Safrin pursued his first head job with vigor. One of his great advocates was Herbert Jaques III, whose father and grandfather both served as USGA presidents. He was a member of both Myopia and Gasparilla, and told him that though the search committee was comprised of Myopia's 'next generation' of members, and were in the process of interviewing some 60 candidates for the position, he would put in a good word.

Safrin was remiss to leave the Gulph Mills family. His wife Kathy, though a schoolteacher by profession, had been moonlighting as a waitress there intermittently for a decade. Her mother Bernadette had been the bookkeeper for 25 years. This 'clubhouse romance' begat a wedding attended by dozens of Gulph Mills members, and no one would have figured that in a few short months, the newlyweds would be irrevocably Boston-bound.

It's a wonder they didn't turn around upon arrival, and high-tail it back to Philadelphia. They found the pro shop a few hundred yards straight uphill from the clubhouse proper, and Safrin wasn't sure if he was in his new office and retail domain, or if he had inadvertently wandered into the caddie shack. "It was small, grimy, with cement floors, fly strips everywhere, and virtually no merchandise. One of the powers-that-be told me not to worry; nobody makes the trek up to the pro shop anyway, so it didn't really matter!"

There was no real driving range. Helmeted caddies, often squinting into the sun, stood in the 17th fairway shagging range balls hit by members outside the pro shop door. Safrin reminisces about a golf culture that was almost nonexistent some 35 years ago. "Tennis was far more popular than golf when I arrived. We did $5,000 in pro shop sales that first year, only played 4,500 rounds of golf, had a season that began in mid May and ended after Labor Day, even though our weather is conducive for a season three times that long. We didn't have to open the pro shop until 9 am on weekends, because nobody showed up until then. When we began in 1980 this was more of a hunting club and polo club than a golf club. The membership was slowly skewing younger, and with our enthusiasm and energies, we began to build the golf program."

"We were in the process of shifting our club's culture somewhat when Bill came onboard," begins Fred Moseley, who was the first incoming president of the club during Safrin's tenure as head professional, taking the reins a couple of years after the pro's arrival. Despite his amazing longevity, Safrin is just a Billy-Come-Lately in comparison to the distinguished Mr. Moseley, who became a member at Myopia more than 20 years before Safrin came aboard as head pro.

"The club was slowly starting to change from an emphasis on being a gentlemen's golf and riding club to a club that was more user-friendly and family oriented. In my opinion Bill was the right man for the job, as we began to be more open and inclusive," continues Moseley, who is also a longtime member of Augusta National. "The

Bill Safrin with members of his staff

women loved him, the kids gravitated towards him, and he was a key component as Myopia became a more fully-faceted club. He's very personable and considerate, an astute businessman and an excellent instructor. I've been around golf and fine clubs for many decades, and while there are likely better instructors out there, and probably better merchandisers, in sum total I have never been around a golf professional who fully encompasses the spectrum of the position any better than Bill Safrin."

His total compensation in year one was less than he made as an assistant pro at Gulph Mills. "But I knew it was a great opportunity regardless. The club had so much potential. We needed more members, enthusiastic members, and golf-lovers. I thought then and am convinced now this could and would become the finest job in the nation."

It was an uphill battle for years, and not just the walk to the pro shop.

Early on as his salary crept up imperceptibly, he became aware that some colleagues around the North Shore were making three times what he was. He mentioned as much to the club president, who told him, "while I'm in charge, no golf professional here will ever make as much as $30,000."

Despite his fiscal predicament, Safrin persevered, and soon enough began to thrive. The years rolled by, Bill and Kathy's family grew, they established deep roots in the area, and business increased dramatically. His pro shop eventually did 100 times the revenue it did initially, thanks in great part to the unique fox-and-horn club logo he commissioned an artist to create. Lesson revenue cracked six figures. The golf season tripled in length, to about nine months, and rounds tripled commensurately. He bought acreage adjacent to the club, with views of the polo fields, and built a home.

Escaping the stark New England winters, Safrin and wife Kathy made a beeline for Florida for seven consecutive winters before children Will and Katey came along, usually to Vero Beach. He was, depending on the year and the situation, a real estate agent, a membership director at a high-end country club, and a Director of Golf. "Beautiful as it is north of Boston from spring through autumn I've always liked the warmer weather. It's also easier for me to stay active down south, as Myopia is extremely quiet over the winter months."

Safrin has enjoyed long term contracts that are practically unprecedented in golf. He went from a one-year deal initially to a two-year deal, then a mammoth 15-year deal, followed by eight more, and now eight more. "The club has always thrived on continuity. Presidents hold the position as long as they'd like, the golf chairmen have long tenures, and we've always agreed that this was where we wanted to be. Kathy has been running a playgroup for 3-year olds for 30 years. Kids she had in the group during those early years now bring their own kids to the group!"

Safrin replaced another thirty-year man, John Thoren, but only after a couple of interim years when the club really waned. "The timing was excellent," offers the former New England Section PGA Professional of the Year. "I was ambitious and hardworking, and the club was truly at a low point when I arrived. We both managed to thrive and grow simultaneously."

It's more than just his work ethic that sets him apart, according to Fred Moseley. "Bill is a perfect gentleman, with the highest ethical standards, and these qualities go way above and beyond his skills as a golf professional," offers the former investment banker. "At the same time, he is great fun to be around, an outstanding individual, and because we have traveled together many times, including overseas jaunts on several occasions, I can also add that he is a fantastic companion."

After a 20-year hiatus from heading south in winter, to give the children stability and continuity while they grew up, once he and Kathy became empty-nesters Safrin took another winter job at the ultra-posh Naples National Golf Club in 2010, with its impressive Hurdzan-Fry-designed golf course. It was full circle for the 60-something Safrin. It was the Myopia connections he had made all those years ago at Gasparilla that lead him up to Massachusetts, and here again, it was Myopia member and Naples National Ladies Golf Chairman Mary Jo Bovich who enticed him to southwest Florida. The differences between his clubs are stark: One is ancient, understated, multi-generational, with deep New England (and specifically Harvard) roots, peopled by members in traditional professional disciplines.

The other is new, grand in scope, luxurious, with many entrepreneurial-oriented members who created their own fortunes, many of whom call either the Midwest or the Northeast home. "Driving in my first day on the job I was struck by how meticulous the grounds are," relates Safrin. "Not a blade of grass out of place. The Italian Renaissance clubhouse is magnificent, well-appointed, but not overdone. The course is exceptional, but so is everything else; the valets, the caddies, the locker room, the practice facility, the food is amazing, it's considered the best in town, and Naples is known for it's exceptional cuisine."

His clubs are 1,500 miles apart and are different in so many ways, but the golf pro focuses on their respective commonalities. "The common denominator is that everyone is there to enjoy their golf experience and have a good time. If my staff maintains their enthusiasm and passion for the job, and all of us together continue to make the members happy, and insure they take pleasure in coming to their club, then we are doing our jobs properly."

"Naples National is extraordinary, and I love my affiliation there. But there are a number of reasons as to why I consider Myopia the best job in the country," concludes the four-time winner of the PGA's Horton Smith Award, given to those who make outstanding and continuing contributions to PGA education.

"Our infrastructure is so unique, with these old New England farmhouse outbuildings, which remain fully functional. The course is just as unique, and one of the most fun and memorable courses you can play. There's no micromanaging, and I have the latitude to run my part of the operation as I see fit, hire and train who I like, and be invigorated by their successes when they go onto their own jobs. I've been well compensated over the years, despite the lean times when I first began. And finally, it's the quality of the members, the deepness of the friendships we've developed over the years. All of these reasons in combination are why I truly feel this is the premier job, at least for me, anywhere."

The final irony is that even at the beginning of his tenure, when things were far from ideal, with infrastructure problems in the pro shop, too few members and an overall malaise regarding the golf program in general, Safrin could see the job's incredible potential.

What are the odds? A club that takes its name from the self-parody of four nearsighted brothers was lucky enough to hire a golf professional with incredible long-range vision.

CURRENT OR FORMER HEAD GOLF PROFESSIONALS WHO WORKED FOR BILL SAFRIN INCLUDE:

- Mark Ashton
- Mike Bemis
- Patrick Berry
- Peter Bronson
- J.P. Connelly
- Mike Corcoran
- Jeff Fraim
- Greg McFee
- Tom O'Brien
- Tom Roberts
- Erik Sorensen
- Tim Talbot
- Tom Thornton
- Jean Waters
- Tom Waters

Bill Safrin's tip for fellow golfers:

As someone who has suffered missing more than his share of three-foot putts I have discovered secrets to solving this problem. They are:

1) take the putter slowly away from the ball

2) make a short backswing

3) follow through twice as far as you take the club back

4) listen for the ball to go in

The tendency is for players to be quick due to anxiety that results in a short follow through and premature movement of the head, thus missing the putt. Do the above and your percentage of made putts will increase substantially.

Bill Safrin's tip for fellow golf professionals:

The impressions that you make on the people you meet can have far reaching effects on your career and the career of others. As Golf Professionals we are introduced to prominent, successful and powerful individuals that have a passion for golf.

A good lesson, shared experiences, helpful advice, correcting a problem or even concerned listening can lead to developing relationships that can help you or your assistant professional land a job. Relationship building and networking are keys towards becoming successful and helping others get ahead. Most people genuinely like to help others they know and respect. Once you earn this respect your word can be used to help others.

Randy Smith
Dallas, Texas

Texas is the largest state in the Union, and no state looms larger in terms of contributions to golf. The list of Lone Star luminaries would span the Rio Grande. Ten major (and Major) names would include Hogan, Nelson, Crenshaw, Kite, Trevino, Jimmy Demaret, Lloyd Mangrum, Jackie

Randy Smith and longtime student Justin Leonard

Burke Jr., Kathy Whitworth and "Babe" Zaharias, with 385 victories on the PGA and LPGA Tours combined. Add the name Justin Leonard to the list (more about him shortly) and the number pushes right up towards 400.

Texas also has a legacy of producing superb club professionals, most notably the late Harvey Penick of Austin Country Club, who passed away in 1995. One of the leading lights of the current generation is the highly regarded, long-enduring Randy Smith, approaching 40 years of tenure at Royal Oaks Country Club in Dallas, where he has served as the club's head professional since 1980.

Smith hails from the west Texas town of Odessa, which is known for oil and football, not necessarily in that order. But it's a little-known hotbed for golf professionals. When he was honored as National PGA Professional of the Year in 1996, Smith was actually the third Odessa native to win the most prestigious award available to a club pro. Jerry Cozby and David Price preceded him, honored in the same capacity.

Despite his numerous achievements and the accolades bestowed upon him, Smith has a great sense of his place in the scheme of things. Call it the Texas Timeline, and he attributes much of his success to those who came before him and those who mentored him, just at Messrs. Cozby and Price preceded him in winning the PGA's ultimate award.

"I have had several mentors that helped shape me into the professional I became, and I begin with Harvey Penick. His thumbprint is on so many club professionals in Texas and beyond, and he taught me lessons in kindness and attentiveness that are indelibly etched to this day."

Smith graduated from Texas Tech, where he spent his first two years on the golf team before going to work for professionals Gene Mitchell Sr. and his son, Gene Mitchell Jr., at Lubbock Country Club, while still an undergrad. His first post-college job was as an assistant pro at Tulsa Country Club, which is when he called Penick and asked for help with his short game. He made the six hour drive south where the icon had served the membership of Austin Country Club for fifty years, and was still teaching. "I hit balls for about three hours," reminisces Smith, still marveling at the memory. "Mr. Penick only offered about four pieces of advice the whole time, and did so in simple, easy-to-understand language. He would make a slight grip modification, for example, watch me hit a dozen balls, and then get in the range picker, and let me hit balls with this new adjustment for 30-odd minutes."

The scene repeated itself several more times. Penick would make another suggestion based on the ball flight Smith was hoping to achieve, watch him hit a dozen, then let him imprint the new alteration as he went back out to pick up the range. "He taught me 'less is more.' He used simple analogies with me, like trying to get the feeling of swinging a scythe. He was emphasizing reducing tension in the body, and the swing. I'm a talker by nature, but I learned that day to say far less during lessons, keep it simple, and keep repeating the key points so they will really sink in. He taught based on the student's wants, needs and limitations. "

As importantly as anything else, Smith learned true kindness and selflessness. At lesson's end, he was profusely thanking Penick for his time and expertise, and then casually mentioned they never discussed the short game, which was his primary concern. "He was mortified," recalls Smith, named on four separate occasions as the North Texas Section Teacher of the Year. "Even though his club was closed the next day, he insisted on meeting me at 8 am regardless, and we spent 90 minutes on my short game the following morning. It was an amazing experience for me, and I've never forgotten it."

Randy Smith went to Permian High, immortalized in the best-selling expose on high school football, Friday Night Lights. Much as he loved the game he quickly realized there wasn't much demand for a 115-pound freshman linebacker, and furthermore, he didn't have the 'hell bent for leather' mindset that allows undersized-but-game competitors to hold their own. "I was always concerned with breaking a finger, hurting my wrist, and derailing my golf game," explains Smith, who was a junior golfer of note. "When I separated my shoulder in spring football practice it was my last day in pads."

Perhaps it was malaise over his fizzled football career, but moping around Odessa Country Club one afternoon, wanting to avoid an important junior event, Smith received a vital lesson from another essential mentor. "Jake Bechtold was the head pro at the club, and he was surprised I wasn't entered in the tournament," recalls the 2005 inductee into the PGA of America's Hall of Fame. "I told him I didn't have the $10 entry fee, which was my lame excuse, because I was down on myself and my game. He reached into the cash register, took out $10, and told me I was on the tee in 30 minutes. He believed in me, and taught me the value of tenacity, and never quitting. I also learned that the best pros have their tentacles in lots of different places. They are concerned with all their members, even sulky juniors, and not just the club's power brokers," says Smith, who surprised himself, but not the pro, by winning that very event. "That small gesture by Jake Bechtold, urging me into the event, jump-started me again, and might have been the catalyst for my eventual career in golf. Who knows? If he hadn't done what he did, I could be a pipeline fitter in west Texas instead of the head professional at Royal Oaks in Dallas."

Later on, as a promising junior player, another soon-to-be-mentor delivered another unforgettable lesson. "I shot 80 at a junior event, and was dismayed with my performance. I convinced one of my playing companions that it was actually 79, which looks better on the scoreboard, but wasn't nearly competitive, nor did it fool some other players who knew what I had actually shot. I was sick about it on the ride home, couldn't sleep a wink, and the next morning back at the event I admitted what I had done to the pro, Mr. S.A. Smith, and asked him to disqualify me," recalls Smith.

The words spoken to him by the wise and compassionate pro were never forgotten. "Son, I can tell by looking at you that you've already paid for this transgression. We'll raise your score to what it should be, and then I want you to go out and finish the tournament."

Former British Open champion and Ryder Cup hero Justin Leonard
under the watchful eye of his instructor Randy Smith

In the ensuing decades, throughout his long career at Royal Oaks, Smith has run into similar situations with junior players half-a-dozen times or more. "Mr. S.A. Smith taught me that day that the 'letter of the law' is less important than looking at the big picture, observing who the kid is, his character, his potential. The long-term ramifications are what matters, not the final scoreboard in a junior tournament. I've applied this crucial lesson of keeping things in perspective, and feel strongly that the young golfers in question were far better off than if I had just brusquely disqualified them."

One junior player who never came into question was eventual British Open champion and Ryder Cup hero Justin Leonard, who has been under Smith's tutelage since elementary school. "We were euphoric when Justin mentioned Royal Oaks in his thank you speech as he held the Claret Jug aloft," reminisces Smith, thinking about that magical summer day in 1997. "To think back to when he was a skinny six year old with legs like toothpicks, who first came for golf lessons, to what he turned into, is remarkable. I was just as overjoyed when Harrison Frazar, finally won his first Tour event in 2011, in his 355th attempt. Like Justin, Harrison has also been a member at Royal Oaks since he was a kid. It's hard to compare and contrast the feelings I had, maybe because I was 15 years older and that much more established in my job when Harrison won. But the feeling each time was amazingly gratifying."

Smith distinguishes between "Royal Oaks guys" like the aforementioned, along with former US Amateur winner Colt Knost, up-and-coming PGA Tour player Martin Flores, and other stars-in-the-making like Matt Weibring and Paul Haley. "I am their swing coach and also their head professional," explains Smith, "as they have all been around the club a long time. I also have taught or continue to teach touring professionals like John Rollins, Ryan Palmer, Gary Woodland and others, but in those cases I am their instructor only, not their head pro."

"Randy has been instrumental in everything I've done in the game of golf." So begins Justin Leonard, who has a dozen Tour wins and more than 30 million dollars in career earnings. "There was never any over-coaching or over-teaching, but he gave me just the right amount of information, which is so critical when you are young. I've now been a professional for about 20 years, and he still makes things exciting. He is a feel-oriented instructor, which is crucial because when you are on the golf course all you can rely on is your feel."

"He's incredible with junior golfers," continues Leonard, who has represented the United States a dozen different times as a member of various Ryder Cup, President's Cup, Walker Cup, Dunhill Cup and World Cup teams. "He takes as much pride in helping a member lower their 15 handicap down to single digits as he does when one of his professionals wins on the PGA Tour. In my opinion he's the reason Royal Oaks is the great club that it is. I joke with him that he must live there, because he has this beautiful golf shop, puts on first-class tournaments, yet seems to be on the range teaching eight hours a day. It's like Randy has two full-time jobs, and he excels at both."

Buddy Cook was another key mentor to Smith, and helped imbue his incredible work ethic. "I've been working for him in one capacity or another since I was 13 years old, and continue to do so," states the acclaimed instructor, whose various students have received more than a hundred college golf scholarships around the country. "I caddied for him as a kid back in Odessa, helped him sell fireworks so he could get through college, he hired me to work for him in Tulsa, and when he got the top job at Royal Oaks he brought me along as his assistant," recounts Smith, who took the reins about four years later when Cook left to pursue other opportunities.

"Buddy basically taught me everything about the golf business, including how hard you have to be willing to work to become successful, and even more importantly, the value of interpersonal relationships," continues the former President of the Northern Texas PGA Section. "Buddy cared for and about his members and their families so deeply and so sincerely. He treated them like family, and the affection was returned in kind."

Cook taught Smith about effective merchandising to the point that the latter eventually gave seminars on the subject to other professionals. But soon enough he realized that concentrating on golf instruction was the real key to success. "By teaching and assisting members with their games, whether they are PGA Tour champions, club champions or high handicappers, they get more excited about golf, get more invested in the game, come to the club more often, play more, and it naturally has a positive effect on the entire operation—food and beverage, the pro shop, the whole club."

Comparisons have been made between Smith's tutelage of Leonard and Frazar, and his great mentor Harvey Penick's similar role in the Hall-of-Fame careers of Ben Crenshaw and Tom Kite. "I suppose there are some similarities," concludes Smith, "but I will be the first to tell you that I am no Harvey Penick. Nobody has ever been quite like him."

Truthfully spoken. But owing to his unique status as a respected, admired and long-serving club professional, coach and counselor to two generations of PGA Tour players, and more awards and accolades than any other member of his profession has ever amassed to date, there is nobody quite like Randy Smith, either.

CURRENT OR FORMER HEAD GOLF PROFESSIONALS WHO WORKED FOR RANDY SMITH INCLUDE:

- Phillip Bleakney
- Abe Hernandez
- Kevin Hood
- Glenn Lee
- Mark Mai
- Bruce McNee
- Mike Nedrow
- Doug Smith

Randy Smith's tip for fellow golfers:

To help make your golf swing a usable tool on the golf course you need to specifically practice shots you encounter on your home course. Practice tee shots you'll need on left-to-right holes, and vice-versa. Hit high iron shots, low iron shots, and three-quarter shots. Vary the ball movement and height to an array of different targets, not a single target. Just as importantly, never neglect the short game! Take six balls and start working on all the short shots you need at your course. You'll probably come to realize that pretty much every short shot you need occurs within 15 feet of the green, but they are all vitally important in a round of golf to saving one stroke here, and another one there.

Randy Smith's tip for fellow golf professionals:

Get involved in the entire operation, don't just work there. Even if you are an employee, have the attitude that you have an ownership interest. Take the same pride in the entire club as you do in your own home. Promote the facility, promote the members, develop relationships, and get to know not just your main customers, but also their spouses and their kids. Know where they go to school, know when they are sick, and be aware of their accomplishments. Get totally invested in the operation, not just on the golf side, and over time you'll benefit personally and professionally.

Bill Tindall
Seattle, Washington

A man in demand. How better to describe Bill Tindall, who several times in his storied career decided to leave plum positions at some of the finest clubs in the Northwest. It makes sense in a way, this native of the so-called Emerald City occasionally urged by others towards what they considered greener pastures. "I never thought I would leave Broadmoor Golf Club," begins the soft-spoken pro, now just past 70. "Many of my friends and my peers thought I was

Bill Tindall concentrating at the U.S. Senior Open

crazy to do so, and I questioned myself, because its one of the greatest jobs on the west coast. But everything has worked out in retrospect."

The son of a long-time Seattle area pro named Bob Tindall, things have been working out golf-wise for Bill Tindall since his youth. He was just 14 when he captured the Seattle Men's Amateur Championship, a precursor to winning the USGA Boys Junior Championship three years later in 1960. (His opponent in that final was Laurie Hammer, profiled in Chapter Six.) That was the first of Tindall's ten USGA appearances, and one of his fondest mementos came from the famed "Massacre at Winged Foot," the 1974 US Open, which marked his only appearance in our national championship. "I have a photo of the scoreboard after round one," recalls Tindall with a chuckle. "It shows me at 75, with Jack Nicklaus and Johnny Miller a shot behind at 76. Too bad the next day when I needed three pars coming home to make the cut I made three triple bogeys instead! After the first triple, I lost my enthusiasm."

He's never lost his enthusiasm for competitive golf, first as a scholarship player at the University of Washington, and throughout a long career that featured a trio of successful appearances in the U.S. Senior Open, the cut made every time. But Tindall's true legacy is as a first-rate club professional at first-class clubs, and though he had early dalliances after his 1965 college graduation as a schoolteacher, a management trainee for a grocery chain and an ill-fated, one-year PGA Tour career (26 times a Monday qualifier, 13 times in the field, one made cut) it is his service to the posh and prestigious Broadmoor Golf Club in downtown Seattle when his star truly began to rise.

Years before returning to the city of his birth, his career as a club pro began at Longview Country Club in southern Washington, just north of Portland, Oregon. The owners managed to forgive the fact that Tindall had yet to obtain his Class 'A' PGA membership because, according to the pro, "they loved my wife, Linda." After eight years at that initial post, he was tapped to take over at Broadmoor Golf Club, where he was happily ensconced for the succeeding 22 years.

"Broadmoor is one of the true classic clubs in the northwest," explains Tindall, who also moonlighted for nearly a decade as the golf coach at his alma mater, located just a short distance from his fulltime job. "It's a beautiful old Vernon Macan design from the 1920s, and the membership is made up primarily of the city's business elite, mostly professional and entrepreneurial types, and they couldn't have been nicer. It was and remains a delightful place to work, and will always be very special to me. Practically the whole time I was there I never gave a thought to leaving. It's the type of job you keep for a lifetime, the type of job you retire from."

However when one of his members recruited him to come aboard at a brand-new club under construction, the pro began to ponder. "Aldarra was being built east of the city, on land that was originally part of the Boeing family farm," explains the pro, referencing the famed aerospace company whose roots are in Seattle. "This was a totally different club, only individual memberships allowed, not family memberships. It was an extremely high-end Tom Fazio design, well out in the woods, meant to have a Pine Valley-like feel, because one of the founders was a member of Pine Valley himself. More importantly, it allowed me to get involved with a start-up operation from Day One, which was a new experience for me. I was 56 at the time, and thought if I was ever going to take on something so ambitious, I better get to it!"

Aldarra succeeded in spectacular fashion, and would have been a great capper and "curtain call" to a successful career. It didn't quite work out that way. After six non-stop years building and establishing the club, now past his 60th birthday, Tindall decided to retire to his Puget Sound vacation home on Camano Island, about 90 minutes north of Seattle, do a bit of teaching on the side, and spend more time with his wife and family. "I was tending my chickens, enjoying our three acres, but the phone rang again a year-and-a-half later."

This time it was the Tumble Creek Golf Club, an attention-getting Tom Doak design. This new private club was part of the Suncadia Resort, in a small town called Cle Elum, some 90 minutes east of Seattle and on the other side of the Cascade Mountains. Much of the appeal stemmed from the fact it was just a seven-month season over on the 'snowy side' of the Cascades, unlike the year-round play that is standard around Seattle. "I guess I missed the action," admits the former Oregon Open champion. "I also thought it would be a nice change of pace for us to live in a sunny climate, have a season that began in spring and ended in early autumn." He spent a fruitful three-and-a-half years there, and loved his duties, but eventually had enough.

"Our grandchildren were getting a bit older, and we decided we wanted be back closer to the city." Life was good back in Seattle, the kids and grandkids close at hand, a bit of teaching on the side, with playing privileges due to the honorary memberships bestowed by both of his former clubs in town. Then the phone rang. After their Director of Golf left suddenly, Aldarra wanted him back. "I said, 'are you crazy?' I'm almost 70 years old!" They assuaged his reluctance by turning a twelve month job into a seven month commitment, the better for Bill and Linda to spend time at their winter hideaway in Palm Desert, California. So he took back the reins in 2011. "This is definitely my last job," he exclaims, only semi-convincingly, doing a spot-on impersonation of the Pro who cried Wolf.

"It's not surprising that Bill has been so heavily recruited," offers his great friend and University of Washington golf teammate Bruce Richards. "We have been friends for nearly 60 years, and he is an absolutely great guy, and consummate club pro," continues the two-time Washington Senior Amateur Champion. "Bill has been the preeminent club professional in the northwest over the 40-year duration of his career. He's got incredible people skills,

Bill Tindall, longtime coach of the University of Washington Golf Team

and you'd be hard-pressed to find someone with a bad word to say about him, which stems in large part because he loves what he does so much," continues Richards, an insurance executive who also is a partial owner of three public-access golf courses around Seattle. "Even to this day, despite his stature, he'll be out to the car to help a member or their guest with their golf bag as quick as anybody else on his staff."

The service element comes naturally to the pro. "I love to help people, whether it's working with them and improving their game, making a call and gaining them access to a private club, whatever I can do. Helping my assistants move up in their careers has also been a source of great satisfaction." Bruce Richards, who has competed in almost as many USGA Championships as Tindall, picks up the same thread. "Bill has enjoyed success in part because he has always attracted great assistants. Everyone wants to work for him and learn from him, because they know it will lead to greater advancements in their own careers. It's a self-perpetuating scenario; Bill gets good young assistants, makes them better, they go on to upper-echelon jobs, and the next wave of bright kids is dying to come work for him."

Despite his many successes, Tindall's major regret is the toll his profession took on family life. "It's practically a schizophrenic profession, non-stop from the beginning of April through October. All the years I was immersed it didn't faze me much, it was my job. I worked like my dad did before me. But looking back I wish I had managed my time better, and given more of myself to my wife, son and daughter, and not been so focused at the club, but those are lessons that come late. Thankfully my wife did a wonderful job with our children when I was spending all those hours, year after year, on the job."

Looking back at a love of golf spanning 60-plus years gives the pro a unique perspective on what the game was, how it has evolved, and where it's going. "Golf needs to be simplified, in my opinion. The rules need to be simpler, the courses need to be shorter, it would be nice to rein in equipment, belly putters, space age equipment and the like, but that train has left the station. I think the "tee it forward" initiative is a great step, encouraging players to move up a tee box or even two. Putting tees in the fairway, 150 yards from the greens is a fine idea, because it encourages families to play together, kids are playing the 'big course' with their parents, and in this way you can groom the next generation, which is the future of the game."

Looking back at his own legacy, Tindall sums things up thusly: "Making these career decisions over the last 15 years has had tremendous benefits, despite the fact that on the surface, leaving

Broadmoor Golf Club when I did seemed like such an unorthodox move. At Aldarra and at Suncadia I have met and befriended hundreds of wonderful people from all walks of life that I would have never been exposed to otherwise. It was an uncommon path that I chose to follow, but I feel fortunate to have chosen it."

CURRENT OR FORMER HEAD GOLF PROFESSIONALS WHO WORKED FOR BILL TINDALL INCLUDE:

- Eric Bowen
- Bruce Condon
- Tad Davis
- Doug Doxsie
- Dan Hill
- Craig Hunter
- Doug Kauffman
- Mahlon Moe
- Steve Solomon
- Mark Sursely

Bill Tindall's tip for fellow golfers:

The bunker shot is intimidating to many golfers, but it doesn't have to be. Remember to work your feet into the sand and use an open stance with your weight fairly evenly distributed. Let the arms hang straight down and position the ball left of center in the stance. Thus your sternum is over the spot where you want to hit the sand. Open the clubface only slightly unless you have a very short shot. The swing path should be slightly out-to-in, and never in-to-out.

As you swing your arms back have your hands lift the club head up, and let the club "hang" at the top of the swing, thus encouraging a smooth swing (we don't want to work hard---let the club splash the ball out using the bounce of the club.) Have the feeling of throwing a watermelon up into a truck, and allow your eyes to follow the ball up onto the green.

Bill Tindall's tip for fellow golf professionals:

It took me a long time to truly believe that our amateur golfers really do look up to us (it is a big deal to be asked to play with the pro). We must earn that respect and maintain it by conducting ourselves each day (whether on the clock or not) in such a way that someone who knows you would go out of his way to introduce his pro to a friend. You never know who your next boss might be.

Remember that the last person you see each day or the last phone call you answer deserves and expects the same attention and enthusiasm that you gave to the first person who came in the door or who called. Likewise the shop should remain tidy all day- not just in the morning. Everyone can be on board with "touching things up."

You must remember that not a single person owes you his business. You must earn it by doing the extra things that makes that person want to support you. Be proactive by being someone who goes the extra bit to make each golfer's day at the course special. He will be proud of his club and want to share the experience with his friends. You are a Professional and respect and enjoy the responsibility that comes with that title.

JD Turner
Savannah, Georgia

Despite wide-ranging playing success and a long stint as head professional at one of his home state's most venerable golf clubs, Iowa native JD Turner is probably best known for the innovative manner in which he sought to educate golfers. It's not hard to understand; his first and most significant role model was a coach and educator himself for 45 years.

"My father John was a high school teacher and coach his entire adult life," reminisces

JD Turner (right) with Lee Trevino

the PGA Master Professional. "Ironically, he never coached golf though, nor was he much of a player. He would keep his fishing gear with his golf clubs, and pretty much every time he played golf he would also do some fishing. The other quirk was he would only take 41 shots. It didn't matter where he was; on the seventh, eighth, or ninth hole, once he struck the ball 41 times he was ready to drop a line into the creek that abutted the golf course. But my mother Edie was a different story, she won the club championship at our little 9-hole club 22 times over the years!"

While the son admired his dad, fortunately he emulated his mom, eventually winning the Iowa Open on five separate occasions. "I grew up in the polio years of the '40s and '50s," recalls Turner. "There was no public swimming allowed. There was no little league, or tennis, but we had our little golf course. It was nothing for my friends and me to go round and round, 36, even 45 holes a day in summer."

Turner was mostly self-taught, mainly because professional golf instruction in the little railroad burgh of Perry, Iowa was almost as rare as a sea breeze. His high school golf coaches were science or social studies teachers who liked the game, and passed around the coaching duties, which were equal parts cheerleader, chaperone and shuttle driver. It was more of the same after graduation. Recruited in both golf and basketball at Iowa's Graceland University, his golf coach's real vocation was as dean of the music department.

It was only upon transferring to the University of Iowa for his final two years of eligibility that he finally came under the tutelage of a bona-fide, full-time golf coach. Good thing, as he needed all the help he could muster competing against conference rivals Jack Nicklaus and Tom Weiskopf at Ohio State. Just like those future PGA Tour stars Turner was also named to the All Big Ten golf squad, and was named captain of his college team. But despite his on-course success he was thinking about ways to improve the flow of solid information from coach to student, and slowly began to develop the entrepreneurial instinct that brought him to prominence some years later.

Following in his dad's footsteps, the future pro began as a schoolteacher, but with a growing family, became an insurance agent after four years in the classroom. Impressing a prospective client with an eye-popping score of 59 in a casual afternoon golf round, Turner (who explained away the remarkable score by noting the golf course was a powder-puff) was offered and accepted a sponsorship opportunity to take his game to the next level, practicing and competing full time. This is when he began winning Iowa Open titles, but after two years of middling results trying to find a place on the PGA Tour, Turner and his sponsor entered into another business arrangement.

"He had just built a 9-hole course that came with excess acreage which was earmarked for a real estate component, and happened to have an old farmhouse on property," recounts one of the youngest members ever inducted into the Iowa Golf Hall of Fame. "The concept of junior golf camp was all but unheard of, certainly in the early 1970s in our part of the world. But we refurbished the farmhouse, bought bunk-beds and basic furnishings from the University of Iowa, and opened up a golf camp that summer for aspiring juniors."

Turner barnstormed his way across the state in springtime, identifying prospective campers in dozens of small towns. When the summer roster was full, he became chief counselor, lead instructor and camp director concurrently, spending all day teaching his 20 or 30 weekly charges the game's fundamentals. On the last day of the last camp, two teenage brothers were so enamored of the program they had just completed they urged Turner to replace the departing pro at their country club in Council Bluffs.

"I only knew one person in Council Bluffs. It was pure serendipity that he was not only a member of the club, but also the one-man search committee for the new pro!" The on-course job interview ended with Turner shooting a round in the mid-60s, and without ever having spent a day as an assistant pro, he took the reins at Lakeshore Country Club on the first day of 1972.

The modern golf professional is usually a business-savvy merchandising whiz, with a wide-ranging expertise that might include accounting, payroll and computer skills. But 45-odd years ago in Iowa, there was a basic prerequisite: Knowing how to golf your ball. "I had observed that the best jobs in the state were held by excellent players who were all in their later 50s or 60s," says Turner, twice a participant in the U.S. Senior Open. "My playing record was very solid, but I needed club experience to land a top job. Lakeshore was a great proving ground for me, and I spent eight years at the helm. Then just as I had hoped, I was eventually offered the head professional's position at Des Moines Country Club."

Iowa has more courses per capita than almost any other state, and Des Moines CC is one of the best-known golf clubs in the Midwest. It features a pair of Pete Dye-designed courses, and once served as host venue for the US Senior Open. In the 14 years Turner held the reins, from 1980 to 1994, the club's membership almost doubled, from over 500 to nearly a thousand. But despite the demands on his time, and the attentiveness he showed to his burgeoning membership, Turner was intent on bringing quality golf instruction to all corners of the state.

More than a dozen years before Golf Channel initially flickered into select living rooms nationwide, Turner conceived, produced, directed, sold and starred in The Iowa Golf Show, later renamed JD Turner's Golf University. The show was an unrehearsed, real-time golf lesson, and has run for 27 consecutive years, reaching an enthusiastic audience throughout his home state and beyond. One of his early television guests was acclaimed short-game guru Dave Pelz, whose has taught ten Major championship winners include Phil Mickelson, a 2012 inductee in the World Golf Hall of Fame.

JD Turner (2nd from right) with fellow instructors in the Turner Golf Group

"JD Turner is a *great* PGA Professional," offers Pelz, another former Big Ten golfer, who played at the University of Indiana. "He is a really fine player, has a wonderful personality, ran an incredible club operation for his members, and was an ideal mentor to his staff and assistant professionals. And this is before even mentioning his skills and credentials as a teacher."

"I have worked directly with JD Turner in the teaching environment and appeared on several of his instructional television shows. He has an extensive knowledge and understanding of the game, and is one of the best communicators I have ever seen," states the author of numerous popular instruction books. "His golf schools are excellent because he truly cares about his students' problems and efforts, and their games improve as a result of his work. It has been an honor and a privilege to know and work with JD."

It was this innovative cable television show with 850,000 subscribers, which brought Turner to the attention of GOLF Magazine, which tapped him as one of their inaugural Top Teachers. Now the list is 100, but when Turner was selected the list was just the Top 50.

He wasn't done innovating. After a couple years on-air, he had amassed quite a bit of instructional material. He realized he could put together a coaching blueprint for all those math and science teachers-turned golf coaches from Davenport to Dubuque, not to mention little hamlets like Pocahontas and Prairie City, and help them teach their charges in a methodical and effective manner. He distilled the TV show archives down to the essentials, and created a pair of 2 ½ hour videotapes called the My Pro Series. It began in Iowa but soon spread well beyond the state line. The total package was geared to physical education departments in school systems, libraries, and both high school and college golf teams.

Over time the idea was sharpened and sophisticated. Now the program is called "Be the Golf Coach," and the original two videotapes became eight DVD's. The accompanying workbooks are laminated, professional and concise. The system Turner created eventually reached many thousands of coaches, teachers and golf students in the nation. It included numerous lesson plans for effective practice, a Q&A directed towards golf as taught in a classroom environment and specific fixes for faults in the swing. "For example, if a college wants to offer golf as a PE elective this system will demonstrate to the instructor how to teach their students all aspects of the game. Another example: You often see a husband attempting to instruct his wife, or a parent trying to teach a child. This system is effective in that regard also," explains Turner, now a resident of coastal Georgia.

Longing to leave a half-century of frigid Midwest winters behind, the enterprising pro formed the Turner Golf Group in the mid-'90s, bidding adieu to the rewarding, but ultra-demanding life of the club professional. His new endeavor was a variation on his traditional theme of bringing quality instruction to an eager, but potentially underserved clientele: Corporate America.

"I hand-picked a wide range of professional colleagues I've met over time that are terrific teachers, fine players and great communicators. We set up a rotating series of three-to-four day schools based mostly in Arizona, where the weather is ideal. Our typical students were key executives, incentive winners or valued customers of blue chip companies like Martin-Marietta, AC-Delco, BASF, Gatorade, Monsanto, Bayer, Helena Chemical, and a range of agricultural concerns," continues Turner, whose wife, Brenda is a widely admired golf-themed artist. "I know pros from the north whose clubs shut down in the fall and are available for winter schools. I have colleagues in the south who want to teach in summer during their slow period, so it all works out nicely."

The parallels between his rudimentary summer golf camp and his posh corporate golf schools are clear, despite the passing of 40-plus years. "Now we feature cocktail parties and fine dining instead of franks and beans, and beautiful hotel suites instead of dormitory bunk beds," concludes Turner, three times a featured speaker at the PGA World Teaching Summit. "Not everyone is driven to improve their golf game, and put in the work needed to do so. But in all my years of teaching, I've yet to encounter anybody who wanted to get worse!"

CURRENT OR FORMER HEAD GOLF PROFESSIONALS WHO WORKED FOR JD TURNER INCLUDE:

- Damon Anderson
- John Bermel
- Mark Boggs
- Mark Christensen
- Gary Claypool
- Chris Foley
- Steve Fuller
- Bill Gaukel
- Jay Horton
- Scott Howe
- Scotty Larson
- Chad Lydiatt
- Charlie Mahon
- Melea Mullaly
- Tom Nelson
- Gary Ridgeway
- Curt Schnell
- Kyle Stierwalt
- Stan Truhlsen
- Rick Werner
- Greg Wilson
- Mark Young

JD Turner's tip for fellow golfers:

Most players hold the club too tightly. The vast majority do not sense where the clubface is because of extreme grip pressure. If the player can't feel the head, how can they create speed, maneuver the ball, or be in balance? By squeezing the grip, rhythm, speed, and balance are replaced by heave, lunge, and slug. Effort becomes the system and consistent, repetitive results are questionable.

An effective exercise to learn proper grip pressure is to play catch underhanded with a golf ball. Toss the ball back and forth, changing the distance several times. You will toss it the perfect distance, height, and speed every time. This is because you automatically hold the ball softly in the fingers. If you hold the ball as you do the club, the tension in the arms, wrists, and hands is immediate. The contrast is huge. If you attempt to play catch with the tighter grip you have no chance. Over control loses again.

JD Turner's tip for fellow golf professionals:

Here are some thoughts on how to increase teaching revenues. As in most businesses, golf professionals need to identify potential markets, specific groups, and clusters where classes can be organized. Examples of these include: Breakfast clubs, service clubs, fraternal organizations, ladies auxiliaries, couples, families, working women, corporate wellness programs, college alumni groups, graduates, dinner and luncheon clubs, charitable and philanthropic organizations, fine arts and museum enthusiasts, 9 and 18 hole ladies groups, left-handed players and new members.

Also consider occupation-specific groups such as doctors, dentists, pharmacists, attorneys, accountants, architects and corporate customer schools. Even though the golf business is very challenging in the current era you can still increase your chances of success.

Brett Upper

Phoenix, Arizona

The percentage of club professionals working today who at one juncture didn't entertain at least a passing fancy of making a living on Tour, is microscopic. In most cases it was likely long ago and far away, once upon a time, etc. but there are very few PGA professionals who didn't consider the concept, perhaps fantasy might be a better descriptive, of making a livelihood solely with their sticks.

Former PGA Tour player Brett Upper

The irony surrounding Brett Upper, the longtime Director of Golf at the prestigious Arizona Country Club in Phoenix, is that he claims he was part of that distinct minority. The Pennsylvanian's early ambition was to develop into a well-established club pro, with an enthusiastic membership at a prominent private club. Being around the game, teaching, spending time in the outdoors, working with and for people who were just as enamored of golf as he was, it sounded like a great career path. Never in his imaginings did he see himself as a bona-fide member of the PGA Tour, but that's exactly what transpired, and Upper had more than that proverbial 'cup of coffee' in the Big Leagues; he stayed on Tour for seven full seasons.

"My first job in golf was at Lancaster Country Club, not far from where I grew up," begins Upper, now in his mid-50s. "I was the third of three assistants and routinely worked 60, sometimes 80 hours a week for a hundred dollars," he recalls, shaking his head at the memory. "But then I made about $350 for shooting 73 at the first pro tournament I ever entered. I spent four hours doing what I loved best, which netted me almost four weeks pay. I thought it would be smart to really devote myself to playing, and see how far it would take me."

At first, it didn't take him far from the shop. His boss was John Abernathy, a stern-but-fair taskmaster who didn't want his lowly assistant playing or practicing during working hours, which were pretty much all hours. "He owned the shop, paid his assistants out of his own pocket, and was very demanding in regards to our time. But I got extra motivation to get the most out of my limited practice time, and when I eventually become a head pro I learned to delegate responsibilities from what Mr. Abernathy had taught me."

That first season Upper got in the habit of practicing from daybreak until shop duty commenced at 7 am. He would then zip through as many holes as possible after the last golfers straggled in near dusk, allowing the fledgling pro a precious chance to take some on-course swings in the waning light. Some years later his boss acquiesced in allowing him to play the Pennsylvania Open, but wouldn't let him off duty for a practice round. Doing a reconnaissance mission towards dusk the evening before the event, Upper ran into Oakmont assistant pro Bob Ford, who he knew from their days playing sports around Valley Forge. "Bob has been like an older brother to me over the years," explains Upper. Ford, who ended up winning that state Open, told him Oakmont was in need of an assistant, and Upper went to work for head professional (and former US Open champion) Lew Worsham shortly thereafter.

"Not only was it a chance to move to an incredible club, but Mr. Worsham told me I could live in the clubhouse rent-free, and work everyday from noon until dark, which afforded me the entire morning to work on my game." An added bonus was the fact that Worsham took his new protégé along to his winter job in Florida, at Coral Ridge CC in Fort Lauderdale, where Upper was in charge of the driving range, and presumably beat more balls than the next two most avid range devotees combined.

The work ethic that soon landed him on golf's main stage was evident from an early age. Upper had begun caddying at age eight, and before too long added bellhop, busboy, office cleaner and dishwasher to his resume, which also included lawn-cutting, driveway shoveling and keg party administrative duties. Anything to make a buck. "My dad was a successful salesman, he loved golf, and that love was passed on to me. But nothing was handed to him, he grew up in the Depression and worked hard for everything he had, and I came up the same way."

Iconic Philadelphia-area pro Pete Trenham can speak better than most about Upper's work ethic. "I think Brett was probably my fourth best junior player as he was coming to the latter stages of high school," offers this original inductee in the Philadelphia PGA Section Hall of Fame. "No way would I have figured him for any type of Tour career, never mind a solid seven-year run like he had. But he outworked everyone, made fundamental changes in his game, and made it all the way," explains Trenham, whose career spans in excess of 50 years in the area. "When I began at St. Davids Golf Club in the mid-'60s, Brett's father Maynard, who was known as Mac, was my golf chairman, and Brett was in grade school. That's how far back I go with the family," offers Trenham, who spent a shade under 30 years as the club's head professional.

Upper's one-year stint on Florida's Space Coast Tour wasn't very fruitful. He managed but a single check in 15 tries, going broke in the process, but proved to himself with that singular payday that he did in fact have what it took to compete with some of the best players in the nation, because in those pre-Nike, pre-Nationwide Tour days, the Space Coast Tour was the finest proving grounds outside of the PGA Tour.

He went back to Lancaster CC after several years at Oakmont, now as more of an established player, on my own terms, with appropriate time to practice and compete. He was fortunate to find a wonderful sponsor in Bob Graybill, a wealthy Lancaster CC member, a 36-handicap player who greatly admired the young assistant who could shoot in the mid-60s. Explains the pro, "Mr. Graybill had daughters, no sons, and wanted to provide me with a financial lift. He initially offered me a four-year college education, which I foolishly turned down. Instead we entered into a ten-year playing agreement, with him paying my expenses, a small salary, and the use of a car. Early on he took 85% of what I won, and eventually the balance shifted to me taking home 85% of what I won. I'm happy to say that the agreement worked out over time, he kept me afloat through the lean years, and in the end he was fully repaid, and in possession of a modest profit. We remained friends until he passed away years later."

The investment began to pay dividends in 1983, when Upper received his Tour card after finishing second in Qualifying School, held at TPC Sawgrass outside of Jacksonville. It was this same venue where he found his greatest success on the PGA Tour, with a third place finish in the Players Championship several years after. "I had missed my card by two shots the year prior, which breaks down to one third of a shot per round over six rounds. I decided then and there to prepare myself as though there were

Brett Upper shows the form that kept him on the PGA Tour
for seven seasons.

only ten spots available to get on Tour, as opposed to the 50 that there actually were. The psychology and the preparation paid off, because I was runner-up the following year."

He held onto his Tour card after his rookie year by the slimmest margin possible—he made a seven-foot putt on the final hole of the final round of the year's final tournament, thereby securing the 125th and final spot on the money list. His second year was his most successful, vaulting up to 61st place on the money list, with several top 3 and top 5 finishes, most notably at the Players Championship.

Upper fell to 89th on the money list the following year, and then began a struggle to stay exempt. Family demands and the weariness of travel conspired to whittle away at his ability to focus, and though he held his card for several years thereafter, deep down he knew that his was not to be a long-term career on the PGA Tour.

"I wish I had played a few years longer on Tour, I could have used more discipline. I was having fun, and fun sometimes turns into stupidity. But there's also a lot to be said about coming home to your own house and family every night, too. Once we're gone, and the kids don't remember you being there for them, what does it really matter?"

"I was very foolish not to have taken advantage of the opportunity to attend college when it was offered to me by my sponsor," recounts the pro, ruefully. "But one of my great sources of pride is that all three of our children graduated from college themselves, and are doing great in their respective careers."

One of the main reasons Upper has done so well in his post-PGA Tour career is due to a longtime relationship with fellow Pennsylvanian Arnold Palmer. "We first met while playing a practice round together in advance of his participation in the 1978 PGA Championship at Oakmont, where I was working at the time," recalls Upper. "I was fortunate enough to birdie the first two holes, and even though I didn't play that well the rest of the round, he always remembered that. Add in the fact that I worked for Lew Worsham, whose brother Bubby had been Mr. Palmer's roommate at Wake Forest, and we had a solid connection."

Palmer not only offered him playing and practicing privileges at Bay Hill in Orlando during Upper's years on the PGA Tour, but also helped him land all three of his head professional appointments once he gave up the Tour life. Upper credits both Lew Worsham and Arnold Palmer for leading by example, showing him the right way to be a club pro and Tour pro respectively, being both a diplomat for and an emissary of the game.

Upper began his career as a head golf professional at Feather Sound CC on Florida's Gulf Coast in the early '90s, nearly ten years after he had left that end of the business. "It was a smooth transition, other than the fact that I now had bosses to answer to, and wasn't calling my own shots and making my own schedule." He adds with a small chuckle, "I'm happy I learned quickly the art of making a superior think that your good idea was actually their good idea, so things can progress and improve at a club!"

Three year later he went back to his old stomping grounds, a brand-new club called Bent Creek, not far from his original digs at Lancaster CC. "In the back of my mind I thought I might end up back over at Lancaster as the head pro someday," recalls Upper. Bent Creek opened with a full membership and waiting list on Day One, reflective of the 'go-go' golf market of the time, and the fact there was a dearth of viable private options in the area. Six years later, the pro didn't relocate 15 minutes, as he had surmised, but more like 2,300 miles, when he took over at The Arizona Country Club, where he has been firmly ensconced for some 15 years, and where he plans on finishing his career.

Scottsdale is one of the most golf-rich locales in the world, but when The Arizona Country Club was established in 1909, the area was, pardon the expression, a real golf desert. "Our club has tremendous reverence for golf history and tradition," explains the Director of Golf. "It's a golf club first, but with tremendous country club amenities. It's the type of old-school club that cannot be created or conjured, but has to evolve over the decades. I can't foresee leaving here. The membership is passionate and knowledgeable, and they revere the game like I do. It is my pleasure, along with my first-rate staff, to provide the utmost service we can to further their pleasure in the game."

The Arizona Country Club, which in the middle of the past century served for nearly twenty years as the host venue for the PGA Tour's Phoenix Open, is anomalous in its location in terms of the layout and design. Located on a flattish parcel at the base of famed Camelback Mountain, the course is wall-to-wall grass with huge specimen trees throughout. It is the antithesis of the target golf sensibility which has sprung in this desert landscape like so much jumping cholla in the last 30-odd years, where the golf topography heaves and rolls, and wayward shots often come to rest among the cacti and the creosote bushes. "Our course is so wonderful, and the club itself so popular, in part because it's basically a parkland course like the kind you find in the Northeast, but in this wonderful desert climate," states Upper.

All of his post-Tour career successes come as no surprise to his boyhood pro, Pete Trenham. "Brett has street smarts, despite his lack of formal education," continues the former Philadelphia PGA's Golf Professional of the Year. "He's smart enough to know what he doesn't know, and smart enough to hire the right people to do the things he cannot, or would rather not do. Add in the fact he's likeable, personable, outgoing, the way he looks and his ability to play great golf, it's no real surprise he's made a wonderful career for himself as a club pro. He was determined, he was focused, and the fact he's done as well as he has shouldn't be a shock to those of us who really know him."

Because of his playing background, Upper has an overall perspective on golf that 99% of his club pro colleagues don't. "In regards to the PGA Tour, I had a long drink at the trough, far greater than most club professionals ever experience. Add in those years with the 25-or-so I have spent subsequently in the club capacity, and I feel I have a deep understanding of the game and where it stands. I will say this: If every club pro and every PGA Tour professional felt as I do, that all the golfers out there, strong players or high handicaps, the juniors, the fans, the potential players, etc. are all potential allies, all potential assets, all potentially contributing in some way for us to earn a living and support us in our endeavors, then the game would be far better off. We could have millions more golfers playing regularly if all the professionals were more encouraging and projected more enthusiasm to those who do or might support golf."

"People can tell when someone really loves and lives their job," concludes Upper. "For the most caring professionals, it's a passion and a privilege, and not just a way to support themselves. Customers can feel and sense that. For me, earning a living is a byproduct of being around the game I have loved for so long."

CURRENT OR FORMER HEAD PROFESSIONALS WHO WORKED FOR BRETT UPPER INCLUDE:

- Charlie Bolling
- Paul Coe
- Devin Hillman
- Nick Hodge
- Chris Morrison
- Paul Ogelsby
- Rob Sheuy
- Steve Talentino
- Doug Wolfgang

Brett Upper's tip for fellow golfers

Far too many golfers have a misconception about alignment. A large percentage of the people I have taught through the years believe that the body, feet, hips, and shoulders are to be aimed at the target. This could not be further from the truth.

Only the leading edge of the club face, or the club head is aimed at the target. The body, feet, hips and shoulders are aimed parallel left. In my opinion correct alignment is an absolute must. Visualize railroad tracks, and put the inside track at your foot line, the outside track acts as your target line.

Brett Upper's tip for fellow golf professionals

Every PGA Professional needs to understand that each and every golfer they meet--man, woman or child, that has taken the time to formally establish a handicap, is the sole reason they have a career, and are able to make a living and support their families. Therefore it is a privilege to promote the game of golf and openly share our love for it. As professionals we need to help golfers learn to score better and encourage new players to take up the game.

Don't get overly wrapped up in swing theory with your students. The key is to help them score better, because lower scores bring more enjoyment and increased enthusiasm. Be less concerned with technique, particularly if it's repeatable, and more concerned with results.

Rick Vershure
Scarsdale, New York

Longtime Quaker Ridge head professional Rick Vershure

Yogi Berra said it best, albeit ambiguously: "When you come to a fork in the road, take it."

Rick Vershure was ready to stick a fork in his competitive golf career a dozen different times over the years. Brief flashes of success with a rent-saving paycheck were the exception. Missed cuts, failures at Qualifying School, and a general frustration with his lack of progress were the rule.

He was in his mid-30s and finally beginning to see real progress in the one pursuit he truly loved. Until then he had mostly spun his wheels even more fruitlessly than in the muscle car he roared around in during his disenfranchised youth in Pontiac, Michigan. Squirrel away money all spring, summer and fall working as an assistant pro, then squander everything he had earned on mini-tour entry fees in winter. He had few permanent relationships, no real home, or even a piece of furniture to call his own.

It was January 1988 and he was chasing the white ball and the dream concurrently in South Africa when his fork in the road appeared. Vershure received the type of phone call that 99% of golf professionals will never have the pleasure of getting, particularly golf professionals that have never held a head pro job a day in their life.

Quaker Ridge Golf Club was calling to ask him to become their head professional. This sublime and ultra-prestigious club, tucked amid the stately hardwoods in the leafy hamlet of Scarsdale, in the middle of swanky Westchester County, New York, wanted him to take over. Quaker Ridge is one of the greatest-yet-understated clubs in the country, with a very genteel, educated and accomplished membership. They enjoy a magnificent A.W. Tillinghast-designed golf course, located very nearby historic Winged Foot Golf Club, which is probably Tillie's best known creation. It is by any definition a top 100 club and they were offering their one-year assistant pro the top job. He should have been elated. Instead, he was conflicted.

After years of trying to keep his head above water with his competitive golf game, he was finally sailing. He had missed his PGA Tour card by a single, slender stroke at Qualifying School just a month earlier, and had left plenty of shots on the table. One single shot saved on any of the 108 holes he had played during the final stage and he would have been on the tour; his lifelong dream. His game was never better, he had never been closer, and he had to give the matter some serious thought.

Hours later he called the club back and accepted the position. The next day he left Africa, and his playing dreams behind. That was the day he flipped a switch in his head, and would no longer be a professional golfer. Instead, he would be a golf professional.

With his father out of the picture from the age of eight, Vershure had come to the game via his schoolteacher mom, Evelyn, who despite the burden of raising three kids was an avid golfer in her limited spare time. The future golf pro was single-minded about baseball with an occasional summer time dalliance for nine holes with his mother or baseball teammates. But an ex-Marine of a baseball coach was a bit heavy-handed in terms of discipline, and after one pre-season dressing down, the rebellious fifteen year-old decided that if he was destined to wear a glove on his left hand, it would be supple and skin tight. So he abandoned his thick leather mitt and turned to golf full time.

Vershure had begun caddying at age 13, and "sealed his fate in golf" as he puts it, when as a scrawny high school sophomore, barely able to break 80, he played way above his head in his high school regional championship, and shot 74. "I made every putt I looked at, and from that day on I never wanted to be anything but the greatest player in the world."

Would the sophisticated and refined membership of Quaker Ridge have been so quick to embrace a nascent pro had they been aware he had, for a time, been a high school dropout, earning a piddling buck an hour in a car wash, no less? "When I turned sixteen, I wanted a 'muscle' car, like every other testosterone-fueled teenage boy around Pontiac in the late '60s, and needed to pay for it," explains Vershure. "It was a hard time to grow up, lots of trouble in and around the 'Motor City,' and without a dad to rein me in, I had a tendency to run amok. Maybe the best way to say it, was that I always wanted to see what was around the next corner, try the next thing, and I wasn't too interested in listening to anyone who wanted to tell me not to do so."

Eventually he went back to high school though his indifference to academics never truly subsided. His golf improved, and he soon wangled an invite to join the locally renowned Oakland Community College golf team, which went 60 – 0 over the course of two regular seasons, managing high finishes in two National Junior College Championships despite seasonal weather disadvantages.

The University of South Florida took notice, and offered him a conditional scholarship, and Vershure continued to improve as a player through the final two years of his college eligibility. He played in two U.S. Amateurs and was runner up in the 1976 Michigan Amateur. "Those modest successes provided little hint that I would ever become the world-class golfer that I had been envisioning for years, but no one was holding my feet to the fire and I continued to ignore any and all evidence to the contrary."

His initial success on a Florida mini-tour, post-college, was illusory and short-lived. He had some high finishes and doubled, even tripled his modest seed money, but by season's end, he was broke. It was March, 1977 and he needed work.

His first club job was offered to him by Don Barber, who had been the head professional at Indianwood Golf and Country Club in Lake Orion, Michigan, the club where his mother had belonged, and where Vershure had played in his late teens and early twenties. "Don had moved south to become the first head professional at Feather Sound Country Club in Clearwater, Florida, and he hired me in April of 1977." There, he was able to learn at the hip of a top-shelf club professional. "Don insisted that I enter the PGA apprentice program, thereby building a bridge that I would ultimately take full advantage of." It was a hectic three years, as the neophyte was working 70 hours weekly at the club. He began giving lessons which he billed at $8.00 per half hour. From there it was but an hour's commute to Orlando to play on the Space Coast mini-tour. "Although, I had some success, ultimately I was spending more than I was making. There were fewer than 10 guys out of 150 or so that were actually in the black while playing that tour. It was a good thing I had a job."

Vershure made what would eventually become a permanent move to New York and the Metropolitan Section of the PGA in 1981, having learned that assistant pros made three or four times as much as their Floridian counterparts, in a season little more than half as long. He began as an assistant at Middle Bay Country Club on Long Island's south shore.

It was his first taste of the Met Section, which he feels is unparalleled. "It's not just the incredible clubs, history and tradition, though that is a large part of it. It's the fact that terrific players and club pros from all over the country come to work there and compete. And the pay scale is attractive."

He also loves the fact that the traditional golf club model, while disappearing elsewhere, is alive and well in the Metropolitan area. "In our section of the PGA you still have phenomenal courses with virtually no real estate influence. The members still take pride in both the playing and teaching ability of their professionals. Most of my colleagues still own their golf shops, which is not always the case elsewhere. Our profession has moved more toward administrators, bookkeepers, general managers, and number-crunchers in recent decades, but not so much in the Met Section."

Like careless drivers do regularly around the city, Vershure quickly hit a major pothole. His job at Middle Bay Country Club was short lived, his interest and shop clerk capabilities called into question by his boss, Doug Steffen, now the outstanding Head Professional at New Jersey's Baltusrol Golf Club. Luckily an old mini-tour competitor named Bob Lendzion, the 1986 National Club Pro Champion, hired him at the Stratton Mountain Golf School in Vermont. "I loved it up there, learned a great deal from a terrific guy in a fun atmosphere, and my teaching improved dramatically. However that winter, I again spent every dime I had saved on tournament expenses."

Rick Vershure will be retiring at the end of the 2013 golf season

The following year, after another failed effort at the final stage of Qualifying School, the frustrated pro was ready to throw in the golf towel. He headed back to Tampa to live with his sister and nephew, planning to pick up the last few college credits needed for his business degree, and to get on with his post-golf life. But when he heard that two Winged Foot assistants had left simultaneously to take head jobs at other clubs he contacted their legendary boss, Tom Nieporte. Tom remembered him from a U.S. Open qualifier where they had been paired together, and Vershure had played like the world beater that he had always hoped to be. The good news: Nieporte hired him on the spot. The bad news: The job only lasted a year.

"Tom wanted to bring his son Joe into the golf business, and as the last man in I was the first man out. That could not have been easy for Tom, not because I was any superstar, but because he may be the single kindest man I have ever met," explains Vershure, whose only year at Winged Foot was 1983, one year before an old junior college co-competitor, Fuzzy Zoeller, won the U.S. Open on the grounds.

He then spent three years working for a Met legend named Joe Moresco at Woodmere Country Club in the Five Towns section of Long Island. He left the club without another job, but with the confidence to land one. He was quickly hired by Jim McLean, at the time Head Professional at Quaker Ridge, but now known as one of the preeminent teaching professionals in the world. "We were both golf swing junkies," offers Vershure by way of explanation. "We tended to be the last guys hitting balls at section events, and we had become friends when I was working at nearby Winged Foot."

That season was a golden one for the brand-new Quaker Ridge assistant. He captured the prestigious Met Section Player of the Year award, his lesson book was full, and he was warmly embraced by the membership. His game was at its apex, and he would come tantalizingly close to getting his tour card at this, his eighth, and what turned out to be final Q-School appearance. "Jim's encouragement was great for my confidence. When tour pros and top area players came to the club, Jim would remind me that I hit the ball better than any of them. He was likely telling them the same thing, but that didn't matter to me."

There were rumors afoot that McLean might be leaving Quaker Ridge, and club insiders suggested Vershure stick close by for the call that might be coming his way. Ever the iconoclast, he was a mere 8,000 miles away in Johannesburg, South Africa, when he received the fateful phone call. "I actually felt ill when I got the message to call the club. I knew there was a life changing decision to be made," recalls the hesitant pro. "If my game was lousy, and I was down on myself, it would have been easy to say yes. If it was a second-tier club calling, I would likely have turned it down. But I was offered one of the best jobs in the country without a day's experience as a Head Pro. After two wrenching hours, I knew I needed to accept."

The man who had pin-balled about for a dozen years was finally tethered. The years spun by, became decades, and despite his relative youth he has chosen to retire at the end of 2013, nearly 30 years after first coming to Quaker Ridge. "There could not have been a better job for me. It has been a wonderful fit for my skill set and personality. I've been fortunate to have visited many of the great clubs around the world, and there is nowhere I would have rather worked than right here."

Part of his deep connection is the fact that he met his wife Maureen, now the Golf Shop Director, while at Quaker Ridge. Part of it is the life-long friendships he has made with different generations of club members. "I never lose sight of the fact that I'm 'the help.' But my long tenure and the mutual respect that I have developed with my membership has allowed me to communicate through friendship and I believe they appreciate that. I feel I've earned the right to be honest and not simply say what my members want to hear."

Just as he left Woodmere Country Club all those years ago without another job in the offing, Vershure is leaving Quaker Ridge without a concrete plan for what's next. "I'm not sure what it will be, but I'm excited to get after it." He and Maureen have lived well but simply, and even though they'll always be welcome at Quaker Ridge, and have been given Honorary Membership status at the club, they will likely spend a greater amount of time at their second home, in La Quinta, California.

Over his tenure, Quaker Ridge has become more family friendly, and many younger people with children have joined. "Twenty or twenty-five years ago, legacy children did not take advantage of the opportunity to join because they were never encouraged as youngsters. I also feel that the Tiger Woods era may have had more influence on golf becoming cool for that generation. The recent economic crunch, while devastating to many clubs, has actually brought in another younger, more active element, and Quaker Ridge is better for it."

Vershure is also better for the life-altering decision he made back in Johannesburg more than a quarter century past. When he talks about the final stage of Q-School in 1987, which occurred just two months before the Quaker Ridge opportunity, he reminisces like it's been 25 minutes, not 25 plus years since he was in those final, crucial moments.

"The penultimate hole was a par five. I hit a good drive and a three iron to 20 feet. The putt was flat as a billiard table and I ran my eagle try over the edge of the hole, maybe two feet past. I wasn't careless with the birdie try but somehow missed it. There were no leader boards but I had a sinking feeling that it might be the difference."

"I would love to have made it onto the PGA Tour," concludes the 60-year old. "But who knows how I would have fared, or if I even would have kept my card for a second year. All I know is that if it had happened, I would have declined the job at Quaker Ridge to take my chances on the tour and the position would never again have been an option. This is not the type of job anyone is going to leave quickly," concludes the one-time reluctant club professional, who has managed to amass 27 years of tenure as Quaker Ridge's head man, looking back fondly on the greatest three-putt of his life.

CURRENT OR FORMER HEAD GOLF PROFESSIONALS WHO WORKED FOR RICK VERSHURE INCLUDE:

- Ray Ford
- Scott Hawkins
- Chris Klaffer
- Shaun Powers
- Jim Wahl
- Andy Zullo

Rick Vershure's tip for fellow golfers:

For a golfer, the word 'transition' likely conjures an image of the point in a swing when the backswing becomes the downswing. Now, consider a different 'transition' - the point at which a pre-shot routine becomes the beginning of your backswing.

Some players almost seem to be on 'GO' when they begin their backswings, while others seem to be on 'STOP.' It is almost like the pre-swing rituals of the latter have little to do with the 'event' itself, whereas the 'GO' player's routine tends to become part of their takeaway.

A golfer is an action creator or actor as opposed to a reactor - much as is a pitcher in baseball, a server in a racquet sport or football's place kicker, etc. The batter, return of server, or defensive football player is a reactor.

The next time you have a chance to observe a top level athlete/actor doing their thing, notice that none are disconnected or static as they prepare to begin their motion. They will have a 'ritual' that repeats itself unerringly. They will be relaxing their bodies, aligning, and finding rhythm – as should golfers.

Rick Vershure's tip for fellow golf professionals:

Golf professionals wear many hats. At any moment we may be on the golf course, at the lesson tee, behind a computer, doing paperwork, attending meetings with the GM, superintendent, staff, or committees. We may be conversing privately with a member or composing a notice to the entire membership, but we are rarely idle. In nearly every one of these cases, we may well be invisible to 95% of our membership. There is one crucial period in my week – Saturday morning– when I should be in none of those locations.

Saturday morning presents a unique opportunity. It is my busiest morning and for many of our members it may be the only time I see them. It is in my best interest, for several reasons, to be on or around the first tee at that time. This simple activity may well be the most productive thing I'll do all week, and here's why:

- I get to see and interact with 100 or so of my members in those hours.
- Perhaps more importantly, those same 100 people see me present and fully engaged with the membership.
- I have a chance to observe them giving their best effort on that stressful opening tee shot.
- I have a chance to give reassurance or comfort to a stressed player or to remind them of their personal commitment for the day.
- An amazing number of these golfers will turn to give/get a reaction to/from their 'pro.' Our opinion of them and their games clearly matters to our members.

Nicole Weller
Savannah, Georgia

Nicole Weller is different than almost anyone else showcased within these pages, and not just due to her gender. It's also goes beyond her relative youth. Though it would be disingenuous to claim she's young enough to be any of these other pros daughter, it's not a stretch to say she's young enough to be anyone's niece. Her distinction is not that she's a black belt in karate, or that she is an accomplished pianist. No, what sets Nicole Weller apart from her peers within this text is the facility where she practices her craft.

Nicole Weller is one of the brightest young stars in golf instruction

Referring to the Landings Club in Savannah, Georgia as just another golf-real estate community is like calling Buckingham just another palace.

It's not one or two courses, but half-a-dozen. Not one clubhouse, but a quartet. Not just a head pro and a couple of assistants, but all told some 15 different PGA professionals employed in varying capacities. Not just a couple of hundred members, but nearly 1,600 golf memberships which translates into some 2,500 golfers.

While golf instruction has been readily available and sought out by some during the club's 40 year existence, it has become an absolute priority for many hundreds—neophytes, kids, women, beginners, decent players and par shooters alike—since Nicole Weller became the head teaching professional.

"The instructional component of this club has grown significantly and measurably since Nicole took over, it's practically night and day," offers Director of Golf Tad Sanders, who has 25 years of tenure at the facility. "I began here as an assistant pro right out of college in 1987, and haven't seen anyone here who brings such a passion to teaching, with such a love of instruction, and to the junior golfers in particular. She has really elevated the instructional programs here, and is on the cutting-edge of all the latest developments."

Sanders' boss is Landings Club General Manager Steven Freund, who spent more than 20 years at golf properties in the Ritz-Carlton organization before taking the reins at The Landings Club in 2010. He is equally impressed, offering that, "Nicole has inquisitiveness and a curiosity unlike anyone I've ever seen. She's not complacent with where she's at, she is constantly scouring the world to find new and creative ways to help our members, whatever age, experience level or ability, learn how to improve, and accelerate the learning process in an enjoyable manner."

A Massachusetts native now in her early 40s, Weller was introduced to the game by her dad, who had her wandering the golf course chasing butterflies and swinging the club in earnest at age 4. She was playing competitively at 11, played in three US Girls Junior Championships, captured the first AJGA event she played in, was an Honorable Mention for the AJGA Rolex All-American team and was awarded a four-year golf scholarship to Wake Forest University. "I studied psychology at Wake Forest, and then earned my Masters in Sports Psychology at the University of Tennessee. I became a golf professional almost by default, and started concentrating on teaching. It wasn't long before I realized I had found my calling," begins Weller.

In her ten years in Tennessee, Weller began as an assistant professional at a Donald Ross gem called Cherokee Country Club, and then moved into full time teaching at Fairways and Greens Golf Center in greater Knoxville. It was there she met her future husband Ty Weller at a PGA training seminar, where they were both studying to obtain their Class 'A' card. Portending her future, as local president and site director she grew the LPGA-USGA Girls Golf program from 15 girls to 80.

Ty and Nicole married in 2000, honeymooned at Kiawah Island and fell hard for the Low Country, moving over from Tennessee to Savannah and the Landings Club in 2005 as assistant professionals, where both advanced quickly. Ty is now one of the head professionals at the club, and Nicole was elevated to head teaching professional within a year and a half of her arrival.

All things being equal, each of the 15 PGA golf professionals working at The Landings would command a bit less than 7% of the lesson revenue. Nicole Weller does nearly five times that amount, or about one third of total lesson revenue. She is quick to use the "right time, right place, right circumstance" explanation for her unprecedented success. After all, she is a teacher first and last with the latitude to simply teach and create programs, without the golf operations and shop responsibility that most of her colleagues have. As the only woman on the golf staff, the many hundreds of avid women golfers in The Landings have a natural affinity for her. (The LWGA, or Landings Women's Golf Association, is literally one of the largest women's golf organizations in the world.) But it goes beyond these natural advantages, compelling as they might be.

"Her results have been wonderful," continues Tad Sanders. "It's her marketing savvy, her enthusiasm and dedication to service, the fact that she genuinely cares, not just about her own students but about all the members and their progress in the game. It is no wonder our lesson revenues and interest in instructional programs and seminars have never before approached the level they are at now."

"I think part of the success I've enjoyed is that I've been fortunate enough to attend numerous education seminars and bring these ideas back to Savannah, that I'm willing to try new teaching techniques to enthuse our members about the game," states Weller. "I love to teach anyone who is willing, but I have a particular affinity for women and juniors, and those two categories make up approximately 70% of my students. Perhaps the women find me very approachable and open, receptive to their concerns, or fears about the game. As for juniors, maybe the little kids sense how much I love to be around them, am willing to get down on the ground with them, make it fun for them and have a silly time whether we are actually doing active drills on the range, or inside making cupcakes or our own golf visors as a rainy-day project. And any accomplishment, no matter how minor, is a cause for celebration. I blow it up big, they get more enthusiastic, and want to come back again," continues Weller, who recently published an appealing sticker-and-activities book geared to introduce very young children to the joys of the game, called *Stick to Sports: Let's Play Golf.*

The Landings is unique in that attracts a large percentage of residents who have had limited, and in some cases, virtually no exposure to the game before they decided to relocate to a golf Shangri-La. "I love the 'never-evers' as much as any other type of student," states Weller, honored in 2010 as one of Golf Digest's "Top 40 under 40" instructors. "To see the spark when they grasp a concept, hit a solid shot in the intended direction, get the ball airborne, whatever it might be. It's also an opportunity to teach life skills in a golf context, things like strategizing, controlling the emotions, overcoming fear and doubt. They are all endemic to the game, and life outside the game, and it's great to be able to impart some wisdom in this manner. We are opening up a whole new world for these people by virtue of this incredible game, and I absolutely love it."

"One of the things that really impresses me about Nicole is that she is so much more than an on-course or driving range instructor," continues GM Freund, who has nearly 400 employees at the club, but few who are capable of generating revenue like Weller. "She looks at the totality of a member, and is capable of helping not only with mechanics, but due to her martial-arts background, can help with the mental and psychological demands of the game. Her combination approach of physical, mechanical and mental aspects of golf is something I've never encountered to this degree previously."

Weller finds success because she doesn't wrap herself entirely in swing technique, but uses a holistic approach to the game, encompassing fitness, flexibility, emotional strength, mental strength and strategy. "I am a big fan of PGA Professional Bob Day, my coach when I was growing up in Massachusetts, and also the work of Pia Nilsson and Lynn Marriott, whose books and seminars

Teaching fundamentals to kids is one of Nicole Weller's favorite parts of golf instruction

have as much to do with reaching your potential in golf and beyond, as they do with any technical jargon or swing mechanics."

She spends at least six to seven hours a day teaching, sometimes more, and spends several additional hours setting up and breaking down the training stations, and several more hours with the behind-the-scenes office work on marketing, phone calls, emails, equipment maintenance, follow-ups, upcoming multiple program preparation and more. Often there's additional planning she brings home at day's end and during time off. The workday sometimes stretches to twelve hours or more, but the time flies by. "I try and fit six days of work into a five or five-and-a-half day schedule, so even though I work about 60 hours weekly, it's more than just my job, it's a career and a passion. I use my time off to recharge and spend time with my husband, because even though we work out of the same pro shop, we are always going in different directions."

The vast network of amenities on Skidaway Island, not to mention the deep vein of human resources, are two of the reasons Weller relishes coming to work each day. "If one driving range happens to be closed for maintenance, there are three others I can teach on," she continues. "Where else is that possible? The diversity of backgrounds, geographies, experiences, professions and age groups of our members is remarkable, as is the fact that women are so empowered here, so welcomed and encouraged to learn golf and play with regularity."

The synergy that exists between Weller and her students reflects her success. "I have a great desire to learn and improve my teaching, and so many members have this deep thirst for knowledge, which I am able to provide. It works as well as it does because ultimately we are both after the same thing—a greater understanding of golf, and how we can play better and improve ourselves, on and off the course."

"I love to educate golfers and enhance their lives, get them moving, get them thinking, and get them to enjoy themselves more through this wonderful game. I stay motivated every day and night thinking about breakthroughs with individuals, them understanding a concept, and beaming after success. I get a great sense of accomplishment as they find the same sense of accomplishment by improving. I've actually shed a tear on the range watching a student make a major breakthrough."

Weller believes for the game to shake off its decades-long doldrums and thrive once again, kids should start as early as she did—introduced to the game as early as two or three, with simple and fun instruction and golf learning games commencing at four or five years old. She also believes a non-traditional approach to beginners will ultimately pay dividends. Her philosophy is that it's easier to wean people from playing "relaxed rules" to playing traditional golf, than it is to continuously recruit brand-new candidates to the game. In other words, because golf can be so punitive, so challenging, she bases her relaxed rules on the PGA Get Golf Ready 'It's OK Guidelines' and thinks beginners should, for example, be able to hit a mulligan on the first tee, and on any tee, time permitting.

Ground the club in the bunker, and if the ball refuses to be extricated, then toss it onto the green. Don't keep score, and if you do, then a swing-and-miss doesn't count, because you didn't hit it. "If they fall under the game's spell, start to love it, and take it more seriously then of course they need to learn to play by the rules," continues Weller, a 2010 and 2011 U.S. Kids Golf Top 50 Teacher. "But why run the risk of driving them away from the get-go, because the demands of "real golf" are so overwhelming to those who have never played previously? We need to grow the game, and not scare people away or turn them off right from the start."

Other than her musings on traditional versus non-traditional philosophy, Weller differs from the other professionals showcased here in one other respect. Most every other professional within these pages has a long and storied legacy. They are celebrated here because of who they are, and what they've already achieved. Nicole Weller has already accomplished a great deal in the game. But because of her enthusiasm, dedication and sheer delight of teaching golf, she's featured not only because of what she has done to date, but also because of the great things she will assuredly accomplish going forward.

Nicole Weller's tip for fellow golfers:

Greater consistency can be achieved by finding ways to narrow the differences between the practice range and the course. Golf is one of the only sports that isn't learned in the same area where it's played. Basketball, soccer, tennis and football are great examples of games that train and scrimmage in the same performance arena. Golf is practiced one way but then played in another way.

When practicing, go through the same walk-up routine to each shot. How you approach the ball on the range shouldn't be any different than on the course. Walking into the ball and settling into the shot is part of the entire shot. Be consistent. Practicing under transfer conditions make success easier to attain on the course. If one just learns an idea and can repeat it on a flat surface without any pressure, does that mean it will hold up on the course? Most likely not. So seek out side-hill lies on the range if they are available, or hit balls out of old divots. Try and replicate conditions you will actually encounter on the course. Repeat motions to gain an understanding of cause and effect but then build that skill in a play/practice setting. If you can practice it under pressure and it holds up, you'll have a better chance of that on the course!

Nicole Weller's tip for fellow golf professionals:

If you're looking to grow the game of golf, consider capturing the imagination and interest of youngsters ages three through eight. This has been one of the fastest growing and most rewarding customer bases of mine. The key to attracting such youngsters to our wonderful sport is FUN! While it's up to you to market to adults who provide finance, equipment, transport and help, instructors must be very animated, fast-paced, creative and be able to have silly moments while actually getting down to the child's level.

Engaging activities and tools include SNAG Golf, stickers, reward prize boxes, pool noodles, bubbles, fitness equipment and games, hula hoops, ribbons, marshmallows and much more. I published many of my creative ideas in *Stick to Sports: Let's Play Golf* as a vehicle for adults in need of guidance with very young golfers. Using colorful clubs like The Littlest Golfer's First Set to get children interested and then feeding them into SNAG and US Kids Golf clubs and programs can provide great structure. Organizing birthday parties, Family Golf, Teeny Tiny Tots (age 3), Tiny Tots (ages 4-6), Holiday and Summer Camps are just a few lucrative ways to reach out to this population.

Suzy Whaley
Farmington, Connecticut

Unlike professional golfers, golf professionals are mostly an anonymous bunch, little-known outside their clubs or communities. There are exceptions to the rule, as the best and most successful become more prominent, with a far-reaching reputation. But true celebrity? That's reserved for Tiger, Phil and Freddie.

Suzy Whaley flanked by her teaching colleagues Martin Hall (left) and Laird Small

With one exception.

It was a decade ago that esteemed teaching professional Suzy Whaley received her '15 minutes of fame' which stretched out far longer than the allotted quarter-hour. When she qualified for the PGA Tour's 2003 Greater Hartford Open by virtue of winning the 2002 Connecticut Section PGA Championship, she set off a media firestorm that raged for the better part of nine months. "That first day alone my husband and I must have received about 700 phone calls," recalls the vivacious pro, now in her mid-40s. "It was Newsweek, Time, USA Today, U.S. News and World Report, inquiries from Japan, China, Australia, Sweden, throughout Europe. It was overwhelming!"

Equally overwhelming was the turnout when Whaley stepped to the first tee at TPC River Highlands that July morning for the tournament's opening round, surrounded ten deep, with thousands of patrons lining the fairway. "I popped up my drive about 200 yards down the middle, and I was thrilled to have managed that much!"

It would be easy to surmise that her opening tee shot was the most nerve-wracking of her career, but that's incorrect. At least she managed to get the ball on a peg. Twenty years earlier as a 16 year-old, in her first and only U.S. Women's Open appearance, Suzy McGuire was joined on the first tee in a practice round by LPGA legend JoAnne Carner, one of her idols. "On the first hole I was literally too nervous to put the ball on a tee, so I hit driver off the deck! She mentored and coached me the entire round, and that day remains one of my fondest golf memories."

One of little Miss McGuire's earliest golf memories was as a nine year-old, hitting balls on the range in her bathing suit. "Our family golf dynamic was unusual. My mother loved the game, my older sister hated it, and my dad was terrible at it! Mom was fearful of introducing me to golf, because of my sister's attitude. But when mom found me hitting balls with the boys that day she thought she might have a convert!"

Her first 'glass ceiling' occurred in grade school. With little course or tournament access at their club, her family thought more opportunities would be available elsewhere, so they changed affiliation to Onondaga CC in Syracuse, where little Suzy played in the Ladies League, along with her mother's friends. "In the late '70s, there was no IJGA or AJGA circuit, and when I got to high school I played on the boy's team." With a strong lower body developed from competitive ski racing, and attempting to keep up with her golf teammates, the teenager was hitting her tee shots some 250 yards, all the more impressive with a persimmon driver. "I hit it long, but not too straight, and my short game wasn't much, either!"

Her Olympic ski racing aspirations took a backseat to golf, which to that point was her part-time sport, after her 16th summer, the year she qualified for the U.S. Open. After a single college semester in Boulder, Colorado, Whaley was enticed back east by famed University of North Carolina women's golf coach Dot Gunnells. She was soon to make the acquaintance of her fellow Tarheel athletes Davis Love III and Michael Jordan, and went on to excel in Chapel Hill, with a stellar four-year career, both on and off the golf course.

Law School was looming post-college, but some financial backers wanted her to take a run at LPGA Qualifying School, impressed as they were with her appearance in the LPGA Championship, and her run to the semifinals in the prestigious North-South Championship, among other high profile events. "My mom encouraged me to take a shot," recalls Whaley. She said I could always go to Law School, but this might be your only chance at Tour School."

She surprised herself by making it to the LPGA Tour, albeit with non-exempt status. But because the Tour was thriving in the early '90s, with three-dozen or so events, the rookie had numerous opportunities to play. Unlike the Tour itself, Whaley didn't thrive, earning a measly two grand that season. With no status the following year she worked as a waitress and worked on her game, and despite her mother's admonitions not to date golf pros, she married PGA

Professional Bill Whaley, who was serving as her swing coach, during her one year hiatus from the competitive arena.

Her second stint on Tour, as a newlywed in 1992, was as dismal as her first. So with her husband's encouragement, at the time the head professional at Ibis Country Club in Palm Beach, Florida, she decided to explore teaching the game.

With newborn Jennifer being cared for by a trusted sitter, the young mother became, in her words, "an unpaid and unappreciated apprentice" at the Nicklaus-Flick Golf School, not far from their home in Palm Beach Gardens. "In 1995 I spent almost the whole year sitting in a chair, observing this amazing group of teachers give lessons: Jim Flick, Bob Toski, Laird Small, Martin Hall, Mike Malaska, Dean Reinmuth, Mark Wood and Charlie Epps, among others."

The irony is that though she was amidst this Mount Rushmore of instructors, it was Whaley herself who was as quiet and still as a mountainside carving, absorbing the nuance and subtlety of communication that brought these instructors to the top of the profession. "I listened and learned, and when Jim Flick eventually asked my opinion on an instructional technique and didn't like my answer, I was banished back to my chair for another couple of months," recalls Whaley, smiling at the memory.

Lunchtime was when the instructors sat together and debated swing technique, and these interludes were the most fascinating for their patient apprentice. "I had never given much thought to swing technique when I was playing," offers the former New York Junior Girls Champion. "I was strong and athletic, so I walked up to the ball and belted it. They made me really think about the science of the golf swing, and I was just as impressed with the passion and dedication they had to their craft, it had a huge impact on me. I

Suzy Whaley was the center of attention at the PGA Tour's Greater Hartford Open in 2003
Photo Courtesy Montana Pritchard--PGA of America

didn't mind that I was unpaid. I feel I should have been paying them for such an amazing education."

Jim Flick offered her a real job a year later, and despite being confined to the putting green for another entire year, Whaley spent almost eight years as an instructor in the school, mostly doing contract work at Desert Mountain in Arizona, with daughter Kelly coming along three years after her older sister.

"The key to being a good teacher is connecting with the individual on an interpersonal level," suggests Whaley, one of Golf Digest's 50 Top Instructors. "If you can connect, you can change their behavior. It's imperative that you let students know how much you value their time. The trick is being able to assist people with different abilities, egos, ages, athleticism, attitudes and experience who all want the same thing—to play better golf. If everyone was the same the job would be far simpler!"

Whaley found it simple to land a new job after employing a simple technique to do so when she followed her husband Bill up to Hartford, Connecticut, when he was named the General Manager of TPC River Highlands in 1997. She moved north six months after Bill got settled, and just six weeks after Kelly was born. "I put together a basic resume, drove around the area and handed out copies at five different clubs, and by the time I got home, all five clubs had called me."

Bill Whaley, a 30-year PGA Professional, explains his wife's magnetic personality. "Suzy has this unique ability to make whoever she is talking to feel like the most important person she has seen all day," states the Philadelphia native, who was eventually promoted to National Director of Golf for the 19 TPC golf properties nationwide. "She is such a wonderful communicator, whether it's giving a lesson, a clinic or a speech. People are engrossed by her, she's very charismatic."

Her first Connecticut interview stop turned out to be her last. Whaley was hired on the spot to be the teaching professional at Tumble Brook CC in the suburb of Bloomfield, and the lengths the club went to in regards to retaining her services included allowing her to make her own hours, and keep every dime of lesson revenue. "I loved the club and never would have left, but four years later I was recruited by a woman named Lisa Wilson Foley to run her public golf course called Blue Fox Run in nearby Avon. I had never been a head professional before, so I wanted to explore that side of the business," explains the three-time winner of the Connecticut Open.

"It is rare for a woman to own a golf course, and Lisa wanted a woman head pro at her club, so I came onboard, and had to learn every aspect of running a golf operation, trying to make a modest daily fee facility (about $25 per player at the time) the most fabulous experience it could be."

Hectic doesn't begin to describe the pace that ensued, with both Bill and Suzy working 70-plus hours at their respective positions, with two little ones at home. At least Bill was a seasoned pro. His wife was embroiled in trial and error, emphasis on the latter, never more apparent then after her approval and purchase of 30,000 new scorecards emblazoned with the incorrect phone number. "The learning curve was steep," admits the two-time Connecticut Section Teacher of the Year. "I had never run a men's league, women's league, corporate league, ordered merchandise, hired a staff, or done the books. I never would have survived without Bill, I called him at least ten times a day for months!"

Amidst all the craziness, Whaley found some time to play competitively, and when she won the Connecticut Section PGA Championship in September 2002, she had punched her ticket to the GHO the following June. "I was never even thinking about that exemption when I entered. I was playing great that summer, and had won the LPGA National Tournament and Club Professional Championship by a record nine shots a few months earlier. I was just focusing on a high finish, and collecting a nice check." Whaley shot five under par for the 54-hole event, winning by a couple of shots. She was allowed to play at 90% of the men's distance, about 6,300 yards compared to the men at 7,000 yards. Of course there would be no such distance dispensation granted by the PGA Tour in regards to the GHO, which was one of the main reasons she thought long and hard before accepting the challenge confronting her.

"Other than in my profession I was a person of obscurity, working a fulltime job, with two small girls at home," recalls Whaley, still with a sense of wonderment. "And then overnight the phone started ringing, and didn't stop! Everyone wanted to know one thing: Would I take part in the tournament."

Hamlet-like, she pondered the question endlessly: 'To play or not to play?' It was three entire months before she decided to plunge into the abyss. "I needed to decide what was right for my family, my employer, and the PGA of America, which I would be representing. I continually emphasized that my real job was to insure that other people were having fun and enjoying the game, and not spend all my time playing golf myself. I also knew that once I committed there would be no turning back, so I had to be 100% sure I could give it my best."

Her best meant 4 a.m. wakeup calls preceding three hours of strength training, flexibility and cardio work, Christmas included, all before waking her girls, getting them ready for school, and then going off to work ten-hour days. As the winter turned to spring, her employer brought on additional staff, her husband took on more responsibilities with the kids, and Suzy, crediting the team effort surrounding her, hit thousands of balls in preparation. "I couldn't take on the world's finest Tour professionals without putting my best foot forward, and preparing as best I could."

Nothing could prepare her for the throngs that awaited her on the first tee. The record shows she shot rounds of 75 and 78 on the 6,800 yard, par-70 course, missing the cut handily, but beating three men, and only one shot in arrears of former U.S. Open champion Scott Simpson. She is quick to credit Dr. Richard Coop, a sports psychologist from her alma mater, the University of North Carolina, who helped her navigate all the obstacles she would face. "I was never focused on score. I wanted to stay in the moment, enjoy the experience, avoid distractions, and maintain my focus. That was how I determined success."

It was a heady time for women's golf. Annika Sorenstam played The Colonial two months earlier. Precocious 13 year-old Michelle Wie played in the final group at an LPGA Major that spring, carding a top ten finish. There were magazine covers, photo shoots, TV interviews, and comprehensive publicity the likes of which that women's golf had never received previously. "My goals were much different than Annika's," continues Whaley. "She expected to compete, and was striving for a high finish. I wanted to serve as an example to women to grab an opportunity, prepare yourself, give it your best and don't fear failure. I wanted to get more women aware of, thinking about and taking up golf. And I think in those regards we were greatly successful."

Suzy and Bill Whaley have been just as successful raising their daughters. Jennifer is on a full golf scholarship at Quinnipiac College, and will be pursuing an MBA. Her little sister Kelly, already a three-time Connecticut Section Junior PGA champion and the Connecticut Women's Amateur Champion, is enrolled in a prestigious golf academy on Hilton Head Island. "It took plenty of guts for her to leave home and go to boarding school in South Carolina, almost a thousand miles away," continues Whaley. "But she wants to push herself, gain more discipline and maximize her potential."

Bill Whaley gives much of the parenting credit to his wife. "She's a wonderful mother and a great role model for our daughters. She's shown them, and countless others, both in words and deeds, to not play it safe, to go out on a limb, and get out of your comfort zone. Don't fear failure, but embrace the chance to get to the next level."

"The utmost satisfaction for me is, partially because of the whole GHO experience, my teenage daughters have no fear," concludes the winner of the 2012 LPGA National Nancy Lopez Achievement Award, and since 2006 one of the teaching professionals at TPC River Highlands. "Our girls embrace opportunity and are willing to put in the work to be successful. They know it's OK to trip or stumble, but to keep their head up, and jump right back in. Looking back I cannot imagine having forgone that amazing, electrifying experience. It took me months to make up my mind, but I definitely made the right choice in playing. It was easily worth all the hard work, sacrifice and preparation needed to participate."

They have been married for more than 20 years, but Bill Whaley, unofficial President of his wife's fan club, lends great perspective. "The GHO appearance was just a brief blip on the radar, but even though it's a decade later, her profile is still raised. Suzy has parlayed that once-in-a-lifetime experience to help charities in need, junior golfers, women golfers, and shown everyone that breaking out of your comfort zone is possible. If a female teaching pro can accept the challenge of competing against the finest male Tour professionals in the world, then it's possible for anyone who wants it badly enough to work hard, strive for results, and find improvement, in aspects of life that go far beyond golf. In my opinion that's truly the lasting lesson."

With her charisma and communication skills, her raised profile and interest in growing the game, particularly among women and kids, it's been a natural progression to turn towards PGA of America politics. Having served on numerous committees both regionally and nationally, she's become more immersed in the process over time. Those who know her well wouldn't be shocked to see a day in the foreseeable future when Suzy Whaley becomes the first female officer, indeed, maybe the first female president, of the PGA of America. Both on course and off, she continues her trailblazing ways.

Suzy Whaley's tip for fellow golfers:

Striking the golf ball solidly is one of the best feelings in golf. There are plenty of ways to score well, and we all know and admire players who have great short games, putt the eyes out, and consistently turn three shots into two. But hitting it flush never gets old. Improve your ball striking by working on your impact position. At impact check to be sure that the handle and the shaft arrive prior to the club head. This will produce a descending blow and create more powerful strikes.

Suzy Whaley's tip for fellow golf professionals

Impact, influence and inspire those around you and your job as a golf professional will become very clear. As teachers and coaches, we have the ability each day to significantly impact someone's life through golf. Take that opportunity and listen more to your students than you speak. Understanding their motivations will allow you to pass on information in a manner that will help the student change behavior to enhance their experience and ultimately their daily life.

Brad Worthington
Fairfield, Connecticut

Brad Worthington (left) with his protégé Randy Taylor

There is likely no greater concentration of fine golf courses in one geographic area then what is found in the Metropolitan Section of the PGA of America, in and around New York City. The assemblage of courses is so deep and powerful it's akin to the "Murderers Row" lineup of the 1927 Yankees, assuming that in addition to Babe Ruth, Lou Gehrig, and Tony Lazzeri, that famed roster also included their Hall of Fame contemporaries Roger Hornsby, George Sisler, Tris Speaker and Ty Cobb.

The section has more than 300 courses in total, including several dozen exquisite, to-die-for clubs within a few hours of Manhattan. Suffice it to say that places like Winged Foot, Shinnecock Hills, National Golf Links of America, Quaker Ridge, Garden City Golf Club, and Bethpage Black, on any expert's list of some of the nation's finest courses, only scratch the surface of the quality available throughout the Met.

Brooklawn Country Club in Fairfield, Connecticut flies well below the radar in comparison to some of the better-known venues in the region. But it is one of the most delightful golf experiences in the Met, a superb A.W. Tillinghast design dating from 1929 with lots of topographical interest, a great routing, varied elevations, rolling fairway contours, elegant bunkering and daunting greens. The club has a rich history, which includes employing a former assistant pro named Gene Sarazen, who went on to become the first player to complete the modern Grand Slam. The club played host to several USGA events over the years, most notably, the 1987 U.S. Senior Open, where Gary Player, another Grand Slam winner, won the first of what became back-to-back titles in what's considered the most prestigious golf event for the over-50 crowd.

Brad Worthington, now part of the over-50 crowd himself, has held Brooklawn's head professional's position for twenty years. His desire to remain for another twenty has as much to do with his love of the club, its ambience and the longstanding and supportive membership as does the fact that he's also a product of Fairfield County, and prefers to stay in the area, close to family and friends.

The Trumbull native excelled in many sports in his youth and as a teen won the New England Junior Golf Championship by five shots over future PGA Tour stalwart Brad Faxon, among others. He spent a single semester on the University of Houston golf team, teaming briefly with Fred Couples and broadcaster Jim Nantz, before finding his stride at Miami of Ohio, where he won All-Conference honors and the golf team's captaincy his senior season.

Worthington stands a shade less than 6'3" tall and a thimble below 250 lbs. It's easy to envision him orbiting a tee shot 300-plus yards, which he did with great regularity as a younger man. Nowadays a 320-yard drive is de rigueur for every Toms, Rick and

Rory on the PGA Tour, but Worthington was winning long-drive contests at that distance when the distinctive "ping" sound of first-iteration metal-headed drivers still turned heads in curiosity, and balata balls were considered an engineering marvel.

320 off the tee will always be impressive, but 10,000 was a number that was depressive to the would-be touring pro, which was the dollar amount he was slated to receive for a second-place finish, but never actually collected, when the tournament circuit he was playing on went bust in the mid-'80s. "My sponsor was just as unhappy as I when that big check never arrived," begins Worthington, offering a rueful shake of the head and a wry smile at a memory more bitter than sweet. He took it as a sign he was meant for the club life, got his first job in the Met section, has never left, and never plans to.

"I began working at a little-known Tillinghast club on the south shore of Long Island called Rockaway Hunting Club. My boss was Randy Cavanaugh, who was formerly an assistant at Winged Foot, and recommended me to their long time pro, Tom Nieporte. So after two years at Rockaway I was lucky enough to spend the next four years as a Winged Foot assistant."

His first head job came as the first head professional at the brand-new and highly regarded Atlantic Golf Club, in Bridgehampton, Long Island. "Now there are a number of very high end golf clubs that have come into existence in the last 20-odd years," continues Worthington, referring to the 'new wave' at places like Sebonac, Friar's Head, The Bridge, Easthampton Golf Club, Liberty National and Hudson National, among others. "But Atlantic was the first, and it took plenty of long days to get it up and running properly." Not that he was afraid of the sunrise-to-sunset schedule. "Back when I got started almost 30 years ago, if a new assistant asked the boss for his schedule, sometimes he was handed a key. That meant he was to open the shop just past dawn, and close it up after dark!"

Great as the job was, and bright as prospects looked, Worthington's future wife, Gayle, was hours away up in Greenwich, Connecticut. And with an eye towards the family they were planning on starting, the socially-conscious pro wasn't sure the dichotomy between the year-round, local residents and the jet-setting summer visitors that make The Hamptons such a glam destination was the best environment to raise kids. "It seemed to me that raising kids in a more normal environment, where there wasn't such disparity in lifestyles, would be a smart move for us. So when Brooklawn offered me the head professional's position, it was a chance to get closer to home, and raise the kids we were planning on having in a more stable atmosphere."

The irony in his decision to move is that even though Fairfield County is one of the nation's most prosperous, there are deep pockets of poverty and many thousands in need sprinkled among its nearly two dozen towns. Greenwich, Wilton and Westport bring to mind great affluence, but the city of Bridgeport, 60 or 80 years ago the machine tool capital of the nation, continues to decline, and is beset by serious economic woes.

As a longtime member of the Met Section's Executive Committee, including a stint as president, Worthington is keenly aware of the importance of growing the game, particularly among populations that have never been exposed. "I worry for the game's future. My boys, Grant and Mitchell, are in high school and middle school, and they don't spend four straight hours doing *anything*, much less something as hard to learn as golf." Brooklawn has made a concerted effort to attract younger families, and by virtue of junior clinics and programs, not to mention a specified kid's

Brad Worthington with his sons Grant and Mitchell

course contained within the championship course, complete with their own tee markers and scorecard, the game is thriving on the grounds. But Worthington is looking well beyond the grounds.

"We as teachers need to remember how discomforting it can be to learn the game as a rank beginner," he states earnestly. "I forced myself to take dance lessons, and with a male instructor no less, just so I could really feel the same sense of awkwardness and unease that a typical beginning golfer feels when they venture to the course."

One of the ventures that Worthington has deeply embraced is the First Tee Program of Fairchild Wheeler, named not only for the 36-hole municipal facility in Bridgeport where the program is conducted, but originally for an area businessman and philanthropist of the same name, a founding member of Brooklawn, who donated the land for the courses to be built.

The First Tee endeavors to build character and instill life-enhancing values through golf. Responsibility, perseverance, honesty and sportsmanship are among the core values emphasized. "Never mind the golf grip, one of the first things First Tee kids learn is to grip someone's hand correctly when they shake, look them in the eye, and introduce themselves properly," explains Worthington.

The former Program Director of the area First Tee is a young African- American named Randy Taylor, who grew up in one of Bridgeport's roughest neighborhoods, and attended a high school where the expulsion rate, while not as high as the graduation rate, was substantial nonetheless.

"Other than my parents, Brad has been the most positive adult role model I've ever had," begins Taylor, whose parents were born in the West Indies. Taylor, now in his early 30s, had about 1,600 charges in the First Tee program he ran. But when he took the job in his early 20s, there were maybe a hundred kids enrolled. Like his mentor, Taylor wasn't afraid to wade in and build things from the ground up. "I initially came to Brooklawn as part of a local after-school internship program called GOLFWORKS," continues Taylor, who continues to pursue his sports marketing degree at nearby Sacred Heart University while working fulltime.

Created by the Metropolitan Golf Association, GOLFWORKS offers employment opportunities to underprivileged and minority youth by exposing them to the many facets of the golf industry. Beginning as an industrious busboy in the Brooklawn dining room, Taylor quickly came to the attention of the head pro, who had him transferred into the golf shop. Worthington gradually increased his protégé's responsibility, eventually putting him in charge of the juniors, and then the ladies 9-hole golf league.

Imagine the culture shock when Taylor, who had likely never before given instructions to even a single white adult in his life, was handed the microphone by his boss one afternoon, and voice quavering, gave detailed instructions to an expectant crowd when outlining the format for a shotgun tournament. "The three seasons I spent there were wonderful, and Brad was instrumental in recommending I pursue the opportunity at the First Tee. But even though it's been a decade or so since I left Brooklawn," marvels Taylor, "Brad continues to mentor me, counsel me, and remains a great friend. I consider myself very fortunate to have him as part of my life."

Almost as fortunate are the 50-or-so of the most committed and engaged First Tee participants, along with their parents, that were recently invited by Brooklawn's board and Worthington to come over and actually play their pristine golf course, opening their collective eyes to the possibilities and potential their lives may hold. "Many high-end clubs hold First Tee fundraisers," states Worthington, "where the business elite gather in an environment they are familiar with, and donate monies to the organization. But we wanted to actually show the kids, most of whom have never played anywhere but Fairchild Wheeler, and probably couldn't imagine a club or course like this exists so close to where they live, what they can aspire to in life if they work hard and dream big. We've had caddies here who eventually managed to join the club themselves, so this is along the same lines."

Club members and their head professional extend themselves to the surrounding community far beyond their First Tee affiliation. The Day of Gratitude was an initiative that invited more than 50 Iraqi and Afghanistan war veterans out to enjoy the club.

Another worthwhile program that Brooklawn enthusiastically supports is the Nicholas Madaras transitional home for female veterans of the Armed Forces. Veterans make up a disproportionate number of the homeless in general, and there are hundreds of former servicewomen in Connecticut that are without permanent housing. The club has offered more than financial support to the 14-bed residence, where the average length of stay is approximately two years. They have also provided furnishings, appliances, and perhaps most importantly, real-world expertise. Members have counseled the women in residence on a variety of subjects—legal advice, cooking, computer skills and resume-building, among others.

Because Worthington is such an imposing physical presence, the fact that his empathetic nature is also outsized comes as no surprise to those who know him well. "My mother Mary Ann always taught me to give back, and be as generous to others as possible," concludes the pro. "She's in her mid 70s, and she is still picking up bottles and cans on the side of the road, and using the deposit money for charitable purposes. I had a wonderful role model."

Worthington understands that he is privileged to have enjoyed the stability of a great job and the fruits of numerous long-lasting relationships at this fine and historic country club that is both metaphorically and literally at the top of the hill. He feels it's both duty and obligation to venture into the workaday neighborhoods in the valley below the high ground, and do what he can to assist those who haven't been quite as fortunate.

CURRENT OR FORMER HEAD PROFESSIONALS WHO WORKED FOR BRAD WORTHINGTON INCLUDE:

- Sean Busca
- Jimmy DiMarino
- Ben Kristopiet
- Bryan Moran
- Mark Parsons
- Stephen Roach
- Sean Toohey

Brad Worthington's tip for fellow golfers:

When ball contact is uncharacteristically poor most players think too much versus thinking the simple thoughts which got them to be good ball strikers in the first place! Consistent solid contact is obtained through encouraging hand-eye coordination and not regurgitating dozens of different swing thoughts in ones head prior to each golf shot.

Have you ever considered using a practice swing prior to most every shot on the course AND in practice? Swinging through an imaginary ball perceived about four inches inside your ball and focusing on bottoming out on the target side of the ball is a mind freeing pre-shot routine. A simple "sweeping" of that target side grass gives a sense of confidence leading to consistency in your ball striking and simplifies what is in your mind for each and every shot.

Many golfers bottom their swing out too far behind the ball, seldom taking a divot, even with short irons. Setting up with some forward shaft lean (gradually more with a wedge working back to less for a fairway wood) will encourage you to bottom out correctly on the target side of the ball. Since each club is a different length, the unintended but substantial consequences of playing and practicing this way is that your practice swings will "measure" ball position for each lie to determine where best to bottom out. Lining up several golf balls in practice will give feedback as to where the optimum spot for a divot is for each shot.

Brad Worthington's tip for fellow golf professionals:

Long before the self help books which were popular in the '70s and '80s my father attended a work-related seminar where the instructor suddenly appeared with a sign across his chest, reading "Make me Feel Important." Throughout my golf career I have done my best to keep this phrase in mind when serving the many members/customers/guests at the Clubs where I have been fortunate enough to work as a PGA Golf Professional.

The impact from this simple phrase is as invaluable for your Opening Staff Meetings as it is for encouragement during any Performance Evaluation of a staff member. Personally, for each golf lesson I give I point to three positive things I see in each student's game at the start of our lesson. Even a comment on their clothing (hopefully purchased in our golf shop!) sets any student at ease and allows them to look at each lesson as a positive learning experience and not personal criticism.

ABOUT THE AUTHOR

Joel Zuckerman is the author of six other books, including

Pete Dye Golf Courses—*50 Years of Visionary Design,* named as the 2009 Book of the Year by the International Network of Golf.

His features, essays, personality profiles and travel stories have been seen in more than one hundred publications, including Sports Illustrated, GOLF Magazine, LINKS, SKY Magazine and Golfweek. He lives in Savannah, Georgia.

For more information visit: www.vagabondgolfer.com

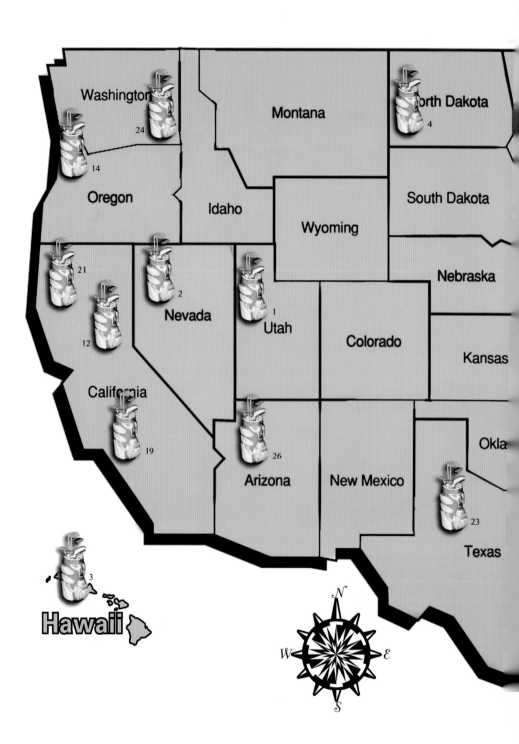

Washington

24

14

Oregon

Idaho

Montana

orth Dakota

4

South Dakota

Wyoming

21

2

Nevada

1

Utah

Nebraska

Colorado

Kansas

12

California

19

26

Arizona

New Mexico

Okla

23

Texas

3

Hawaii

N

W　E

S

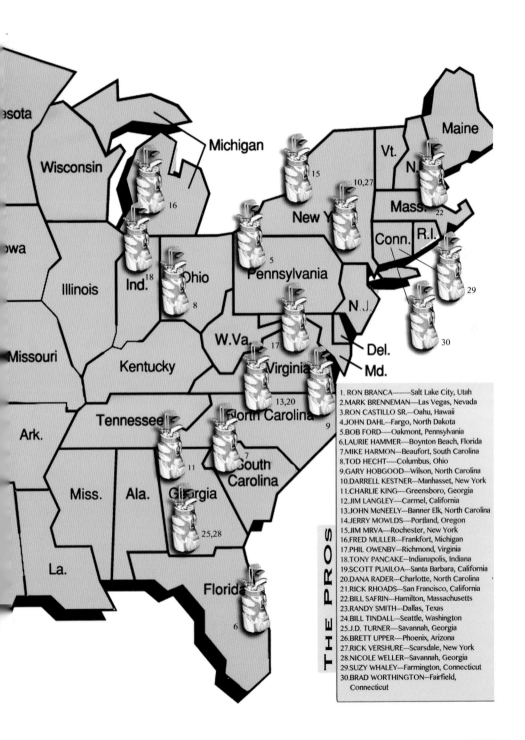

THE PROS

1. RON BRANCA----------Salt Lake City, Utah
2. MARK BRENNEMAN----Las Vegas, Nevada
3. RON CASTILLO SR.---Oahu, Hawaii
4. JOHN DAHL---Fargo, North Dakota
5. BOB FORD-----Oakmont, Pennsylvania
6. LAURIE HAMMER----Boynton Beach, Florida
7. MIKE HARMON---Beaufort, South Carolina
8. TOD HECHT-----Columbus, Ohio
9. GARY HOBGOOD---Wilson, North Carolina
10. DARRELL KESTNER---Manhasset, New York
11. CHARLIE KING-----Greensboro, Georgia
12. JIM LANGLEY----Carmel, California
13. JOHN McNEELY---Banner Elk, North Carolina
14. JERRY MOWLDS---Portland, Oregon
15. JIM MRVA---Rochester, New York
16. FRED MULLER--Frankfort, Michigan
17. PHIL OWENBY---Richmond, Virginia
18. TONY PANCAKE---Indianapolis, Indiana
19. SCOTT PUAILOA----Santa Barbara, California
20. DANA RADER---Charlotte, North Carolina
21. RICK RHOADS---San Francisco, California
22. BILL SAFRIN---Hamilton, Massachusetts
23. RANDY SMITH---Dallas, Texas
24. BILL TINDALL---Seattle, Washington
25. J.D. TURNER----Savannah, Georgia
26. BRETT UPPER----Phoenix, Arizona
27. RICK VERSHURE---Scarsdale, New York
28. NICOLE WELLER---Savannah, Georgia
29. SUZY WHALEY---Farmington, Connecticut
30. BRAD WORTHINGTON---Fairfield, Connecticut

Pro's Pros by Joel Zuckerman   327